WALL STREET'S GREATEST MINDS

A SYSTEMATIC ANALYSIS OF THE STRATEGIES USED BY ELITE TOP INVESTORS

AF704024

Published by Forecortex, 2025.

While every precaution has been taken in the preparation of this book, the publisher assumes no responsibility for errors or omissions, or for damages resulting from the use of the information contained herein.

WALL STREET'S GREATEST MINDS

First edition. November 21, 2025.

Copyright © 2025 Peter Peret Lupo.

ISBN: 978-1069913517

Written by Peter Peret Lupo.

A Note on the Creation of This Book

The creation of this book represents a partnership between human direction and artificial intelligence. I believe in transparency in the creative process, and I want to share how this work came to be.

For the text, I employed a suite of AI as sophisticated tools to assist in structuring and drafting. The process began with my own core concepts, plot points, and detailed chapter outlines. I then directed leading AI models, including ChatGPT 5 Thinking, Claude Opus 4.1, and Gemini 2.5 Pro, to generate initial text based on highly specific instructions and prompts for each section. This AI-generated content served as a creative foundation, which I then extensively edited, rewrote, and refined to ensure the narrative voice, pacing, and thematic depth aligned with my vision. Every word has been weighed and approved by me, and the ultimate authorship of the final prose is my own.

The book's visuals were also created in partnership with AI. The cover art was generated using ChatGPT 5, while the internal illustrations were created with Gemini Pro 2.5 Canvas. For each image, I developed detailed prompts and stylistic guides to direct the AI, and the final selection and curation were entirely my own creative decisions.

My goal in using these technologies was to explore a modern creative workflow, blending human imagination with the capabilities of machine intelligence. This book, in its entirety, is a product of my vision and effort, and I take full responsibility for its content, both written and visual.

— Peter P. Lupo

To my family and friends, especially my wife for her support, and my cousin Harry for the inspiration.

— Peter P. Lupo

Table of Contents

Part I: The Foundations of Greatness

Before we can deconstruct the complex machinery of the world's greatest investors, we must first understand the language they speak and the principles that guide them. This foundational section is your primer—the essential toolkit you will need to appreciate the genius in the chapters that follow. We begin with the very purpose of our journey in "The Quest for Alpha," defining that elusive, almost mythical, quality that separates skill from luck and greatness from mediocrity. We will establish our central thesis: that sustained success in the markets is not an accident, but the product of a well-designed and repeatable framework. Next, in "A Common Lexicon," we will demystify the core concepts that form the bedrock of investment theory, from the "Margin of Safety" to "Reflexivity." Consider these first two chapters your orientation, ensuring that when we step into the minds of the masters, you have the context and vocabulary to understand not just what they do, but why they do it.

Chapter 1: The Quest for Alpha

The Anatomy of Conviction

In the early 1990s, the capitals of Europe were bound by a grand and fragile ambition: the Exchange Rate Mechanism, or ERM. It was a political construct designed to lash the continent's currencies together in preparation for a single monetary union, with the formidable German Deutschmark as its anchor. Britain, seeking to tame its domestic inflation, entered the ERM in 1990 at what many economists privately knew was an unsustainably high exchange rate. This decision tethered a struggling British economy, beset by low productivity and high unemployment, to the powerhouse of a newly reunified Germany. A fundamental, tectonic stress was built into the very foundation of European monetary policy—a crack visible to anyone willing to look.

From their offices in New York, two men were looking with singular intensity. One was George Soros, the philosopher-king of finance, a man who saw markets not as efficient machines but as chaotic, reflexive systems of human bias. The other was his lead portfolio manager, Stanley Druckenmiller, a fiercely analytical mind with an instinct for the market's jugular. They were not gamblers looking for a lucky tip; they were global detectives hunting for systemic flaws. In the ERM's rigid peg of the weak British pound to the mighty Deutschmark, they identified what Soros would call a "fertile fallacy"—a widely held belief that was profoundly at odds with economic reality.

Their developing thesis was not merely that the pound was overvalued, but that the structure of the market offered a uniquely skewed opportunity. The pound was already languishing at the very bottom of its mandated ERM band, artificially propped up by the daily interventions of the Bank of England. The risk of the pound strengthening was therefore minimal; the British government and the central bank were already spending their reserves to prevent it from falling further. The potential reward, however, was a catastrophic devaluation if the peg were to break. It was the quintessential asymmetric bet: limited, quantifiable risk with the potential for an explosive, almost unlimited reward.

For months, their Quantum Fund quietly built a $1.5 billion short position against the pound. Then came the catalyst. In an interview, the president of Germany's own central bank, the Bundesbank, publicly hinted that certain currencies—widely understood to mean the pound—might come under pressure. For Druckenmiller, this was the final confirmation. He presented the case to Soros: they should not just add to their position; they should bet the entire fund. Soros, in a legendary display of conviction, famously told him that was a ridiculous idea—they should bet even more.

On the morning of September 16, 1992—a day that would be immortalized as Black Wednesday—they escalated their wager to a colossal $10 billion short sale of the British pound. The move was so large it acted as a Bat-Signal to every other speculator in the world, signaling that the Bank of England's defenses were about to be breached. A tidal wave of selling followed. The Bank of England fought back, burning through billions of dollars of its foreign reserves in a matter of hours to buy its own currency. In a desperate move, the British government hiked interest rates from 10% to 12%, and then announced a further hike to a staggering 15%. But it was futile. The market's conviction, led by Soros and Druckenmiller, had become a self-fulfilling prophecy. Their bet did not just anticipate the pound's collapse; it helped trigger it, proving Soros's own theory of reflexivity—that markets can and do influence the events they anticipate.

By evening, the British government capitulated. Britain crashed out of the ERM, and the pound went into freefall. The Quantum Fund netted a profit of over $1 billion. Yet the true lesson of Black Wednesday lies not in the staggering profit, but in the triumph of a superior *process*. It was the culmination of deep historical analysis, a clear-eyed understanding of political constraints, and the rare psychological fortitude to act with overwhelming force when a lifetime's opportunity presented itself. It was the antithesis of a lucky spin of the roulette wheel. It was the physical manifestation of a masterfully constructed framework.

Defining Alpha: The Alchemist's Signature

To understand what separates the actions of a Soros or a Druckenmiller from the noise of the everyday market, we must first grasp two fundamental concepts: Beta and Alpha. They are the twin forces that govern the world of returns, one common and accessible to all, the other rare and jealously guarded.

"Beta" (β) is the return you get simply for showing up. It is the measure of a portfolio's sensitivity to the market's overall movement. Imagine the entire stock market as a great ocean tide. When the tide comes in, nearly every boat rises with it—the magnificent yachts and the leaky dinghies alike. This broad, indiscriminate lift is Beta. An investor who buys a simple S&P 500 index fund is capturing pure market Beta. It requires no particular genius, only the capital and the patience to participate in the market's general upward drift over time. It is the reward for taking on systemic market risk.

"Alpha" (α), by contrast, is the alchemist's secret. It is the measure of performance that is *independent* of the market's movement. If Beta is the tide, Alpha is the skill of a master captain—the ability to harness the winds, read the currents, and navigate a course so superior that their vessel arrives at its destination far ahead of the fleet, regardless of whether the tide was high or low. It is the quantifiable evidence of an edge. A positive Alpha signifies that a manager has generated returns above and beyond what would be expected for the amount of market risk they took on. It is, in the simplest terms, the return generated by skill.

To make this distinction vivid, consider the world of gastronomy. Beta is the basket of high-quality, seasonal ingredients available at the public market. Any competent home cook can purchase these ingredients and, by following a standard recipe, produce a perfectly decent meal. This is the market's return, available to everyone. Alpha is the unique contribution of a master chef. It is their proprietary spice blend, their secret technique for searing, their counterintuitive understanding of flavor pairings that no one else can replicate. It is the *process* that transforms those common ingredients into a Michelin-starred dish that commands a vast premium. The investors in this book are the master chefs of capital. They work with the same raw materials as everyone else—stocks, bonds, currencies—but they apply a proprietary process that generates a result that cannot be easily replicated.

The pursuit of Alpha is, therefore, an inherently contrarian act. To generate a stream of returns that is different from the market (Alpha), one must, by definition, think and act differently from the market consensus, which generates the market's return (Beta). This transforms Alpha from a dry financial metric into a measure of something far more profound: intellectual independence, courage, and the discipline to execute a unique vision in an arena governed by herd behavior.

FIGURE 1 - ALPHA IS THE QUANTIFIABLE SKILL THAT SEPARATES ENDURING SUCCESS FROM FLEETING LUCK

The Central Thesis: The Architecture of Outperformance

This brings us to the central question of this book, and indeed, of all investing: Is sustained success the product of skill or merely of luck?

In the short term, the market can feel like a grand casino. A novice investor, making a blind bet on a hot technology stock, can outperform a seasoned professional over a few weeks or months. This is the "fooled by randomness" effect. Imagine an auditorium filled with 10,000 people, each asked to flip a coin ten times. By pure statistical chance, a handful of them will flip ten heads in a row. For that brief moment, they will look like coin-flipping geniuses, but they are merely the beneficiaries of probability. So it is in the markets. In any given year, some managers will beat the market soundly, but for many, it is simply their turn to flip ten heads.

The argument for skill rests on the statistical impossibility of sustained luck. A single year of outperformance can be chance. But the multi-decade, market-crushing, crisis-surviving track records of the investors profiled in these pages defy the laws of probability. Their persistence through bull markets, bear markets, geopolitical shocks, and technological revolutions is overwhelming evidence of a durable, repeatable edge. This is made even more profound by what is known as the "Paradox of Skill". As the average level of talent in any competitive field increases, luck plays a greater role in determining outcomes for the masses. As markets have become more efficient and investors more sophisticated, generating Alpha has become exponentially harder. The fact that these masters continued to deliver extraordinary results in this hyper-competitive environment implies their edge was not just good; it was structurally different, operating on a plane inaccessible to the increasingly skilled crowd.

This book's central thesis is that this durable edge is not the result of a series of brilliant, disconnected "calls" or lucky streaks. It is the output of a coherent, systematic, and deeply personal **framework**—what we will call an "Investment Operating System." This personal OS is the unique architecture of how each master sees the world and translates that vision into profit. It is a combination of four key components:

1. **A Core Philosophy:** A fundamental, deeply held belief about how markets truly work (e.g., "Mr. Market is a manic-depressive," "liquidity is the prime mover," "competition is for losers").
2. **An Analytical Toolkit:** A specific set of methods and processes for identifying opportunities that align with their philosophy (e.g., forensic accounting, reflexivity analysis, scuttlebutt research).
3. **A Risk Management Protocol:** A non-negotiable set of rules for sizing positions, using leverage, and, most importantly, preserving capital.
4. **A Psychological Overlay:** The immense mental and emotional discipline required to execute the system without being swayed by fear, greed, or the roar of the crowd.

The purpose of this book is to deconstruct these personal operating systems. We will move beyond the what—the famous trades and track records—to reverse-engineer the *how*. We will build a schematic of the intellectual machinery that allowed these individuals to achieve what so few have. This is a journey into the architecture of Alpha.

Introducing the Pantheon: A Roadmap of Mastery

To guide us on this journey, we have assembled a pantheon of 15 of the greatest investors in modern history. They come from different eras and employ wildly different methods, but all have demonstrated the sustained, framework-driven success that is the hallmark of true mastery. We have grouped them into four distinct schools of thought, providing a roadmap for the intellectual expedition to come.

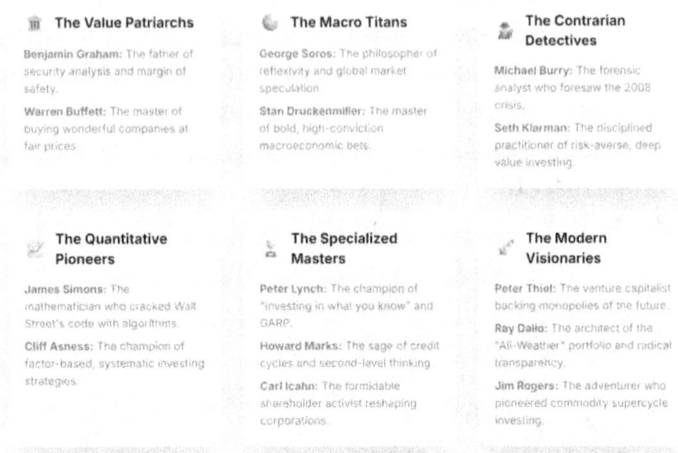

FIGURE 2 - WE WILL DECONSTRUCT THE MENTAL MODELS OF 15 OF HISTORY'S GREATEST INVESTORS, GROUPED BY THEIR CORE PHILOSOPHY.

THE VALUE SCHOOL & ITS DESCENDANTS

This is the bedrock of modern investment analysis, the intellectual lineage that begins with a simple but revolutionary idea: a stock is not a piece of paper, but a piece of a business. We start with the patriarchs, **Benjamin Graham & Warren Buffett**, who taught the world to demand a "margin of safety." We then trace the philosophy's evolution through the "growth at a reasonable price" methodology of **Peter Lynch**; the crisis-hunting contrarianism of **Sir John Templeton & Seth Klarman**; the mastery of credit cycles by **Howard Marks**; the forensic deep-value investigations of **Michael Burry**; and finally, the aggressive, catalyst-creating campaigns of shareholder activists **Carl Icahn & Bill Ackman**.

THE GLOBAL MACRO THINKERS

Here we pivot from the microscope to the telescope. These are the global chess players who analyze the great tides of capital, politics, and human psychology. Our guides are the undisputed titans of the field, **George Soros & Stanley Druckenmiller**, who mastered the feedback loops of reflexivity and the primacy of central bank liquidity. They are joined by a cadre of specialized masters: the adventurer **Jim Rogers**, who rides decade-long commodity supercycles; the wildcatter **T. Boone Pickens**, who brought an oilman's understanding of assets to Wall Street; and the indefatigable pioneer **Mark Mobius**, who charted the volatile but rewarding frontiers of emerging markets.

THE FUTURE & THE ABSTRACT

This group of visionaries is less concerned with valuing what *is* and more obsessed with underwriting what *could be*. They operate at the highest levels of abstraction. We will explore the world of **Peter Thiel**, the philosopher of Silicon Valley who argues that all great value is created in "Zero to One" moments that lead to durable monopolies. Then we enter the mind of **Ray Dalio**, the ultimate systems engineer who, instead of trying to predict *a* future, built an "All-Weather" machine designed to be resilient to *all* possible futures.

THE QUANTITATIVE REVOLUTION

This is the final frontier, where the intuitive human investor is systematically removed from the equation. We enter the cold, hard domain of data, algorithms, and the scientific method. Our journey begins with **Cliff Asness**, the academic-turned-practitioner who codified the systematic harvesting of market "factors" like Value and Momentum. We conclude inside the ultimate black box with **James Simons** and Renaissance Technologies, the secretive firm of mathematicians and codebreakers who abandoned financial theory entirely to find faint, fleeting patterns in petabytes of data, building the most powerful money-making machine the world has ever seen.

Setting the Expectation: The Promise of the Quest

Before we embark, a crucial word of caution. This is not a book of "hot tips" or a list of stocks to buy. There is no magic formula within these pages that can be copied verbatim for instant success. Indeed, the single greatest mistake an investor can make is to adopt a strategy that is fundamentally misaligned with their own personality, time horizon, and circle of competence. To do so is a surefire recipe for disaster.

The true promise of this book is something far more valuable: it is a masterclass in *how to think*. By dissecting the frameworks of these 15 masters, you will learn the art of:

- **Analysis:** How to deconstruct a complex problem from first principles and develop a unique, variant perception.
- **Risk Management:** How to think in probabilities, structure asymmetric bets, and protect your

capital from the permanent loss that ends the game.

- **Psychological Discipline:** How to recognize and master the powerful emotional and cognitive biases that derail the vast majority of market participants.

The ultimate goal is not to become the next Warren Buffett or George Soros. It is to understand the universal principles of process, patience, and intellectual honesty that connect every one of them. It is to borrow their tools, learn from their mistakes, and be inspired by their courage. This book is the apprenticeship. The final challenge—the one that awaits you at the end of this journey—is to use these lessons to become the architect of your own framework, to build an operating system for success that is uniquely and powerfully your own.

The quest for Alpha begins now.

Chapter 2: A Common Lexicon

Before we can deconstruct the complex machinery of the world's greatest investors, we must first understand the language they speak and the principles that guide them. Investing is a discipline built upon a foundation of powerful, interconnected ideas. To the novice, these terms can seem like an impenetrable jargon; to the master, they are the essential mental models for navigating the chaos of the markets.

This chapter is your primer. It is not a simple glossary to be memorized, but an introduction to a set of profound concepts that, once understood, will permanently change the way you view risk, price, and value. Mastering this lexicon is the prerequisite for understanding not just *what* the masters do in the chapters that follow, but *why* they do it. These are the building blocks of the repeatable frameworks that separate sustainable success from fleeting luck.

The Value Investor's Toolkit — Principles of Business Analysis

The journey begins with the foundational principles of value investing, a philosophy that demands we think like business owners, not speculators. These concepts teach us how to manage risk, maintain psychological discipline, and conduct deep, investigative research.

MARGIN OF SAFETY

Definition: The Margin of Safety is the foundational principle of value investing, first articulated by Benjamin Graham. It is the deliberate act of purchasing a security at a significant discount to its underlying, or "intrinsic," value. This discount acts as a financial cushion, protecting an investor against errors in judgment, unforeseen negative events, or the simple irrationality of the market.

Analogy: The Bridge Warren Buffett, Graham's most famous student, provided the ultimate analogy for this concept. He explained that when you build a bridge, you design it to hold 30,000 pounds, but you only ever drive 10,000-pound trucks across it. That 20,000-pound difference is the margin of safety. In investing, you might calculate a business to be worth $100 per share, but you will only buy it when the market offers it to you for $60. That $40 discount is your margin of safety. It is an admission that valuation is an "art rather than science," and that the future is inherently uncertain.

This principle is not merely a defensive tactic; it is the structural mechanism by which a value investor engineers a favorable risk-to-reward profile. Buying an asset for 50 cents that is believed to be worth a dollar does more than just protect against a 50-cent loss. While the downside is mathematically capped at the purchase price (the stock can only go to zero), the upside is not. If the underlying business performs well, its intrinsic value can grow over time, meaning the potential for gain is theoretically unlimited. By systematically demanding a large margin of safety, an investor is not just buying cheap; they are constructing a portfolio where the potential magnitude of the wins can dramatically outweigh the capped, quantifiable losses. This transforms a simple rule into a sophisticated strategy for creating positive asymmetry.

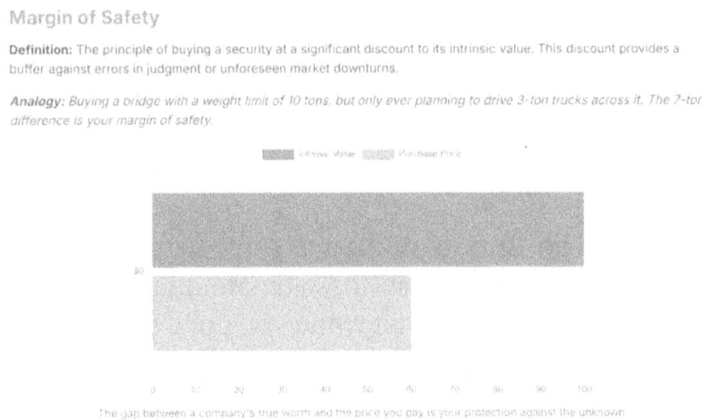

FIGURE 3 - MARGIN OF SAFETY: THE PRINCIPLE OF BUYING A SECURITY AT A SIGNIFICANT DISCOUNT TO ITS INTRINSIC VALUE.

MR. MARKET

Definition: In his book *The Intelligent Investor*, Benjamin Graham introduced a brilliant allegory to explain the proper attitude an investor should have toward market fluctuations. He asks you to imagine that you are partners in a private business with a man named Mr. Market.

Analogy: The Manic-Depressive Partner Mr. Market is a very obliging but deeply unstable partner. Every day, he shows up and offers to either buy your share of the business or sell you his, at a specific price. The problem is, Mr. Market is a manic-depressive. On some days, he is euphoric about the future and quotes a ridiculously high price. On other days, he is gripped by pessimism and offers to sell you his shares for pennies on the dollar.

Graham's crucial insight is this: Mr. Market is there to *serve* you, not to *guide* you. You are free to ignore his nonsensical offers and focus on the actual performance of your business. However, if his mood swings to an extreme, you can take advantage of him—buying from him when he is terrified and selling to him when he is ecstatic. This allegory teaches the investor to view market volatility not as a risk, but as an opportunity.

The Mr. Market story is more than just a memorable parable; it is a powerful cognitive tool for creating emotional distance. Behavioral finance has proven that investors are susceptible to fear, greed, and herding behavior. These are internal, often overwhelming, emotional responses. By personifying the market's irrationality as this "crazy guy," Graham allows the investor to reframe the source of the turmoil. It is not *you* who is panicking because a stock is down; it is the external, flawed entity "Mr. Market" making you a ridiculous offer. This act of personification creates a psychological "circuit breaker," helping an investor shift from an emotional, reactive state to a detached, analytical one. It becomes easier to say, "Mr. Market is being a fool today," than it is to admit, "My own emotional response to this price drop is irrational."

Mr. Market

Definition: A fictional character from Benjamin Graham's work who represents the stock market's irrational, often manic-depressive behavior. His mood swings offer prices that fluctuate wildly around a company's true value.

Analogy: *Your business partner, Mr. Market, shows up daily, offering to either buy your shares or sell you his at wildly different prices, driven by his mood, not by reality.*

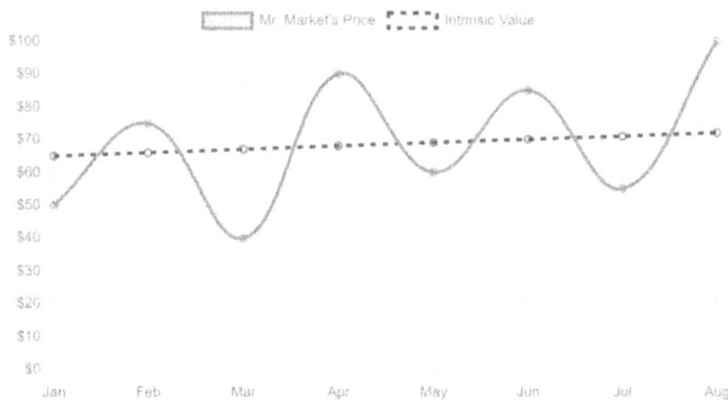

FIGURE 4 - THE INTELLIGENT INVESTOR USES MR. MARKET'S MOODS, BUYING WHEN HE IS PESSIMISTIC AND SELLING WHEN HE IS EUPHORIC.

CIRCLE OF COMPETENCE

Definition: A concept championed by Warren Buffett and his partner Charlie Munger, the Circle of Competence is the principle that an investor must have the discipline to only invest in businesses they can genuinely and deeply understand. As Buffett has stated, the size of that circle is not important; knowing its boundaries, however, is vital.

Analogy: The Baseball Player's Strike Zone The legendary baseball player Ted Williams was famous for his incredible discipline at the plate. He mentally divided the strike zone into 77 baseball-sized squares and knew his batting average for a pitch in each one. He learned to only swing at pitches in his "sweet spot," where his probability of getting a hit was highest. Swinging at a pitch on the edge of the strike zone, even if it was technically a strike, would dramatically lower his performance. Similarly, an investor must define their own intellectual "sweet spot"—the industries and business models they know intimately—and refuse to swing at investment "pitches" that fall outside of it.

This principle serves as a crucial guardrail against intellectual arrogance. It is not just about avoiding mistakes; it is a proactive strategy to ensure that the investor is always operating with an informational or analytical advantage. Financial markets are intensely competitive. To consistently outperform, one needs an edge. By strictly defining a circle of competence, an investor is implicitly choosing to play only in those areas where they can develop a deeper, more nuanced understanding than the average market participant. A doctor analyzing a medical device company or a software engineer evaluating a cloud computing firm can see subtleties and process information in a way that a generalist Wall Street analyst cannot. The principle, therefore, is not merely a defensive rule to "stay safe." It is an offensive strategy that dictates you should only play games you are uniquely equipped to win, thereby actively seeking out and exploiting a positive informational advantage.

Circle of Competence

Definition: The boundary separating the businesses and industries an investor understands deeply from those they do not. A disciplined investor only makes investments that fall within this circle.

Analogy: *A professional baseball player sticking to the strike zone. They know which pitches they can hit well and patiently wait for them, ignoring the ones they can't.*

FIGURE 5 - YOU DON'T HAVE TO BE AN EXPERT ON EVERYTHING, BUT YOU MUST KNOW THE PERIMETER OF YOUR OWN EXPERTISE.

ECONOMIC MOAT

Definition: Popularized by Warren Buffett, an Economic Moat refers to a durable competitive advantage that protects a company's profits and market share from competitors. It is a structural feature of a business that makes it difficult for rivals to attack and capture its success.

Analogy: The Castle and Moat The analogy is as simple as it is powerful. Think of a business as a valuable economic castle. The profits it generates are the treasures inside. Competitors, like marauding armies, are constantly trying to breach the walls and plunder those treasures. A great business is not just a strong castle; it is a strong castle surrounded by a wide, deep, and treacherous moat that keeps invaders at bay.

Economic Moat

Definition: A sustainable competitive advantage that protects a company's long-term profits from being eroded by competitors. Common moats include brand identity, network effects, and cost advantages.

Analogy: *The deep, crocodile-infested trench around a medieval castle that protects it from invaders. It makes attacking the castle costly and difficult.*

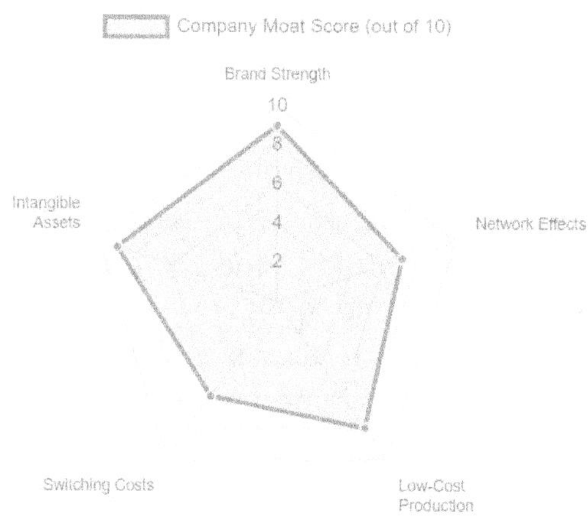

FIGURE 6 - A STRONG MOAT ALLOWS A COMPANY TO FEND OFF COMPETITION AND EARN HIGH RETURNS ON CAPITAL FOR MANY YEARS.

There are several primary sources of these moats:

- **Intangible Assets:** Powerful brands (like Coca-Cola), patents that protect intellectual property (like a pharmaceutical drug), or regulatory licenses that are difficult to obtain.
- **Switching Costs:** The pain, expense, or hassle a customer would have to endure to switch from the company's product to a competitor's. Apple's

integrated ecosystem of hardware and software is a classic example.
- **Network Effects:** This occurs when a product or service becomes more valuable as more people use it. Social media platforms like Facebook or payment networks like Visa become more useful to each user as the total number of users grows.
- **Cost Advantages:** The ability to produce a product or service at a lower cost than competitors, often due to massive economies of scale (like Walmart) or unique access to a cheap resource.

The true value of an economic moat lies not just in protecting today's profits, but in determining the *duration* and *rate* of future value compounding. In a competitive capitalist system, high profits naturally attract competition, which tends to erode those profits over time. An economic moat is a structural barrier that defies this tendency. It allows a company to sustain a high return on its invested capital for many years, enabling it to reinvest its earnings at that high rate. This sustained, high-rate compounding is the mathematical engine of long-term wealth creation and is the key difference between a temporarily cheap "cigar butt" investment and a truly "wonderful company".

SCUTTLEBUTT

Definition: Coined by the legendary investor Philip Fisher, the "scuttlebutt" method is an investigative, on-the-ground research process. It involves going beyond the official corporate documents like annual reports and press releases to build a complete, qualitative picture of a company.

Analogy: The Diligent Car Buyer Imagine you are about to buy a used car. A prudent buyer would not simply read the dealer's brochure and take their word for it. You would look under the hood. You would take it for a test drive. More importantly, you would do your scuttlebutt: you would talk to mechanics who have worked on that specific model, read online forums to hear from current owners about common problems, and maybe even check consumer reports to see how it stacks up against its competitors. This process of gathering informal, real-world intelligence is precisely what the scuttlebutt method applies to buying a piece of a business.

Scuttlebutt Method

Definition: An investigative approach to investing, popularized by Philip Fisher. It involves gathering information about a company from a wide range of sources, not just official company reports.

Analogy: *Before buying a car, you don't just read the brochure. You talk to mechanics, existing owners, and even people who own competing cars to get the full picture.*

1. Talk to Customers
2. Interview Suppliers
3. Analyze Competitors

✓ Make Informed Decision

FIGURE 7 - SCUTTLEBUTT PROVIDES ACCESS TO OFF-THE-RECORD INFORMATION FROM STAKEHOLDERS WHO HAVE NO INCENTIVE TO MAINTAIN THAT OFFICIAL STORY.

This is the practical fieldwork required to truly understand a company's **Economic Moat** and to operate confidently within one's **Circle of Competence**. The method involves talking to a wide network of sources—customers, suppliers, competitors, former employees, and trade association executives—to gather unfiltered information. This provides the qualitative data on things like company morale, management integrity, and customer loyalty that numbers alone can never reveal. In an age of sophisticated corporate communications, scuttlebutt serves as a critical defense against carefully crafted narratives. Companies invest heavily in investor relations to present the "rosiest picture possible". Scuttlebutt provides access to off-the-record information from stakeholders who have no incentive to maintain that official story. It is a qualitative triangulation process designed to validate or invalidate the narrative presented by management, making it an essential tool for forensic analysis.

The Macro Thinker's Lens — Understanding Market Dynamics

Having established the tools for analyzing individual businesses, we now pivot to the macro-level forces that shape the entire investment landscape. These concepts explain the powerful dynamics of psychology and capital flows that can overwhelm even the best-run companies.

REFLEXIVITY

Definition: A theory most associated with the legendary macro investor George Soros, Reflexivity posits that there is a two-way feedback loop between market participants' beliefs and the underlying economic fundamentals. In this view, investors are not passive observers of reality; their perceptions and actions actively shape and alter that reality.

Analogy: The 2008 Housing Crisis The 2008 global financial crisis is the quintessential real-world example of a reflexive boom-bust cycle. It began with a prevailing belief: "house prices always go up." This perception led banks to relax their lending standards (a change in fundamentals). The resulting flood of easy credit allowed more people to buy homes, which pushed prices higher, thus reinforcing the original belief. This created a self-reinforcing upward spiral. The bust was equally reflexive. When prices began to fall, the perception shifted. This led to tighter credit and foreclosures (fundamentals), which forced more selling and drove prices down even further, creating a vicious, self-reinforcing downward spiral.

Reflexivity is a direct challenge to the classical economic theory of efficient markets, which assumes that prices gravitate toward a rational equilibrium. Instead, Soros argues that markets are inherently unstable and prone to these powerful boom-bust cycles. This framework reveals how risk in financial markets is often *endogenous*—created from within the system itself—rather than being caused by external shocks. During the boom phase of a reflexive cycle, the collective actions of market participants, driven by a flawed belief, create systemic fragility. Perceived risk appears low, which encourages more leverage and risk-taking. This very behavior increases the *actual*, hidden risk in the system. The subsequent bust is therefore not an external accident but the inevitable consequence of the risk that was created and masked during the boom.

FIGURE 8 - REFLEXIVITY POSITS THAT THERE IS A TWO-WAY FEEDBACK LOOP BETWEEN MARKET PARTICIPANTS' BELIEFS AND THE UNDERLYING ECONOMIC FUNDAMENTALS.

LIQUIDITY PRIMACY

Definition: This is the principle, most closely identified with investor Stanley Druckenmiller, that the flow of liquidity—meaning the amount of money and credit in the financial system, primarily driven by central bank policy—is the single most important determinant of asset prices, often overriding company-specific fundamentals in the short to medium term.

Analogy: The Ocean Tide Think of central bank liquidity as the tide of the ocean. When the tide is coming in—that is, when a central bank is pursuing an "easy money" policy by lowering interest rates and increasing the money supply—all boats (asset classes like stocks, bonds, real estate, and cryptocurrencies) tend to rise, regardless of their individual quality. Conversely, when the tide goes out—when the central bank "tightens" policy to fight inflation—even the most seaworthy vessels can find themselves stranded on the sand.

This concept provides the overarching context for all investing. Central banks, like the U.S. Federal Reserve, manage the economy by adjusting the supply of money, which directly influences interest rates and the overall availability of credit. This "funding liquidity" is the fuel for financial markets. Understanding the direction of central bank policy is therefore critical to knowing whether you are investing with a powerful tailwind at your back or fighting against a stiff headwind. Furthermore, the level of liquidity acts as the primary conductor of market correlation. In a high-liquidity environment, the flood of money can cause historically uncorrelated assets to rise in unison, undermining traditional diversification. In a liquidity crisis, a desperate "dash for cash" can cause all assets to fall together. This makes central bank policy arguably the most important single variable for any investor to monitor.

Liquidity Primacy

Definition: The concept that the flow of money (liquidity) from central banks is a primary driver of asset prices, sometimes even more so than underlying fundamentals.

Analogy: *The tide of the ocean. When the tide of central bank money is coming in, all boats (assets) rise, regardless of their individual quality. When the tide goes out, all boats fall.*

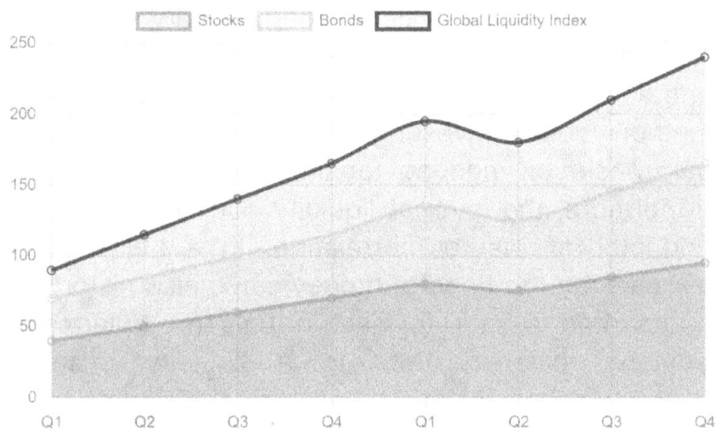

FIGURE 9 - UNDERSTANDING THE MACRO TIDE OF LIQUIDITY CAN PROVIDE CRUCIAL CONTEXT FOR INDIVIDUAL SECURITY SELECTION.

The Portfolio Architect's Blueprint — Strategies for Structuring Success

The final section moves from analysis to application, covering the concepts that guide how investors structure their portfolios, position themselves strategically, and systematically capture returns.

ASYMMETRIC RISK/REWARD (CONVEXITY)

Definition: An asymmetric risk/reward profile is an investment opportunity where the potential for gain is orders of magnitude greater than the potential for loss. It is the art of finding bets where the downside is small, fixed, and known, while the upside is large and potentially unlimited.

Analogy: The Movie Ticket Buying a ticket to a movie offers a perfectly asymmetric payoff. Your maximum possible loss is fixed and known in advance—the $15 price of the ticket. That is your capped downside. The potential upside, however, is immense and uncapped. The film could provide a cherished memory that lasts a lifetime, inspire a life-changing idea, or spark a new passion. The emotional and intellectual reward could be a thousand times greater than the financial cost.

This is the unifying mathematical goal behind many of the other concepts in this lexicon. A **Margin of Safety** is a tool to create it. **Contrarian Investing** in a hated stock seeks it. Venture capital is built entirely upon it, where one massive winner is expected to pay for a portfolio of many small losers. The objective is to build a portfolio that benefits more from positive surprises and volatility than it is hurt by negative ones. This approach is the most robust strategy for navigating a world that is fundamentally unpredictable. Rather than attempting to be right about the future, an investor focused on asymmetry structures their portfolio to be profitable even if they are wrong most of the time, so long as the magnitude of their few correct bets is sufficiently large. The focus shifts from the *frequency* of being right to the *magnitude* of the payoff.

Asymmetric Risk/Reward

Definition: An investment where the potential upside is significantly greater than the potential downside. This is also known as a convex payoff profile.

Analogy: *A movie ticket. The most you can lose is the $15 price of the ticket, but the potential emotional or intellectual reward from a brilliant film could be immense and last a lifetime.*

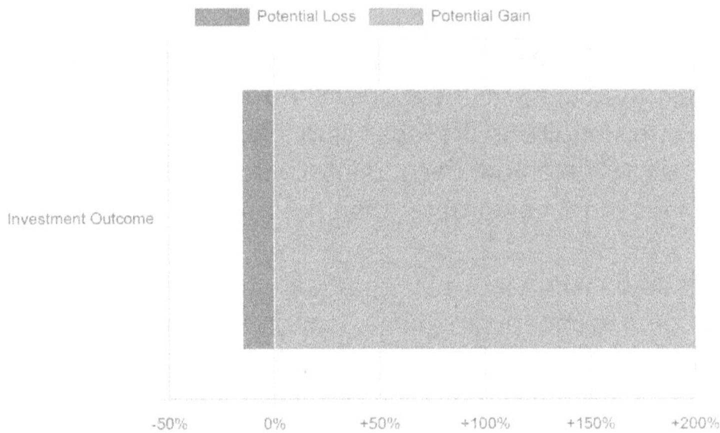

FIGURE 10 - SEEK OPPORTUNITIES WHERE HEADS YOU WIN BIG, AND TAILS YOU DON'T LOSE MUCH.

CONTRARIAN INVESTING

Definition: Contrarian investing is a strategy characterized by deliberately acting against the prevailing market sentiment. It means buying assets when the overwhelming consensus is pessimistic and selling when the consensus is euphoric. The core belief is that the herding behavior of crowds, driven by fear and greed, leads to predictable and exploitable mispricings.

Analogy: The Unpopular Restaurant Imagine you are on a street lined with restaurants. One is packed, with a long line of people waiting outside; this is the popular, "hot" stock. Next to it is an identical-looking restaurant that is completely empty; this is the unpopular, "hated" stock. The crowd assumes the line is a sign of quality and waits patiently. The contrarian, however, has done their own research. They have read the reviews and know that the empty restaurant secretly employs a world-class chef. They walk right in, get the best table, and enjoy a spectacular meal at a reasonable price, while the crowd is still waiting in line for an average meal at an inflated price.

Contrarian Investing

Definition: An investment strategy characterized by going against prevailing market trends. A contrarian buys when others are selling (and assets are unpopular) and sells when others are buying (and assets are popular).

Analogy: *Walking into an empty, unpopular restaurant because you've done the research and know they secretly have the best chef in town, long before the crowds arrive.*

"Be fearful when others are greedy, and greedy when others are fearful."

- Warren Buffett

FIGURE 11 - CONTRARIAN INVESTING IS A STRATEGY CHARACTERIZED BY DELIBERATELY ACTING AGAINST THE PREVAILING MARKET SENTIMENT.

This strategy is the psychological application of the **Mr. Market** allegory and is famously summarized by Warren Buffett's maxim: "Be fearful when others are greedy, and greedy when others are fearful". However, successful contrarianism is not merely about betting against the current price trend; it is about betting against the prevailing *narrative*. A cheap stock can always become cheaper if the negative story the market is telling about it is true. True contrarian insight comes from conducting deep research (**Scuttlebutt**, for example) and concluding that the market's pessimistic narrative is exaggerated or false. The most profitable contrarian investments are not just bets against a price, but bets against a flawed story.

FACTOR INVESTING

Definition: Factor investing is a systematic, evidence-based approach to investing that moves beyond traditional asset classes (stocks, bonds) to target specific, well-documented drivers of return known as "factors". Instead of picking individual stocks based on discretionary analysis, factor investing seeks to build a portfolio with diversified exposure to these broad characteristics.

Analogy: Dietary Factors Building a healthy diet is not about trying to pick individual "superfoods" that will be popular this year. It is about ensuring your body gets consistent exposure to essential nutritional factors like protein, healthy fats, fiber, and vitamins. Similarly, factor investing is not about trying to pick the next "super stock." It is about systematically constructing a portfolio that has consistent exposure to the proven "nutritional factors" of returns.

Decades of academic research have identified several persistent and pervasive factors. The most prominent include :

- **Value:** The tendency for stocks that are cheap relative to their fundamental value (e.g., earnings, book value) to outperform expensive stocks over the long run. This is the systematic application of the **Margin of Safety** principle.
- **Momentum:** The tendency for assets that have performed well in the recent past (e.g., the last 6-12 months) to continue performing well, and for recent losers to continue losing. This is the systematic opposite of **Contrarian Investing**.
- **Quality:** The tendency for companies with strong financial health—high profitability, stable earnings, and low debt—to deliver superior risk-adjusted returns. This is the systematic search for businesses with an **Economic Moat**.

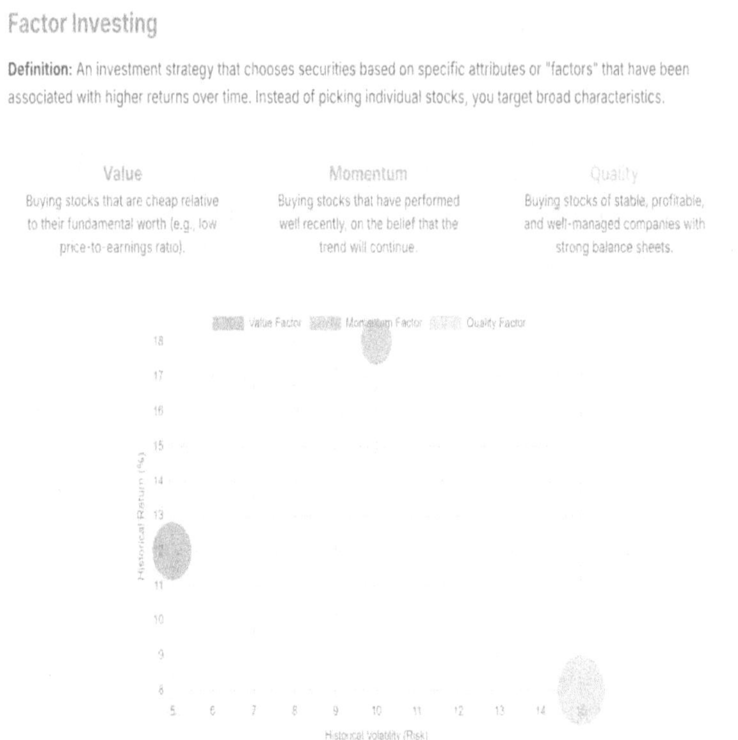

FIGURE 12 - INSTEAD OF PICKING INDIVIDUAL STOCKS BASED ON DISCRETIONARY ANALYSIS, FACTOR INVESTING SEEKS TO BUILD A PORTFOLIO WITH DIVERSIFIED EXPOSURE TO THESE BROAD CHARACTERISTICS.

The existence of these factors reveals a deep truth about markets. The fact that two philosophically opposed strategies—Value (a contrarian, mean-reverting approach) and Momentum (a trend-following approach)—both have strong historical evidence of success is a profound paradox. It suggests the market is not inefficient in one simple way, but in multiple, contradictory ways. This is why combining factors can be so powerful; it creates a more robust portfolio that can profit from different forms of market irrationality at different times.

RISK PARITY

Definition: Risk Parity is a portfolio construction strategy, pioneered by Ray Dalio of Bridgewater Associates, that allocates capital based on risk contribution rather than dollar contribution. The objective is for each asset class in a portfolio—such as stocks, bonds, and commodities—to contribute equally to the portfolio's overall risk.

Analogy: Building a Sports Team A traditional 60/40 stock/bond portfolio is like building a sports team by spending 60% of your budget on a star quarterback and 40% on the rest of the team. Because the quarterback's position is so volatile and high-impact, his performance will dictate nearly 90% of your team's success or failure. Risk Parity, in contrast, is like building a team by allocating resources to ensure that the offense, defense, and special teams are all equally balanced and contribute equally to the final outcome. This often means investing more capital in the less volatile but crucial "defensive" assets (like bonds) to create a more resilient, "all-weather" team.

Risk Parity

Definition: A portfolio allocation strategy that focuses on allocating capital based on risk contribution rather than dollar amounts. The goal is to balance the risk exposure from different asset classes.

Analogy: *Building a sports team not by spending the most on the star quarterback, but by allocating resources to ensure the defense, offense, and special teams are all equally strong and balanced.*

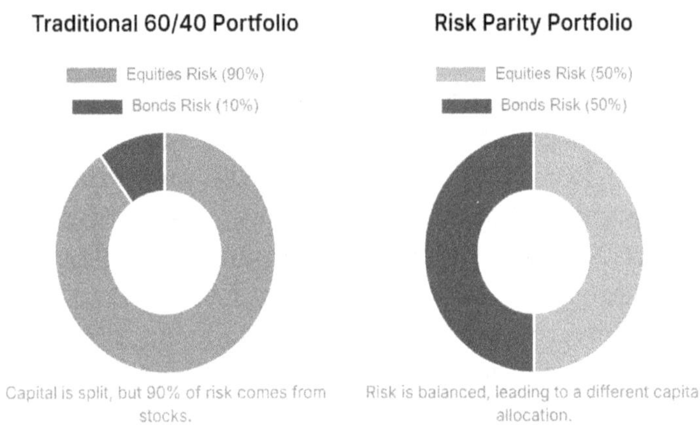

FIGURE 13 - RISK PARITY IS A PORTFOLIO CONSTRUCTION STRATEGY THAT ALLOCATES CAPITAL BASED ON RISK CONTRIBUTION RATHER THAN DOLLAR CONTRIBUTION.

This approach is a direct critique of traditional diversification. A 60/40 portfolio is diversified by capital, but because stocks are so much more volatile than bonds, its risk is highly concentrated in the stock portion. To achieve true risk balance, the strategy often employs leverage on lower-volatility assets like bonds to increase their risk contribution to match that of equities. At its core, however, the strategy's success has historically relied on the negative correlation between stocks and bonds. This relationship, in turn, is a function of central bank credibility in controlling inflation. In periods of high and unpredictable inflation, that negative correlation can break down, causing both stocks and bonds to fall together and challenging the strategy's fundamental diversification mechanism.

From Words to a Worldview

These eleven concepts are more than just vocabulary; they are the essential components of a sophisticated investment worldview. They flow logically from the micro to the macro: from the forensic analysis of a single business, to understanding the powerful economic and psychological environment in which it operates, to the final, crucial step of structuring a resilient portfolio of many such assets.

Viewed not in isolation but as an interconnected toolkit, these ideas provide the intellectual foundation for sound judgment. With this common lexicon established, we are now prepared to see how the masters of the craft combine, weigh, and apply these principles to build their own unique and powerful frameworks for success.

Part II: The Frameworks of the Masters

This is the heart of our expedition. Having established our foundational principles, we now embark on a deep dive into the minds and methods of 15 legendary investors. Each chapter is a detailed schematic, a reverse-engineered blueprint of a unique "architecture of alpha." We have grouped these masters into four distinct schools of thought to guide you on this intellectual journey. We begin with **The Value School**, the bedrock of modern analysis, and trace its evolution from the rigid quantitative rules of Graham to the activist interventions of Icahn. From there, we pivot to **The Global Macro Thinkers**, leaving the world of balance sheets to explore the grand stage of global economics, currencies, and capital flows. Our path then leads us to **The Future & The Abstract**, where visionaries like Peter Thiel and systems-thinkers like Ray Dalio teach us to invest in what *could be* rather than what already is. We conclude with **The Quantitative Revolution**, stepping inside the "black box" to witness how data science and algorithms have forged a new, and profoundly powerful, path to market mastery. Prepare to be challenged, enlightened, and inspired.

The Value School & Its Descendants

Welcome to the bedrock of modern investment theory. The chapters in this section trace the intellectual lineage of the most powerful and enduring investment philosophy ever conceived: **value investing**. It all begins with a simple, yet revolutionary, idea: a stock is not a flickering symbol on a screen, but a fractional ownership in a real business, and it is only worth what that business can produce over its lifetime.

We will start our journey with the patriarchs, **Benjamin Graham and Warren Buffett**, who laid the foundation by teaching us to think like business owners and to demand a "margin of safety" in all that we do. From this solid ground, we will explore the brilliant evolutions and adaptations of their core principles. We'll see how **Peter Lynch** blended value with growth to hunt for "ten-baggers" in plain sight, and how **John Templeton and Seth Klarman** weaponized value investing at the "point of maximum pessimism," turning global crises into generational opportunities.

From there, the philosophy extends into new domains. We will follow **Howard Marks** as he applies these principles to the complex world of credit and distressed debt, and watch as **Michael Burry** takes value investing to its forensic extreme, using it as a tool to uncover not just bargains, but systemic fraud. Finally, we will witness the most aggressive evolution of the discipline with **Carl Icahn and Bill Ackman**, the shareholder activists who prove that when value is trapped, sometimes the only solution is to create the catalyst yourself.

Chapter 3: The Value Investing Continuum: From Cigar Butts to Wonderful Companies (Benjamin Graham & Charlie Munger)

The Two Patriarchs of Value

The history of value investing is not the story of a static doctrine, but of a powerful idea in continuous evolution. It is a philosophy that began as a rigid, quantitative discipline forged in the crucible of the Great Depression and matured into a more nuanced, qualitative art form capable of identifying long-term compounders. This journey can be understood by tracing the intellectual lineage between its two greatest patriarchs: Benjamin Graham, the brilliant teacher who codified its principles, and Warren Buffett, the prodigious student who expanded its boundaries. To study their work is to travel along the "Graham & Buffett Continuum," a path that leads from the statistically cheap to the demonstrably wonderful.

Benjamin Graham, born Benjamin Grossbaum in 1894, was the undisputed father of the discipline. A scholar of immense intellect, he graduated from Columbia University at nineteen and was offered teaching positions in English, mathematics, and philosophy. Financial necessity, however, drove him to Wall Street, where he built a successful career. His defining professional experience was the Wall Street Crash of 1929, an event that ruined his investment firm and instilled in him a profound, lifelong aversion to risk and speculation. In response to the chaos he witnessed,

Graham dedicated himself to creating a rational, systematic framework for investment. He laid out his philosophy in two seminal texts, *Security Analysis* (1934) and *The Intelligent Investor* (1949), in which he drew a hard line in the sand: "An investment operation is one which, upon thorough analysis, promises safety of principal and a satisfactory return. Operations not meeting these requirements are speculative". For Graham, investing was a businesslike endeavor, grounded in facts and figures, designed to protect capital first and seek profits second.[1]

Decades later, a young man in Omaha, Nebraska, discovered Graham's work and found his calling. Warren Buffett, an entrepreneur from childhood who bought his first stock at age eleven, read *The Intelligent Investor* at nineteen and was immediately converted. He has since called it "by far the best book about investing ever written". So profound was Graham's influence that Buffett enrolled at Columbia Business School for the sole purpose of studying under him. After graduating, he went to work for his mentor at the Graham-Newman Corporation, mastering the quantitative techniques of finding undervalued securities. In his early career managing his own investment partnerships, Buffett was a pure Graham disciple, practicing what he would later call "cigar butt" investing—and achieving the highest returns of his legendary career during this period.[2]

Yet, the continuum did not end there. The evolution of value investing thought was spurred by two powerful forces. First, the market itself changed. The deep, statistically obvious bargains that were abundant in the wreckage of the 1930s became scarcer in the more prosperous and researched markets of the postwar era.

Second, and more critically, Buffett faced the problem of scale. The "cigar butt" approach worked well for small sums of money, but as the capital under his management at Berkshire Hathaway swelled into the billions, it became impractical to deploy it in the small, obscure companies that fit Graham's strict criteria.

This practical challenge coincided with the intellectual influence of Buffett's long-time partner, Charlie Munger. It was Munger who convinced Buffett that his focus was misplaced. As Buffett later recounted, Munger's wisdom was simple but profound: "It's far better to buy a wonderful company at a fair price than a fair company at a wonderful price". This was the pivot that defined the modern era of value investing. It was not an abandonment of Graham's core tenets but a sophisticated expansion of them. The definition of "value" was broadened to include intangible assets, durable competitive advantages, and the quality of management. The source of an investor's safety was no longer located solely in the cold, hard numbers of the balance sheet but in the enduring quality and earning power of the business itself.

The Bedrock Principles: Three Mental Models for the Intelligent Investor

Though their methods would diverge, Graham and Buffett were united by a shared set of foundational mental models. These principles form the intellectual bedrock of all value investing, providing the discipline and emotional fortitude necessary to succeed in the often-irrational world of financial markets. They are not complex formulas but timeless ideas that, once mastered, create a virtuous cycle of rational behavior.

THE MARGIN OF SAFETY: THE CORNERSTONE OF INVESTMENT

The single most important concept in value investing, the "three most important words" according to Buffett, is the **Margin of Safety**. In its simplest form, the principle is to purchase a security at a significant discount to its underlying intrinsic value. This gap between price and value serves two critical functions. First, it provides downside protection. Investing is an art, not a science; the future is uncertain, and even the most thorough analysis can be wrong. A margin of safety acts as a buffer, absorbing the impact of human error, bad luck, or unforeseen business challenges. Second, it provides the potential for superior returns. If an investor's valuation is correct, the gap between the low purchase price and the higher intrinsic value will eventually close, generating a profit.

Warren Buffett captured the essence of this principle with his famous bridge analogy:

"When you build a bridge, you insist it can carry 30,000 pounds, but you only drive 10,000 pound trucks across it. And that same principle works in investing".

This simple image is rich with wisdom. It teaches that one must not cut things close. An investor does not try to buy a business worth $83 million for $80 million. The margin must be enormous, so obvious that, as Charlie Munger says, you do not need a calculator to figure it out. The bridge is built to withstand forces far greater than it will likely ever face, and so too must an investment be structured to withstand shocks to the business or the economy. The margin of safety is the ultimate expression of businesslike investing—a systematic effort to maximize the probability of a reasonable return while minimizing the probability of a severe loss.[3]

MR. MARKET: YOUR MANIC-DEPRESSIVE BUSINESS PARTNER

To maintain the discipline required to insist on a margin of safety, an investor must learn to distinguish between the value of a business and its fluctuating stock price. To this end, Benjamin Graham created a brilliant allegory: **Mr. Market**.

Graham asks you to imagine that you are in a business partnership with a man named Mr. Market. Every day, without fail, he shows up and offers to either buy your interest in the business or sell you his, and he names a price. The critical thing to know about your partner is that he is manic-depressive. On some days, gripped by euphoria, he quotes a ridiculously high price. On other days, sunk in despair, he offers to sell his stake for far less than it is worth.[4]

The lesson of the allegory is that you, the intelligent investor, are under no obligation to transact with him. You are free to ignore his daily quotes entirely. His mood should never inform your own view of the business's worth. Instead, you should treat his emotional swings as an opportunity. When he is pessimistic and offers a low price, you can choose to buy. When he is wildly optimistic and quotes a high price, you can choose to sell. Mr. Market is there to *serve* you, not to *guide* you.

This mental model is the investor's primary defense against the psychological pressures of the market. It teaches that volatility is not the same as risk. For the intelligent investor who has done the work to understand a business's value, market downturns are not a cause for panic but an opportunity to buy assets at a discount from a despondent Mr. Market. As Graham famously noted, in the short run, the market is a voting machine, driven by sentiment and popularity contests. In the long run, it is a weighing machine, reflecting the true substance and value of the underlying businesses.

THE CIRCLE OF COMPETENCE: KNOW WHAT YOU OWN

The final bedrock principle serves as the primary guardrail for the entire investment process. Coined by Buffett, the **Circle of Competence** is the simple but vital discipline of investing only in businesses that you can thoroughly understand. An investor does not need to be an expert on every company, or even many. But they must be able to correctly evaluate the select few businesses that fall within their personal area of expertise.[5]

As Buffett has stated, "The size of that circle is not very important; knowing its boundaries, however, is vital". The greatest investment errors are not made by purchasing a mediocre company at a fair price, but by venturing into a field one does not understand and being unable to distinguish a great opportunity from a speculative fad. Operating within one's circle—whether it is defined by one's profession, hobbies, or deep study—confers a powerful advantage. It allows for a more confident and accurate estimation of intrinsic value, which is the necessary prerequisite for all that follows.[6]

These three principles are not independent but are deeply interconnected, forming a virtuous cycle of discipline. The Circle of Competence defines the universe of businesses you are qualified to analyze. Staying within this circle gives you the knowledge to make a rational estimate of a company's intrinsic value. That estimate, in turn, allows you to identify when a sufficient Margin of Safety exists between value and price. Finally, the conviction that comes from understanding the business and knowing you have a margin of safety provides the psychological armor needed to ignore the manic cries of Mr. Market and act only when his folly presents a true opportunity. Without the first step, the others are impossible.

The Foundation: Graham's Quantitative Discipline

Benjamin Graham's approach to investing was a direct reflection of his experience in the Great Depression. He sought a method that was systematic, unemotional, and grounded in the verifiable reality of a company's balance sheet. He wanted to buy assets, not stories, and his methodology was designed to find stocks so cheap that a positive return was nearly a statistical certainty, regardless of the quality of the underlying business.

THE "CIGAR BUTT" PHILOSOPHY: ONE LAST FREE PUFF

Warren Buffett memorably described Graham's core strategy as "cigar butt" investing. The image is vivid: an investor walks down the street and finds a discarded cigar butt, soggy and unpleasant, but with one good puff left in it. He picks it up, takes the final puff for free, and throws it away.[7]

The "cigar butt" is a company that may be in a terrible industry with poor long-term prospects. It might be poorly managed and losing money. However, it is available in the stock market at a price so low that it is worth less than its tangible assets, often less than its net working capital. Graham's insight was that if you buy a stock at a sufficiently deep discount to its liquidation value, you do not need the business to succeed in the long run. You only need "some hiccup in the fortunes of the business" to give you a chance to sell at a decent profit as the price temporarily moves closer to its asset value. That one "puff" is all profit because the purchase was a bargain.

SCREENING FOR CIGAR BUTTS: THE QUANTITATIVE TESTS

To find these cigar butts, Graham employed purely quantitative screens that ignored qualitative factors like management or competitive position. The goal was to find statistical bargains based on asset value.

THE NET CURRENT ASSET VALUE (NCAV) TEST

Graham's most stringent and famous test was to find "net-nets"—companies trading for less than their Net

Current Asset Value. The calculation is a measure of a company's liquidation value in a worst-case scenario.[8]

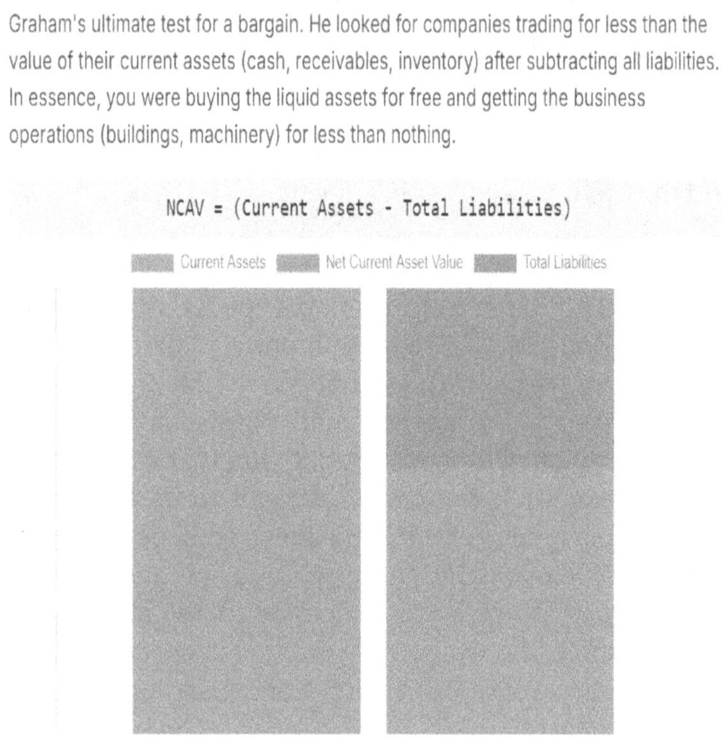

FIGURE 14 - AN INVESTOR BUYING A STOCK FOR LESS THAN ITS NCAV IS EFFECTIVELY GETTING ALL THE COMPANY'S PRODUCTIVE ASSETS FOR FREE, PLUS A MARGIN OF SAFETY EMBEDDED IN THE WORKING CAPITAL.

The formula is:

$$NCAV = \text{Current Assets} - \text{Total Liabilities}$$

This formula is brutally conservative. It takes a company's current assets (cash, receivables, inventory) and subtracts *all* liabilities, both short-term and long-term. In this calculation, all long-term assets—factories, machinery, land, real estate—are valued at zero. An investor buying a stock for less than its NCAV is effectively getting all the company's productive assets for free, plus a margin of safety embedded in the working capital. Graham's rule was to buy stocks at a price of two-thirds of NCAV or less, creating an immense margin of safety.

THE PRICE TO TANGIBLE BOOK VALUE (P/TBV) TEST

A slightly less conservative but still powerful asset-based screen is the Price to Tangible Book Value ratio. This metric compares a company's stock price to the value of its hard, physical assets, stripping out intangibles like goodwill, which can be of questionable value in a liquidation scenario.

The formula is:

$$\text{P/TBV} = \frac{\text{Market Price per Share}}{\text{Tangible Book Value per Share}}$$

where:

$$\text{TBVPS} = \frac{\text{Shares Outstanding}}{\text{Shareholders' Equity} - \text{Goodwill} - \text{Intangible Assets}}$$

A P/TBV ratio below 1.0 indicates that the market values the company at less than the stated value of its tangible assets. For a Grahamite, this suggests the stock is cheap on an asset basis. While not as rigorous as the NCAV test, it provides another quantitative tool for identifying companies whose market price is backed by physical assets.

THE LOGIC OF DIVERSIFICATION: A BASKET OF BUTTS

Graham's strategy is inherently probabilistic. Any individual cigar butt could be a "value trap"—a cheap stock that simply stays cheap or, worse, goes bankrupt before its value can be realized. The investment thesis does not rely on the success of any single company. Instead, it relies on the statistical tendency of a large group of such stocks to, on average, produce excellent returns.[9]

For this reason, Graham insisted on broad diversification. He recommended that an investor using this approach own a portfolio of at least 30 different net-net stocks. This strategy is an explicit defense against ignorance. The investor does not need to know the intimate details of each business or predict its future. The safety and the returns come from the law of large numbers. By owning a large basket, the occasional failure is more than offset by the gains from the rest of the portfolio, allowing the investor to approximate the historically strong returns of the net-net category as a whole.

The Evolution: Buffett's Focus on Quality

As Warren Buffett's capital base grew, he realized the limitations of the cigar butt approach. He could no longer find enough cheap, ugly companies to absorb his funds. Guided by Charlie Munger, he underwent a profound philosophical shift, moving his focus from the balance sheet of today to the earning power of the next several decades. This marked the evolution from buying fair companies at a wonderful price to buying wonderful companies at a fair price.

FROM FAIR COMPANIES TO WONDERFUL COMPANIES

The new approach redefined "value." Value was no longer just a function of assets in place but was primarily derived from a company's ability to generate high and sustainable returns on capital far into the future. This required a new analytical toolkit, one that focused less on what a company *owned* and more on what made it *special*. The key question changed from "What is this company's liquidation value?" to "Does this business possess a durable competitive advantage?".

ECONOMIC MOATS: THE FORTRESS OF PROFITABILITY

Buffett uses the metaphor of an **Economic Moat** to describe the durable competitive advantage that protects a company's profits from competitors, just as a moat protects a castle from invaders. A wide moat allows a company to fend off competition and earn high returns on invested capital for many years. This long-term profitability is the source of a company's intrinsic value. Morningstar has identified five primary sources of economic moats:[10]

1. **Intangible Assets:** These are non-physical assets like brand names, patents, or government licenses that prevent competitors from duplicating a product or service. The brand power of Coca-Cola or the patents held by a pharmaceutical company are powerful moats that allow for premium pricing.[11]

2. **Switching Costs:** When it is expensive, time-consuming, or simply a hassle for a customer to switch from one provider to another, the incumbent company has a moat. These costs can be monetary or psychological and give the company significant pricing power.
3. **Network Effect:** This exists when a product or service becomes more valuable to each user as more people use it. Payment networks like Visa or social media platforms like Meta are classic examples. As the network grows, its competitive position becomes exponentially stronger.
4. **Cost Advantage:** A company that can produce its goods or services at a structurally lower cost than its rivals has a powerful moat. This advantage can stem from economies of scale, superior processes, or access to a unique resource, allowing the company to either undercut competitors on price or earn higher profit margins.[12]
5. **Efficient Scale:** This moat source applies to markets that can only profitably support a small number of competitors. A new entrant knows that its entry would depress industry returns for everyone, including itself, which deters competition. Industries like railroads or utilities often benefit from efficient scale.

THE INDISPENSABLE INGREDIENT: ASSESSING MANAGEMENT QUALITY

If an investor plans to own a business for decades, the people making decisions at the top become critically important. Graham's approach largely ignored management, as the margin of safety was in the assets. For Buffett, assessing management quality is a cornerstone of the analysis. He seeks to partner with managers who exhibit three key characteristics:

1. **Integrity and Honesty:** This is the non-negotiable starting point. Buffett looks for managers who are candid, transparent, and who place the company's reputation above all else. He famously told his managers that if they lose money for the firm, he will be understanding, but if they "lose a shred of reputation for the firm, [he] will be ruthless". Trust is paramount.[13]
2. **Rational Capital Allocation:** The primary job of a CEO is to allocate the company's capital effectively. A great manager consistently reinvests company profits into projects that generate high rates of return. Buffett scrutinizes a management team's track record of capital allocation, looking for a history of high and stable Return on Equity (ROE) and a demonstrated ability to use retained earnings to create more than a dollar of market value for every dollar retained.[14]
3. **Shareholder-Orientation:** Excellent managers think like owners, not employees. They treat shareholders' money as their own. This mindset is revealed in their communications (are they candid about problems?), their compensation (is it tied to long-term performance?), and their actions (do they repurchase shares when they are undervalued and avoid value-destroying acquisitions?).

THE LOGIC OF CONCENTRATION: A PORTFOLIO OF FORTRESSES

The deep, qualitative analysis required to identify a wonderful company with a wide moat and excellent management is an intensive, time-consuming process. It is impossible to develop this level of understanding for hundreds of companies. Therefore, unlike Graham's strategy of broad diversification, the Buffett approach leads to a more concentrated portfolio. When an investor has high conviction in a handful of truly outstanding businesses purchased at fair prices, diversification becomes a hindrance rather than a help. The goal is not to own a basket of average ideas but to make significant, long-term investments in a few exceptional ones.

Case Study: Analyzing Coca-Cola (circa 1988)

To see the value investing continuum in action, there is no better example than Warren Buffett's landmark investment in The Coca-Cola Company (KO) in 1988. By applying both the Graham and Buffett lenses to the company as it existed at that time, we can see precisely why the evolution in thought was so critical.

The business context of 1988 is key. Coca-Cola was just a few years removed from its infamous "New Coke" marketing blunder of 1985. Under the dynamic leadership of CEO Roberto Goizueta, the company had not only reversed that mistake but had used the experience to re-energize its brand. Goizueta was refocusing the company on its high-return core beverage business, having divested its ill-fitting

Columbia Pictures subsidiary in 1987. The company was also aggressively repurchasing its own shares, signaling management's confidence in the future.[15]

THE GRAHAM SCREEN: A CLEAR FAILURE

A strict follower of Benjamin Graham's quantitative discipline would not have given Coca-Cola a second glance in 1988. The analysis would have been swift and decisive.

At the end of 1988, Coca-Cola's market capitalization was approximately $16.3 billion. According to its financial statements from the end of 1987 (the last full year of data available to an investor in early 1988), the company's total shareholders' equity, or book value, was approximately $3.2 billion. This means the company was trading at a Price-to-Book (P/B) ratio of over 5. The Price-to-Tangible-Book-Value (P/TBV) ratio was even higher, as the company's value was not in its physical plants but in its brand—an intangible asset with a book value of zero.[16]

Coca-Cola is a massive, profitable company. Its market price is far above its net current asset value or even its tangible book value. For a deep value investor like Graham, it's an immediate and obvious "pass". There is no quantitative margin of safety in the assets.

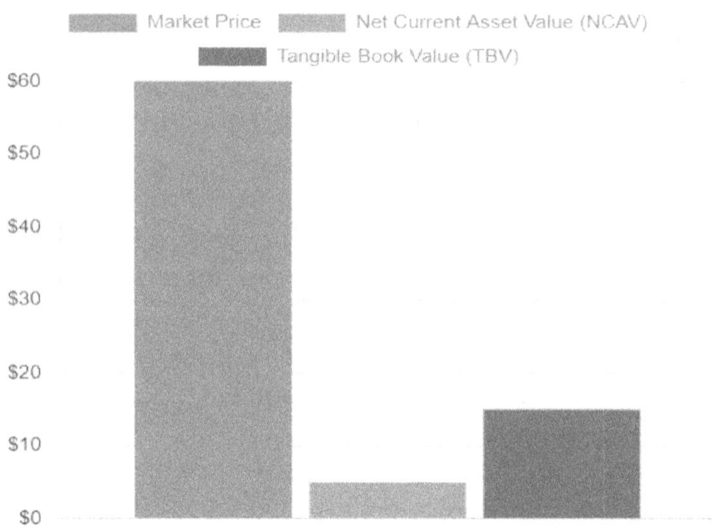

FIGURE 15 - FOR A DEEP VALUE INVESTOR LIKE GRAHAM, COCA-COLA IS AN IMMEDIATE AND OBVIOUS "PASS".

For a Grahamite looking to buy companies for less than their tangible book value or, better yet, their net current asset value, Coca-Cola was the polar opposite of an attractive investment. It was an asset-light business whose market price was many multiples of what its physical assets were worth. The stock would have been immediately discarded as prohibitively expensive. There was no cigar butt to be found.

THE BUFFETT SCREEN: A RESOUNDING SUCCESS

Viewed through the evolved lens of quality, however, Coca-Cola appeared to be one of the finest businesses in the world, available at a reasonable price.

ECONOMIC MOAT ANALYSIS

Coca-Cola's primary economic moat was its **Intangible Asset**: one of the most powerful and recognized brands in human history. The "New Coke" fiasco, far from being a disaster, had paradoxically proven the moat's impregnable strength. When the company changed its 99-year-old formula, the public outcry was immediate and overwhelming, with thousands of protest calls flooding the company's headquarters daily. This revealed a deep, emotional attachment to the brand that no competitor could ever hope to replicate. This brand loyalty gave Coca-Cola immense pricing power; it could consistently raise prices without losing customers, a key trait of a wonderful business. Its global distribution system, reaching over 200 countries, created another formidable barrier to entry.

MANAGEMENT QUALITY ANALYSIS

In Roberto Goizueta, Coca-Cola had a manager of extraordinary talent and integrity. A Cuban immigrant who rose through the company's technical ranks, Goizueta was a brilliant strategist and a rational capital allocator. He took a company that had been drifting and radically refocused it on its core mission: increasing shareholder value. His decision to divest the volatile Columbia Pictures movie studio and concentrate on the high-margin, high-return beverage business was a masterstroke of capital allocation. He was deeply shareholder-oriented, using the company's prodigious cash flow to repurchase stock and consistently increase dividends. During his 16-year tenure as CEO, he increased the market value of Coca-Cola from $4 billion to $145 billion. He was precisely the kind of honest, intelligent, and passionate leader Buffett seeks to partner with.[17]

VALUATION AND THE FINAL DECISION

Buffett's analysis concluded that Coca-Cola was a wonderful business, but the final step was to determine if it was available at a fair price with a sufficient margin of safety.

At the time, Coca-Cola was trading at a Price-to-Earnings (P/E) ratio of around 15 to 18, which was not statistically cheap by the standards of the day. However, its business performance was stellar, with a Return on Equity (ROE) of 27% in 1987 and a demonstrated ability to grow earnings at a high rate.[18]

A conservative discounted cash flow (DCF) valuation, using the financial data from 1987, can provide a reasonable estimate of intrinsic value. Assuming modest revenue growth of around 7-8% and the company's high and stable operating margins, the analysis yields an intrinsic value in the range of $47 to $51 per share. Buffett began accumulating his stake in 1988 at an average price of around $41 to $42 per share.[19]

Comparing his purchase price to the estimated intrinsic value reveals a margin of safety of approximately 15-

20%. This was not the massive 50% discount a Grahamite would demand from the balance sheet, but it was a sufficient buffer. The safety here did not come from tangible assets, but from the high degree of certainty that Coca-Cola's powerful moat and brilliant management would continue to generate growing streams of cash flow far into the future.

The discipline of this final step is absolute. To illustrate, had the analysis yielded an intrinsic value of $47 per share, but Mr. Market, in a state of euphoria, was offering the stock at $50, the decision for a true value investor would be clear and unwavering: **NO-TRADE.** Even for the most wonderful company in the world, the principle cannot be violated. Price is what you pay; value is what you get. Without a margin of safety, there is no investment.

Key Takeaways: The Value Investor's Creed

The journey along the value investing continuum, from Graham's cigar butts to Buffett's wonderful companies, offers a set of timeless lessons for any intelligent investor. These principles form a creed—a declaration of the beliefs that guide rational, businesslike investing.

- An investment must be based on thorough analysis that promises safety of principal and an adequate return; all else is speculation.
- The Margin of Safety—buying a security for significantly less than its intrinsic value—is the central concept of investing and your greatest protection against error.

- Mr. Market is your servant, not your guide. Market fluctuations should be viewed as opportunities to exploit, not as directives to follow.
- You must operate strictly within your Circle of Competence. Knowing the boundaries of what you understand is more important than having a large circle.
- Value can be found in different forms: in the tangible assets of an unloved company (Graham) or in the durable competitive advantages and future earning power of a great one (Buffett).
- For any investment held for the long term, the quality, integrity, and capital allocation skill of management are of paramount importance.
- Price is what you pay; value is what you get. The goal of the intelligent investor is to never confuse the two and to never pay more than a fair price for even the highest quality business.

The two philosophies, while different in application, are branches of the same intellectual tree. The following table crystallizes their defining characteristics, providing a final map of the value investing continuum.

Attribute	Benjamin Graham (The Cigar Butt)	Warren Buffett (The Wonderful Company)
Investment Thesis	Buy fair companies at a wonderful price.	Buy wonderful companies at a fair price.

Attribute	Benjamin Graham (The Cigar Butt)	Warren Buffett (The Wonderful Company)
Source of Value	Tangible assets on the balance sheet (liquidation value).	Durable competitive advantage ("Economic Moat") and future earning power.
Time Horizon	Short-term, until the price reflects asset value.	Very long-term, ideally "forever."
Key Metrics	Price/Net Current Asset Value (P/NCAV), Price/Tangible Book Value (P/TBV).	Return on Equity (ROE), Return on Invested Capital (ROIC), Free Cash Flow.
Management Role	Largely irrelevant; the numbers provide the safety.	Critically important; seeks integrity, rationality, and shareholder-focus.
Diversification	Essential. A broad portfolio (30+) is required to mitigate individual failures.	Not essential. Concentration in a few high-conviction ideas is preferred.

Attribute	Benjamin Graham (The Cigar Butt)	Warren Buffett (The Wonderful Company)
Primary Risk	"Value trap" - a cheap stock that stays cheap or goes bankrupt.	Paying too high a price for a quality business; moat erosion.
Ideal Outcome	A quick, profitable sale as the market recognizes the asset mispricing.	Decades of tax-efficient compounding of capital at a high rate.

Chapter 4: The GARP Framework (Peter Lynch)

One Up on Wall Street: A Common-Sense Guide to Finding "Ten-Baggers"

THE AMATEUR'S ADVANTAGE: A LEGEND'S LEGACY

On Wall Street, legends are forged in the crucible of market chaos, and few are more legendary than Peter Lynch. From 1977 to 1990, Lynch was the maestro behind the Fidelity Magellan Fund, conducting a 13-year symphony of performance that remains the envy of the financial world. When he took the helm, Magellan was an obscure fund with a mere $18 million in assets. By the time he retired at the young age of 46, it had swelled to a colossal $14 billion, holding over 1,000 different stocks and making it the largest mutual fund on the planet.

The numbers behind this growth are staggering. Over his tenure, Lynch delivered an average annual return of 29.2%, a figure that didn't just beat the market; it consistently lapped it. To put that in perspective, he more than doubled the S&P 500's return during the same period. An investment of $1,000 in Magellan on his first day would have been worth $28,000 on his last.

But the most powerful part of Lynch's story isn't just his performance; it's his core belief. He was convinced, and he spent his career proving that the average person has a built-in advantage over the buttoned-up professionals on Wall Street. This "amateur's edge," as he called it, doesn't come from complex financial models or secret sources. It comes from something you already possess:

your "local knowledge." It's the insight you gain from your job, your hobbies, and your everyday trips to the shopping mall. You, as a consumer and a professional, can often spot a great business long before it appears on Wall Street's radar.

However, there is a profound and cautionary tale embedded in the Magellan Fund's success. Despite its world-beating returns, studies showed that the average investor in the fund actually *lost money*. How is this possible? The answer lies not in strategy, but in psychology. Investors, driven by headlines and herd mentality, would pour money into the fund *after* a period of great performance, buying high. Then, when the market inevitably hit a rough patch, they would panic and sell, locking in their losses. They bought on greed and sold on fear.

This paradox reveals the most important lesson Lynch has to teach us: a winning strategy is useless without the right temperament. As he famously said, "Everyone has the brainpower to make money in stocks. Not everyone has the stomach". The framework that follows is not just a set of rules for picking stocks; it is a discipline for managing your own emotions, for staying the course, and for truly capitalizing on the amateur's advantage.

THE LYNCH TRINITY: A THREE-PILLAR PHILOSOPHY

Peter Lynch's investment philosophy can be thought of as a sturdy, three-legged stool. Each leg is a core principle, and together they create a stable and balanced platform for building wealth. Remove any one leg, and the entire structure becomes wobbly and unreliable.

PILLAR 1: "INVEST IN WHAT YOU KNOW"

This is Lynch's most famous mantra, but it's also his most misunderstood. It is not a license to buy stock in your favorite coffee shop just because you like their lattes. It is a directive to use your personal, real-world experience as the *starting point* for serious investigation. If you work in the healthcare industry, you have a head start in understanding a new medical device company. If you're a software developer, you can more easily grasp the competitive advantage of a new enterprise software firm.

This starting point leads to a process Lynch called "scuttlebutt." Popularized by another great investor, Philip Fisher, scuttlebutt is the on-the-ground, investigative work of gathering qualitative intelligence that you'll never find in an annual report. It's about kicking the tires of a business. It means visiting the stores to see if they're crowded, talking to customers to see if they love the product, and even asking the management of one company which competitor they fear the most. This process provides an informational edge because it can uncover unique insights—a superior product, declining customer satisfaction, a brilliant new strategy—that are not yet reflected in the stock price. While the professionals are buried in spreadsheets in a New York skyscraper, you can be gathering the real story on Main Street.

PILLAR 2: GROWTH AT A REASONABLE PRICE (GARP)

Lynch was the great synthesizer, blending two investment philosophies that are often seen as opposites: growth investing and value investing. Growth investors chase companies with explosive earnings, often paying any price to get in on the action. Value investors hunt for bargains, buying downtrodden companies that are trading for less than they are worth. Lynch saw the wisdom in both and the folly in their extremes.

His solution was GARP: Growth at a Reasonable Price. The goal is to find companies with strong, sustainable growth prospects, but to avoid overpaying for them. To achieve this, he popularized a simple but powerful tool: the Price-to-Earnings-Growth (PEG) ratio. It brilliantly connects a company's valuation (its P/E ratio) to its rate of growth. The formula is simple:

$$PEG\ Ratio = \frac{\text{P/E Ratio}}{\text{Annual EPS Growth Rate}}$$

Lynch's rule of thumb was just as simple. A company is fairly priced when its P/E ratio is equal to its growth rate, resulting in a PEG ratio of 1.0.19 A stock is even more attractive when its PEG ratio is below 1.0; a PEG of 0.5, for instance, is a wonderful bargain. A PEG ratio well above 1.0 is a red flag, suggesting that the stock's price has gotten far ahead of its growth prospects. For more mature companies that pay a dividend, he would sometimes use a modified version, now often called the PEGY ratio, which adds the dividend yield to the growth rate in the denominator, giving credit for the total return a company provides to shareholders.

PILLAR 3: FLEXIBILITY AND PRAGMATISM

The final pillar of Lynch's philosophy is the rejection of dogma. He was not a "growth investor" or a "value investor"; he was a successful investor. His portfolio was a testament to this pragmatism. At Magellan, he owned everything from banks (Fannie Mae) and automakers (Ford, Volvo) to retailers (The Gap) and tobacco companies (Philip Morris). He was not confined to a single style or industry.

Lynch believed that the investment approach must be adapted to the company being analyzed. A fast-growing tech startup cannot be judged by the same yardstick as a mature electric utility. Each company has a different "story," and understanding that story is the key to knowing what to look for and what to expect. This flexible mindset is what allowed him to find opportunities in every corner of the market. It is also what led him to develop his most powerful organizational tool for the individual investor: the six stock categories.

THE SIX CATEGORIES: THE INVESTOR'S FIELD GUIDE

Before you look at a single number on a balance sheet, before you calculate a P/E ratio, and before you formulate your "two-minute drill," you must perform one crucial first step: place the company into one of six categories. This act of classification is the foundation of the entire Lynch framework. It tells you what kind of company you're dealing with, sets your expectations for its performance, and focuses your research on the factors that truly matter. Think of this as your investor's field guide to the corporate jungle.

TABLE 1 - INVESTORS SIX CATEGORIES.

Category	Typical Annual Earnings Growth	Key Characteristics	Prime Example
Slow Growers	2-5%	Mature, large companies; generous, regular dividends. Often former Fast Growers.	Electrical Utilities (e.g., Southern Co.)
Stalwarts	10-12%	Large, well-known, quality companies; offer protection in recessions.	Coca-Cola (KO), Procter & Gamble (PG)
Fast Growers	20-25%+	Small, aggressive, new enterprises; the land of the "ten-baggers."	Walmart (in its early days)
Cyclicals	Varies with economy	Sales and profits rise and fall in predictable cycles; timing is everything.	Ford (F), Delta Air Lines (DAL)

Category	Typical Annual Earnings Growth	Key Characteristics	Prime Example
Turnarounds	N/A (recovering)	Battered-down companies with potential to recover; performance is uncorrelated to the broad market.	Chrysler (in the 1980s)
Asset Plays	N/A	Company has valuable assets (e.g., real estate, cash, patents) overlooked by the market.	Pebble Beach, IBM (patents)

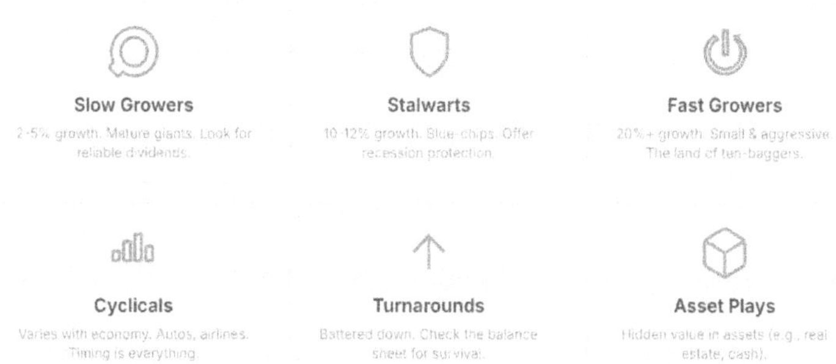

FIGURE 16 - BEFORE ANY ANALYSIS, PLACE THE COMPANY INTO ONE OF SIX CATEGORIES. THIS SETS YOUR EXPECTATIONS AND FOCUSES YOUR RESEARCH.

Slow Growers are the large, aging enterprises of the corporate world. They were once fast growers, but their industry has matured, and now their earnings grow only slightly faster than the overall economy, typically in the 2-5% range. You won't get rich owning these, but that's not their purpose. Their primary attraction is a generous and reliable dividend, which provides a steady income stream and acts as a price support during market downturns. When analyzing a Slow Grower, the key is to check the dividend's safety by looking at the payout ratio (the percentage of earnings paid out as dividends). A low payout ratio means there is a cushion if earnings dip. The biggest risk is that management, desperate to restart growth, engages in a foolish acquisition, a practice Lynch colorfully termed "diworseification".

Stalwarts are the blue-chip, multi-billion-dollar companies that form the backbone of many portfolios, like Coca-Cola or Procter & Gamble. They grow faster than Slow Growers, with annual earnings growth in the 10-12% range. While they are unlikely to be ten-baggers, a 30-50% return over one or two years is an excellent outcome, at which point Lynch would often sell and rotate into another stalwart that hadn't yet moved. Their great virtue is providing protection during recessions; people still buy toothpaste and soda in a downturn. When looking at a Stalwart, check its P/E ratio to make sure you aren't overpaying for its perceived safety and examine how it has performed in past recessions.

Fast Growers were Lynch's favorite hunting ground. These are small, aggressive, and often young companies growing earnings at a blistering pace of 20-25% per year or more. This is where you find the life-changing "ten-baggers" that can make an entire investment career. Lynch particularly loved fast growers in slow-growth industries, where a dominant company like Walmart could expand for years without attracting hordes of competitors. The key is to find one that is already profitable and has a strong balance sheet, ensuring it can finance its own expansion. The PEG ratio is your essential tool here to avoid overpaying. The risks are high: if growth slows even slightly, the stock can get crushed, and their rapid success inevitably attracts competition.

Cyclicals are companies whose sales and profits rise and fall with the broader economic cycle. Think of automakers, airlines, steel companies, and chemical producers. When the economy is booming, these stocks soar. When a recession hits, they get hammered. Timing, therefore, is everything. The biggest mistake an investor can make is to confuse a cyclical with a stalwart and buy it after a long run of prosperity, just as the cycle is about to turn down. The best time to buy cyclicals is at the end of a recession, when public sentiment is at its bleakest and the business is showing the first signs of revival. A key indicator to watch is inventory levels; when inventories that have been building up finally start to shrink, it's a powerful buy signal. Lynch's warning is stark: "Cyclicals are like blackjack: stay in the game too long and it's bound to take back all your profit".

Turnarounds are companies that have been beaten, battered, and left for dead by Wall Street. They may be on the verge of bankruptcy, but they have a chance to recover. A great example was Chrysler in the 1980s, which Lynch invested in successfully. Because they are so hated, the upside can be explosive if they succeed.

Their performance is often completely uncorrelated with the general market, making them a good diversifier. When analyzing a turnaround, the balance sheet is paramount. Does the company have enough cash to survive the next 12-24 months? Is there a clear, credible plan to restore profitability, such as cutting costs or selling off a money-losing division?. The biggest risk is obvious: many turnarounds never turn, and the company goes bankrupt, wiping out your entire investment. For this reason, Lynch advised waiting for concrete evidence of a recovery before buying, not just investing on hope.

Asset Plays are companies that are sitting on a valuable asset that the market has completely overlooked. This is where your "local knowledge" can be a huge advantage. The hidden asset could be anything: valuable real estate, a portfolio of patents, a pile of cash, or even a tax-loss carryforward that can shield future profits. The key is to know the asset, have a good idea of its true worth, and have the patience to wait for that value to be recognized. You must also check the company's debt, because a heavy debt load can cancel out the value of the hidden asset. The risk with asset plays is that without a catalyst—like a takeover bid or an activist investor pushing for change—you could be waiting for years for the market to realize its mistake.

THE LYNCH PLAYBOOK: A STEP-BY-STEP ANALYSIS

With the company properly categorized, you are ready to execute the three-step playbook. This process transforms the broad philosophy into a concrete, repeatable method for making investment decisions.

The 3-Step Playbook

1. **The Story (Two-Minute Drill)**
   Explain the investment case, success factors, and pitfalls simply and concisely.

2. **The Numbers (GARP Check)**
   Verify the story with data. Check valuation (PEG), balance sheet strength, and inventory levels.

3. **The Decision**
   Synthesize. Do the numbers support the narrative? If yes, you may have a winner. If no, walk away.

FIGURE 17 - THE 3-STEP PLAYBOOK

STEP 1: THE STORY - THE TWO-MINUTE DRILL

Before you part with a single dollar, you must be able to articulate the investment case clearly and concisely. Lynch called this the "two-minute drill". It's a simple monologue you should be able to deliver that covers three essential questions 12:

1. **Why am I interested in this company?** This is the qualitative story. What is the product? Why is it great? What is its competitive advantage?
2. **What has to happen for the company to succeed?** These are the key drivers of the story. Does it need to expand into new markets? Launch a new product? Continue gaining market share?

3. **What are the pitfalls that stand in its path?** This is the risk analysis. What could go wrong? A recession? New competition? A change in technology?

If you can't explain the story to a 10-year-old in two minutes, you probably don't understand the business well enough to own the stock. This simple exercise forces clarity, helps you avoid overly complex businesses, and serves as the foundation for your entire analysis.

STEP 2: THE NUMBERS - THE GARP CHECK

A good story is a wonderful start, but it must be backed by solid numbers. This is where you verify the qualitative narrative with quantitative analysis.

- **The PEG Ratio Check:** The first and most important check is valuation. Is the company's growth available at a reasonable price? Calculate the PEG ratio. As a rule, a PEG below 1.0 is attractive, while a PEG below 0.5 is a potential bargain. A PEG well above 1.0 is a warning sign that you might be paying too much for the story.

PEG Ratio =

P/E Ratio ÷ Growth Rate

FIGURE 18 - LYNCH'S KEY TOOL: THE PEG RATIO

- **The Balance Sheet Check:** Next, check for financial strength. Lynch famously warned, "The biggest losses in stocks come from companies with poor balance sheets". The key metric here is the **Debt-to-Equity Ratio**. You want to see that the company has more equity than debt. While acceptable levels vary by industry, a good general rule is to look for a ratio below 0.8 (or 80%), and ideally below 0.5 (or 50%). A company with little or no debt cannot go bankrupt.
- **The Inventory Check:** For any company that makes or sells a physical product, this is a critical, often overlooked, red flag. You must check if inventories are growing faster than sales. If a company's inventory line on the balance sheet is growing at 20% while its sales are only growing at 10%, it's a sign that products are piling up in warehouses and demand may be weakening.

STEP 3: THE DECISION

The final step is to synthesize the story and the numbers. Does the quantitative evidence from Step 2 support the compelling narrative from Step 1?

If you have a great story about a fast-growing company, and the GARP check reveals a PEG ratio of 0.6 and a debt-to-equity ratio of 0.2, you may have found a winner. If, however, the story is exciting but the PEG is 2.5 and debt is soaring, the numbers are telling you to walk away.

This entire process is geared toward finding what Lynch called "ten-baggers"—stocks that go up ten times their original purchase price. Finding just one or two of these in a lifetime can make all the difference. This requires not only doing the homework but also having the patience and conviction to hold on to your big winners. Too many investors get excited by a 50% gain and sell, a practice Lynch compared to "watering the weeds and cutting the flowers". The playbook is designed to give you the confidence to let your flowers grow.

CASE STUDY: ANALYZING THE HOME DEPOT (HD)

Let's put the playbook into action with a real-world example: The Home Depot (HD), a company familiar to millions.

STEP 0: CLASSIFICATION

The first step is always to categorize the company. The Home Depot is the world's largest home improvement retailer, a corporate behemoth with a market capitalization exceeding $400 billion and annual sales of over $150 billion. Looking at its earnings, its five-year average annual EPS growth rate is approximately 7.8%. Given its massive size and a growth rate that falls below the 10-12% threshold, we can confidently classify The Home Depot as a

Stalwart. This immediately sets our expectations: we are looking for a reliable, steady performer that can provide some recession protection, not an explosive ten-bagger.

STEP 1: THE STORY - THE TWO-MINUTE DRILL FOR HD

"I'm interested in The Home Depot because it's a dominant, blue-chip leader in the home improvement industry, a business I understand as a homeowner. For the company to succeed, it needs to continue capitalizing on stable housing market trends and consistent consumer spending on home maintenance, repair, and renovation. Its powerful brand and vast network of over 2,300 stores create a formidable competitive moat. The primary pitfalls would be a severe housing market collapse, a deep recession that crushes consumer discretionary spending, or losing significant market share to its main competitor, Lowe's."

STEP 2: THE NUMBERS - THE GARP CHECK FOR HD

The story is solid and easy to understand. Now, let's see if the numbers support the investment case.

- **PEG Ratio Check:**
    - The Home Depot's Price-to-Earnings (P/E) Ratio is approximately **28.7**.
    - Its five-year average annual EPS growth rate is **7.8%**.
    - We can now calculate the PEG Ratio:

$$PEG\ Ratio = \frac{28.7}{7.8} \approx 3.68$$

- **Analysis:** A PEG ratio of 3.68 is dramatically higher than Lynch's "fair value" target of 1.0. This is a major warning sign, suggesting the stock is priced for a level of growth that far exceeds what it has delivered historically.

- **Balance Sheet Check:**
    - The Home Depot's Debt-to-Equity ratio is approximately **5.75** (or 575%).
    - **Analysis:** This is an exceptionally high level of debt, far exceeding Lynch's preferred maximum of 0.8. For every dollar of equity, the company has $5.75 of debt. While mature retail companies often use leverage, this amount of debt would be a significant red flag for a Lynch-style investor, as it reduces the company's financial flexibility and increases risk during a downturn.

STEP 3: THE DECISION

Now we synthesize. The Home Depot presents a classic dilemma: it's a wonderful business, but is it a good investment at this price?

- **Synthesis:** The story is compelling. The Home Depot is a high-quality Stalwart with a dominant market position. However, the GARP check has uncovered two serious problems. First, the valuation is extremely high, with a PEG ratio of 3.68 suggesting the stock is priced for perfection. Second, the balance sheet is loaded with debt, carrying a much higher risk profile than Lynch would find acceptable.
- **Conclusion:** Based on the Peter Lynch playbook, the decision is clear: **AVOID (at the current price)**. While The Home Depot is an excellent company, the stock is simply too expensive and too leveraged to offer the combination of growth,

value, and safety that the GARP strategy demands.

KEY TAKEAWAYS: LYNCH'S RULES TO INVEST BY

Peter Lynch's wisdom is timeless because it is grounded in common sense, discipline, and a deep respect for the intelligence of the individual investor. As you begin your own journey, keep these essential rules close at hand. They are your compass for navigating the market and finding your own ten-baggers.

- Your edge is not from Wall Street; it's **something you already have.** Use your knowledge from your job and your life to find great companies before the professionals do.
- **Behind every stock is a company. Find out what** it's doing. Don't invest in a stock ticker; invest in a business.
- Never invest in any idea you can't illustrate with **a crayon.** If you can't explain the business simply, you don't understand it well enough to own it.
- **Owning stocks is like having children**—don't **get involved with more than you can handle.** A part-time stock-picker only has time to follow 8-12 companies at most.
- **Never invest in a company without understanding its finances.** The biggest losses come from companies with poor balance sheets.
- **In the stock market, the most important organ** is the stomach. It's not the brain. You need the emotional fortitude to hold on during downturns and not panic-sell.

- **A stock market decline is as routine as a January blizzard in Colorado.** If you are prepared, it can't hurt you. A decline is a great opportunity to buy bargains.
- **Know what you own, and know why you own it.** "This baby is a cinch to go up" doesn't count as a reason.
- **It only takes a handful of big winners to make a lifetime of investing worthwhile.** Don't cut your flowers (winners) and water your weeds (losers).
- **The person that turns over the most rocks wins the game.** Investing is work, but it's fun and exciting. The more companies you investigate, the more opportunities you'll find.

Chapter 5: The Contrarian Framework (John Templeton & Seth Klarman)

The Two Titans of Contrarianism

In the grand pantheon of investment luminaries, few have carved out legacies as distinct yet philosophically aligned as Sir John Templeton and Seth Klarman. They stand as the twin pillars of modern contrarianism, one looking outward to the world with a telescope, the other peering inward at a balance sheet with a microscope. To study their methods is to receive a masterclass in the art of profiting from pessimism, tempered by the science of rigorous risk control.

Sir John Templeton was the quintessential global pioneer. Born in rural Tennessee, his intellect carried him from Yale to Oxford as a Rhodes Scholar, but his vision always extended far beyond the confines of Wall Street or even the United States. Long before "global investing" became a common phrase, Templeton saw a world of opportunity in markets that his American peers dismissed as too foreign, too risky, or too broken. He was a deeply spiritual man whose philanthropic endeavors were as legendary as his financial acumen, and this informed his patient, humble, and optimistic long-term view of human progress. His defining genius was in identifying macro-level dislocations—entire countries or industries gripped by fear—and investing with the serene confidence that crises are, by their nature, temporary.[20]

Seth Klarman, by contrast, is the modern torchbearer of Benjamin Graham's deep value discipline. An alumnus of Cornell and Harvard Business School, Klarman founded the Baupost Group in 1982 and authored the now-legendary (and nearly unobtainable) book, *Margin of Safety: Risk-Averse Value Investing Strategies for the Thoughtful Investor*. His focus is not on the grand sweep of history but on the forensic, bottom-up analysis of specific, often complex and distressed situations where risk can be meticulously calculated and controlled. He operates from a position of profound intellectual humility, assuming that the future is unknowable and that the only reliable defense against error and bad luck is to buy an asset for far less than it is worth.[21]

This chapter's purpose is to fuse these two powerful philosophies into a single, cohesive investment process. We will merge Templeton's top-down "Hunt" for pessimism across the globe with Klarman's bottom-up "Kill," a disciplined execution grounded in a non-negotiable margin of safety. This synthesis addresses a common failing among investors. Macro strategists often identify the correct theme but select the wrong, over-leveraged, or poorly managed asset. Conversely, deep-value specialists can find a statistically cheap security within a market that is destined for permanent economic impairment.

The framework presented here provides a solution. It marries Templeton's long-term optimism—the conviction that moments of maximum pessimism are temporary and that human enterprise ultimately prevails—with Klarman's profound short-term pessimism—the assumption that any single analysis can be wrong and that a discount is the only true protection. This creates the ideal contrarian temperament: the "pessimistic optimist." Templeton's philosophy tells us *where* to hunt for opportunity; Klarman's discipline tells us *how* to hunt with prudence and care.

The Guiding Principles: The Contrarian's Mindset

Before delving into the mechanics of the process, one must first adopt the mindset that underpins it. Contrarianism is not merely the act of doing the opposite of the crowd; it is the disciplined practice of thinking independently, grounded in a set of core principles that provide fortitude when the world is gripped by fear and skepticism when it is euphoric.

THE POINT OF MAXIMUM PESSIMISM: TEMPLETON'S FORTITUDE IN 1939[22]

The foundational parable for this entire framework occurred in 1939. The world stood on the precipice of chaos. Hitler had just invaded Poland, plunging Europe into a war of unknown duration and consequence. Global markets were paralyzed with fear. Headlines screamed of disaster, and the prevailing sentiment was that capital preservation was the only rational goal. This was the very definition of "blood in the streets."

In this environment, a 27-year-old John Templeton saw not just risk, but a generational opportunity. He reasoned that a world war, while tragic, would inevitably ignite America's dormant industrial capacity, pulling the economy from its decade-long slump. This singular, contrarian insight led him to borrow $10,000—a considerable sum at the time—and place an order of breathtaking audacity. He instructed his broker to buy

$100 worth of every single stock listed on the New York and American Stock Exchanges that was trading for less than $1 per share.[23]

The list comprised 104 companies, of which 37 were already in bankruptcy. It was a portfolio of the despised, the broken, and the forgotten. Yet, Templeton's thesis proved prescient. As the war effort ramped up, the tide of industrial production lifted nearly all boats, even the leakiest ones. He held the portfolio for an average of four years, and by the time he sold, he had earned a profit on 100 of the 104 companies. The initial $10,000 investment had grown to roughly $40,000 to $50,000, a return of 400-500% that launched his legendary career.

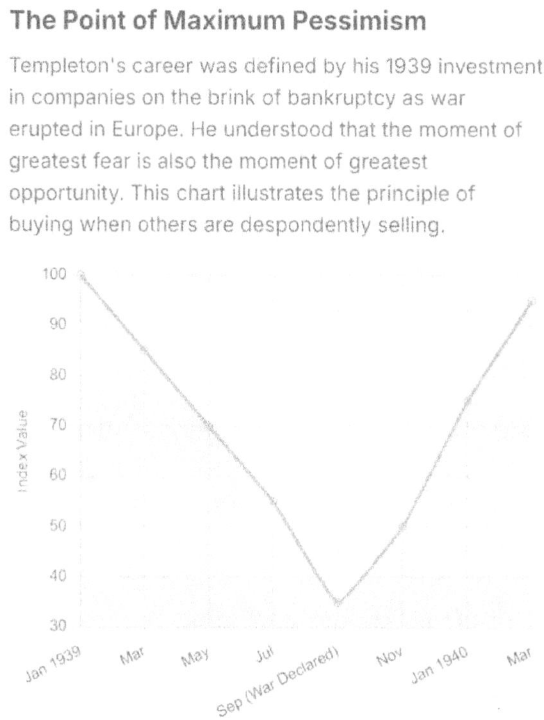

FIGURE 19 - THE TIME OF MAXIMUM PESSIMISM IS THE BEST TIME TO BUY, AND THE TIME OF MAXIMUM OPTIMISM IS THE BEST TIME TO SELL.

The lesson from 1939 is not to gamble on penny stocks. It is to recognize that the market is a manic-depressive beast that overreacts to both good and bad news. At the point of maximum pessimism, it prices in a worst-case scenario as a certainty, offering assets at a fraction of their long-term worth to anyone with the fortitude to act. As Templeton famously summarized: "Bull markets are born on pessimism, grow on skepticism, mature on optimism, and die on euphoria. The time of maximum pessimism is the best time to buy, and the time of maximum optimism is the best time to sell".

THE MARGIN OF SAFETY: KLARMAN'S DEFENSE AGAINST AN UNKNOWABLE FUTURE

While Templeton's grand strategic bet identified the right pond in which to fish, it is Seth Klarman who provides the tools to ensure one does not come home with a boot. The indispensable tool, inherited from his intellectual forefather Benjamin Graham, is the margin of safety.[24]

At its core, the margin of safety is an admission of humility. It is the bedrock principle for investing in a world where the future is unpredictable, information is always incomplete, and we ourselves are fallible, emotional beings prone to analytical error. It is a protective buffer against bad luck, unforeseen events, and the extreme volatility that characterizes markets.[25]

Mathematically, the margin of safety is the significant discount between the price paid for a security and its conservatively estimated intrinsic value. As Graham stated, "The margin of safety is always dependent on the price paid. For any security, it will be large at one price, small at some higher price, nonexistent at some still higher price". The primary goal is not to chase spectacular gains, but to relentlessly focus on the avoidance of permanent capital loss. This is not merely a defensive posture; it is the surest path to long-term wealth creation. A 50% loss requires a 100% gain just to return to the starting point, a mathematical reality that makes loss avoidance paramount. By purchasing assets at a substantial discount, the investor builds in room to be wrong and still achieve a satisfactory result.

CASH AS AN OFFENSIVE WEAPON: THE POWER OF PATIENT OPPORTUNISM

Conventional wisdom treats cash as a drag on performance, a zero-yield asset constantly eroded by inflation. For the contrarian, this view is dangerously shortsighted. Both Templeton and Klarman understood that in an investment world governed by cycles of fear and greed, cash is not a risk-free asset but a strategic one of immense power.[26]

Klarman is famous for his willingness to hold enormous cash reserves—at times exceeding 50% of his fund's assets—when attractive opportunities are scarce. He views it not as a performance drag but as ammunition. Templeton, too, preached flexibility, noting that there are "times to sit on cash, because sometimes cash enables you to take advantage of investment opportunities".[27]

The most effective way to conceptualize this principle is to reframe cash not as a passive position, but as a call option on future volatility. In stable or rising markets, the "cost of carry" for this option is the opportunity cost of forgone returns and the slow erosion from inflation. This is the premium an investor pays. The payoff comes during a crisis. When markets seize up, liquidity vanishes, and forced selling from panicked or over-leveraged investors creates incredible bargains, cash becomes the only tool that allows one to act. Holding cash is therefore not a defensive act of fear, but an offensive strategy of patience. It is the premium paid for the right, but not the obligation, to purchase assets at the "strike price" of maximum pessimism.

The Hunt: Templeton's Global Scan for Pessimism

The first stage of our unified framework is The Hunt. This is a top-down, global process designed to identify the most fertile grounds for investment—not by looking for pockets of optimism, but by systematically searching for pockets of despair. As Templeton advised, the right question is not "Where is the outlook good?" but "Where is the outlook the most miserable?".

STEP 1: FINDING "BLOOD IN THE STREETS" – THE GLOBAL SCREENING PROCESS

The hunt begins with a systematic scan of global markets, industries, and asset classes to find areas suffering from acute crisis, widespread panic, or simple neglect. This requires an open mind and a willingness to look where others refuse to. Templeton was a master of this, pioneering investments in post-war Japan when the country was still ridiculed for producing cheap, low-quality goods. He saw a diligent workforce and a recovering industrial base, while others saw only the rubble of war. He invested when Japanese stocks traded at a price-to-earnings (P/E) ratio of 4, while U.S. stocks were at 19.5, and was rewarded handsomely as the Japanese economy boomed. He then had the discipline to sell out of Japan in the 1980s when it became the darling of the investment world and valuations reached euphoric levels. The goal of this initial screen is to generate a watchlist of geographies or sectors where pessimism is palpable.

STEP 2: QUANTIFYING FEAR – THE MAXIMUM PESSIMISM INDEX (MPI)

To move beyond intuition, we can use a conceptual framework to quantify the level of pessimism in a target market: the Maximum Pessimism Index (MPI). This proprietary index blends behavioral, valuation, and sentiment indicators to create a more objective measure of fear and capitulation. It is designed to measure the gap between what investors are saying (sentiment) and what they are actually doing with their capital (flows).

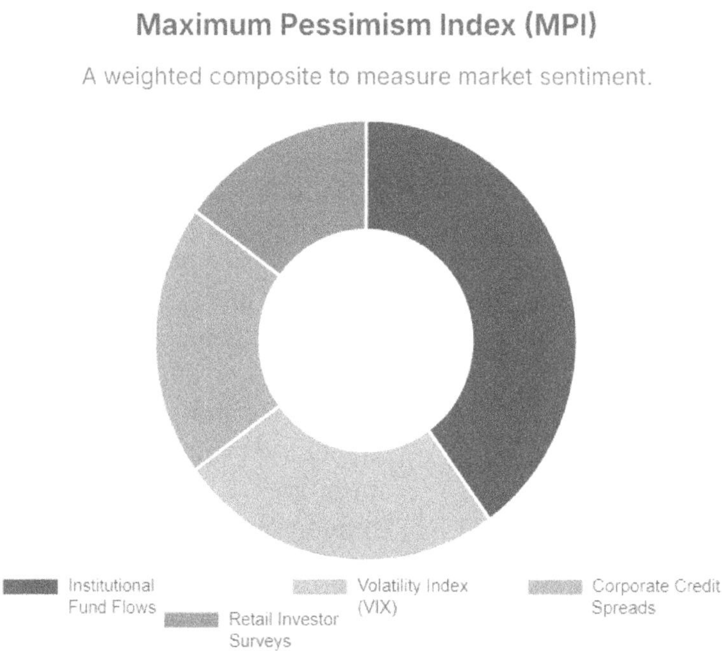

FIGURE 20 - MAXIMUM PESSIMISM INDEX (MPI)

TABLE 2 - MAXIMUM PESSIMISM INDEX (MPI) COMPONENT TABLE

Component	Metric Example	Rationale for Inclusion	Weighting
Capital Flows (Behavioral)	Net Mutual Fund/ETF Outflows (3-month rolling)	Measures actual investor capitulation. "Voting with their feet" is the strongest signal of panic.	40%
Market Valuation (Price)	Shiller P/E Ratio vs. Historical Average	Quantifies how much pessimism is priced into assets. A low valuation reflects low expectations.	25%
Market Volatility (Fear)	Volatility Index (VIX) Level & Trend	A direct "fear gauge" of the market, measuring the expected range of price movements.	20%
Investor Sentiment (Opinion)	AAII Investor Sentiment Survey (Bearish %)	Measures what investors are saying. Extreme bearishness often marks a turning point.	15%

The logic behind the weighting system is crucial. Capital flows receive the heaviest weight because actions speak louder than words. A survey can capture fleeting emotions, but large and sustained fund outflows represent real capital decisions and are the most concrete evidence of capitulation. Valuation is the next most important, as it shows how deeply that fear has been embedded in asset prices. Volatility is a direct measure of market anxiety, while sentiment surveys provide a useful, though less reliable, contrary indicator. A high MPI score for a given market signals that it is a candidate for further investigation.

STEP 3: THE VALUE TRAP FILTER – SEPARATING CRISIS FROM COLLAPSE

This is the most critical and judgmental step in The Hunt. A high MPI score tells us a market is hated, but it does not tell us if that hatred is justified. Not all pessimism is an opportunity; some crises lead not to recovery but to permanent impairment. The investor must distinguish between a **temporary crisis** and a **permanent collapse**. This requires a qualitative overlay to the quantitative MPI score. Key factors to analyze for a country or market include:

- **Rule of Law and Property Rights:** Is private capital safe from expropriation or arbitrary government action? Is the legal system stable, transparent, and predictable? A bargain price is meaningless if an investor cannot eventually realize the value of their asset.
- **Political and Economic Stability:** Is the government fundamentally hostile to free

enterprise? Is inflation running rampant and destroying the value of currency? Templeton actively avoided countries with socialist governments and high-inflation environments, understanding that these conditions are toxic to long-term capital formation.[28]

- **Risk of Structural Disruption:** This is a modern, Klarman-esque consideration that is vital in today's economy. Is an industry in a cyclical downturn, or is it being rendered obsolete by technological innovation? The most dangerous words in investing may be "this time it's different," but an investor must be humble enough to recognize when it truly is. While human psychology remains constant, technological paradigms shift. A newspaper chain trading at two times earnings in 2008 was not a bargain; it was a value trap on the brink of extinction.

Only markets that pass this qualitative filter—those suffering from a temporary, cyclical, or sentiment-driven crisis within a stable long-term framework—become the fertile hunting grounds for the next stage of the process.

The Kill: Klarman's Forensic Margin of Safety

Having identified a promising geography or sector using Templeton's telescope, we now switch to Klarman's microscope. The Kill is a bottom-up, forensic process of selecting specific securities within the target market. The goal is not to find the best company, but the most mispriced security, where the margin of safety is wide enough to protect against the inherent uncertainty of the situation.

STEP 1: ZEROING IN – SCREENING FOR COMPLEXITY AND DISTRESS

Within a crisis-stricken market, the most extreme mispricings are often found in securities that are complex, messy, ignored, or subject to forced selling by institutions. These are the areas where mainstream investors fear to tread, creating a vacuum of demand and, consequently, bargain prices. Prime hunting grounds include:[29]

- **Spinoffs:** When a parent company divests a subsidiary, the new, smaller entity is often poorly understood by the market. The parent's analysts typically do not cover it, and institutional holders of the parent company may sell their new shares indiscriminately, as the spinoff may be too small or outside their investment mandate. This creates a temporary supply/demand imbalance and a potential opportunity for diligent investors.
- **Post-Bankruptcy Equities and Distressed Debt:** This is the ultimate arena of pessimism. In a reorganization, the old equity is often wiped out, and new securities (debt and equity) are issued to creditors. These new instruments are frequently unanalyzed, unwanted, and sold off by original holders who simply want to close the book on a painful experience. For those willing to do the work, this creates fertile ground for bargains.

- **Complex Situations:** Rights offerings, liquidations, and securities with complicated legal structures deter the vast majority of investors, who are unwilling to expend the intellectual effort required to understand them. This complexity itself can be the source of the mispricing.[30]

STEP 2: THE BEDROCK OF VALUE – CONSERVATIVE VALUATION

Once a candidate security is identified, the valuation process must begin. For Klarman, valuation is not about finding a single, precise number; it is an art, not a science. The goal is to determine a conservative *range* of intrinsic value, against which the current market price can be compared. The process must always start with the most tangible and verifiable sources of value.[31]

- **Liquidation Value Analysis:** This is the cornerstone. It asks the question: what would the company's assets be worth if it were shut down today, its assets sold off, and all its liabilities paid? This provides a "rock-bottom appraisal" of value and a powerful margin of safety, as it completely ignores the value of the ongoing business (the "going-concern" value). A quick proxy for this is "Net-Net Working Capital" (NNWC), defined as current assets minus all liabilities (both current and long-term). Buying a stock for less than its NNWC per share is like buying a dollar for fifty cents, with the factory and brand thrown in for free.

A robust analysis triangulates value from multiple conservative perspectives. The following matrix provides a practical template.

TABLE 3 - CONSERVATIVE VALUATION MATRIX (TEMPLATE FOR A HYPOTHETICAL COMPANY)

Valuation Method	Key Assumptions	Estimated Value/Share	Margin of Safety at Current Price of $10.00
1. Liquidation Value	80% recovery on receivables, 50% on inventory, 60% on PP&E.	$15.00	33%
2. Replacement Cost	Cost to replicate key assets and technology in today's market.	$22.00	55%
3. DCF (Pessimistic Case)	0% growth for 3 years, 1% terminal growth, high discount rate.	$18.50	46%

Valuation Method	Key Assumptions	Estimated Value/Share	Margin of Safety at Current Price of $10.00
Conservative Value Range		**$15.00 - $18.50**	

This multi-pronged approach establishes a defensible floor for the company's value, making the margin of safety tangible and explicit.[32]

Step 3: The Survival Check – The Altman Z-Score

A bargain price is irrelevant if the company goes bankrupt before its value can be realized. Therefore, after establishing a margin of safety, the next crucial step is to assess the company's financial stability and its ability to survive the crisis. A powerful quantitative tool for this purpose is the Altman Z-Score[33], a formula developed by Professor Edward Altman in 1968 to predict the probability of a company filing for bankruptcy within two years.

The formula for publicly traded manufacturing firms is:

$$Z = 1.2T_{\{1\}} + 1.4T_{\{2\}} + 3.3T_{\{3\}} + 0.6T_{\{4\}} + 0.999T_{\{5\}}$$

Where:

- $T_{\{1\}} = \frac{\text{Working Capital}}{\text{Total Assets (measures liquidity)}}$
- $T_{\{2\}} = \frac{\text{Retained Earnings}}{\text{Total Assets (measures cumulative profitability)}}$
- $T_{\{3\}} = \frac{\text{Earnings Before Interest and Taxes (EBIT)}}{\text{Total Assets (measures operating efficiency)}}$
- $T_{\{4\}} = \frac{\text{Market Value of Equity}}{\text{Book Value of Total Liabilities (measures leverage)}}$
- $T_{\{5\}} = \frac{\text{Sales}}{\text{Total Assets (measures asset turnover)}}$

The score is interpreted as follows 41:

- **Z > 2.99:** "Safe Zone" - Bankruptcy is unlikely.
- **1.8 < Z < 2.99:** "Grey Zone" - Caution is warranted; further analysis is needed.[34] [35]
- **Z < 1.8:** "Distress Zone" - High probability of bankruptcy.

The Z-Score provides a vital, non-emotional check on a company's solvency, helping to filter out potential bargains that are, in fact, ticking financial time bombs.

STEP 4: FINDING THE ASYMMETRIC BET – CAPITAL STRUCTURE WATERFALL ANALYSIS

This final step is the most sophisticated and often the most profitable. In a distressed situation, the most intelligent investment is frequently not the common stock. To understand why, one must analyze the company's capital structure as a "waterfall".

In a bankruptcy or restructuring, claimholders are paid according to a strict hierarchy of seniority. The company's total enterprise value is the "water" that flows down, filling a series of buckets. Secured senior debt holders are at the top and get paid first. Unsecured bondholders are next, followed by preferred stockholders. Common stockholders are at the very bottom and receive only what is left after everyone else has been paid in full. In most distressed situations, the water runs out long before it reaches the common equity bucket.

The analytical key is to identify the **fulcrum security**. This is the most senior class of debt that is not expected to be paid in full by the company's enterprise value. Because its holders are not made whole, this is the security that is most likely to be converted into the new equity of the reorganized company, giving its owners control.[36]

This creates a powerful investment dynamic. The common stock of a distressed company is effectively a deep out-of-the-money call option; it has a very high probability of expiring worthless, but offers huge upside in a miraculous turnaround. It is a lottery ticket. A senior bond, however, if purchased at a deep discount (e.g., 50 cents on the dollar), offers a profoundly different risk profile. Its downside is capped at the price paid, while its upside can be equity-like if the company recovers and the bond is paid back at par (a 100% return) or, even better, if it becomes the fulcrum security and is converted into a controlling stake in the new, deleveraged company.

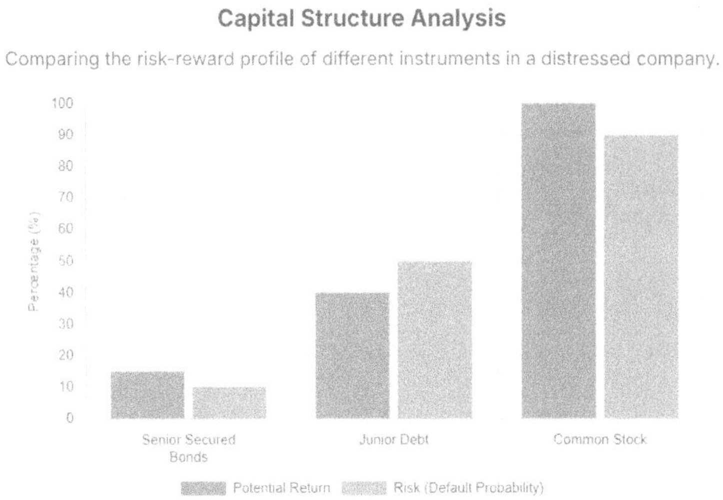

FIGURE 21 - CAPITAL STRUCTURE WATERFALL

This creates a highly **asymmetric risk/reward profile**, the holy grail of investing. The investor gets the potential upside of an equity owner with the structural protection and senior claim of a creditor.

TABLE 4 - INSTRUMENT COMPARISON TABLE (ILLUSTRATIVE DISTRESSED COMPANY)

Instrument	Current Price	Downside Risk (Liquidation)	Upside Potential (Reorganization)	Risk/Reward Profile
Senior Secured Debt	50¢ on the dollar	Capped at -50% (if liquidated for 0)	+100% (paid at par) or converts to controlling equity stake	**Highly Asymmetric**
Unsecured Bonds	20¢ on the dollar	Capped at -100% (likely wiped out)	High (may get some new equity)	Symmetric / Unfavorable

Instrument	Current Price	Downside Risk (Liquidation)	Upside Potential (Reorganization)	Risk/Reward Profile
Common Stock	$1.00 per share	-100% (almost certain wipeout)	Very High (if miraculous turnaround)	Lottery Ticket (Unfavorable)

As the table illustrates, the prudent, risk-averse, and often most profitable investment is in the senior part of the capital structure, where the potential reward vastly outweighs the quantifiable risk.

Key Takeaways: The Contrarian's Code

The synthesis of Templeton's global vision and Klarman's granular discipline yields a powerful and robust framework for navigating the most treacherous market environments. The core tenets can be distilled into a code of conduct for the thoughtful investor.

- **Think Globally, Act Microscopically:** Use a wide-angle lens to find macro pessimism, then a microscope to find micro-level safety.
- **Be a Pessimistic Optimist:** Have the long-term faith to invest in a crisis, but the short-term skepticism to demand a price that protects you from being wrong.
- **Your Temperament is Your Edge:** Emotional discipline, patience, and intellectual honesty are more important than any financial model.
- **Hunt for Forced Sellers, Not Good News:** The best bargains are created by structural selling

pressure—fear, complexity, institutional constraints—not by improving fundamentals.

- **Price is Your Protection:** Value is an estimate; price is a fact. The gap between them is your only true defense against an uncertain future.
- Cash is Not Trash, It's Ammunition: View liquidity as your most valuable strategic asset, allowing you to act when others are paralyzed by fear.
- **Analyze the Capital Structure:** In times of distress, the most profitable and prudent investment is often in the debt, not the equity. Find the asymmetric bet.

Chapter 6: The Most Important Thing: Navigating the Credit Cycle with Second-Level Thinking (Howard Marks)

The Thoughtful Investor: A Portrait of the Author

In the often-cacophonous world of finance, where prognostications are loud and certainty is fleeting, there are a few voices that command attention not through volume, but through the quiet authority of reason and experience. Howard Marks is one such voice. His career, which began at Citicorp in 1969 and led him through senior roles at TCW Group before he co-founded Oaktree Capital Management in 1995, has been a masterclass in navigating the less-traveled, less-efficient corners of the market, such as high-yield bonds and distressed debt. Oaktree, under his guidance, has become the world's largest investor in distressed securities, not by chasing the highest returns, but by adhering to a disciplined, risk-averse philosophy that has proven its mettle across decades of market turmoil.

The core of this philosophy, the unifying principle that animates every decision, is the primacy of risk control. The stated goal is not merely superior investment performance, but superior performance achieved with less-than-commensurate risk. As Marks has often stated, above-average gains in good times are not necessarily proof of skill; they may simply reflect the acceptance of above-average risk. True skill is demonstrated in bad times, through the preservation of capital. This leads to the foundational maxim of the Oaktree approach: "If we avoid the losers, the winners will take care of themselves". This is not a passive statement but an active strategy—a commitment to defensive investing that prioritizes the avoidance of permanent capital loss above all else.

This philosophy was forged in the crucible of market history. Witnessing the collapse of the "Nifty Fifty" era in the early 1970s, a time when the consensus held that certain "good companies" were worth buying at any price, instilled a deep and abiding skepticism of first-level thinking. The painful lesson was that it is not what you buy, but what you pay, that ultimately determines your return. This realization—that even the highest-quality asset can become a source of ruinous risk if its price becomes detached from intrinsic value—is the intellectual seed from which his entire framework has grown. The focus on distressed debt is the logical conclusion of this line of thought: buying assets when pessimism is at its peak and the price is so low that risk is minimized, regardless of the market's perception of the company.

Through his widely read memos, Marks has generously shared the hard-won wisdom of his career, establishing himself not as a guru with a crystal ball, but as a thoughtful teacher and a voice of reason. This chapter is an attempt to distill that wisdom into a cohesive framework—a guide for navigating the treacherous waters of the credit cycle with the intellectual rigor, emotional discipline, and profound humility that define the thoughtful investor.

The Four Pillars of Wisdom: Foundational Mental Models

The investment philosophy of Howard Marks is not a collection of disconnected aphorisms but a self-reinforcing system of thought built upon four interconnected pillars. These mental models work in concert to guide analysis, shape behavior, and govern execution. An understanding of cycles tells you *when* to look for opportunities. Patient opportunism provides the discipline to *wait* for them. Second-level thinking is the analytical tool to *identify* them. And defensive investing is the framework to *capitalize* on them with controlled risk. Together, they form a powerful defense against the psychological errors that so often lead investors astray.

PILLAR 1: SECOND-LEVEL THINKING

The intellectual engine of the entire approach is what Marks calls "second-level thinking." It represents the deep, complex, and often contrarian analysis required to outperform the market consensus. It stands in stark contrast to first-level thinking, which is simplistic, superficial, and accessible to everyone.

First-level thinking says, "It's a good company; let's buy the stock." Second-level thinking retorts, "It's a good company, but everyone thinks it's a great company, and it's not. So the stock's overrated and overpriced; let's sell". First-level thinking says, "The outlook for the economy is rosy, so we should invest aggressively." Second-level thinking asks, "The outlook is rosy, but how much of that optimism is already reflected in asset prices? What is the full range of potential outcomes, and does the current price offer adequate compensation if the future is merely good, not great?".

To achieve superior results, an investor cannot do what everyone else is doing. The market price of any asset reflects the collective wisdom—and folly—of all participants. All widely known information is already discounted in the price. Therefore, an edge can only be gained by interpreting that information differently or more accurately than the consensus. The goal is not merely to be contrarian, but to be contrarian *and correct*, which requires holding a non-consensus view about value that proves to be accurate over time.

In the context of credit, this distinction is critical. A first-level thinker might be attracted by a high yield and immediately purchase the bond. A second-level thinker interrogates that yield. They ask *why* it is high, rigorously assess the probability of default, calculate a conservative recovery value for the bond in a bankruptcy scenario, and only then determine if the offered spread provides adequate compensation for the true, underlying risk—not just the risk perceived by the market. This deep inquiry is the essential prerequisite for outperformance.

PILLAR 2: THE INEVITABILITY OF CYCLES

A central tenet of the philosophy is the recognition that "most things will prove to be cyclical". While it is impossible to predict the timing or amplitude of market cycles with any consistency, superior investors must strive to have a well-founded sense of where we are. This awareness is not for the purpose of market timing—an activity Marks views as a fool's errand—but for adjusting the portfolio's risk posture to align with the prevailing odds.

The primary mental model for understanding cycles is "The Pendulum". This concept describes the perpetual swing of investor psychology between the extremes of euphoria and depression, greed and fear, and risk tolerance and risk aversion. Critically, the market spends the vast majority of its time moving toward or residing at these extremes, and very little time at the "happy medium" of rational valuation. This psychological oscillation is the fundamental engine that drives the credit cycle, causing the "credit window" to swing from wide open to slammed shut.

These cycles are not driven by arcane, mechanical processes but by the timeless and unchanging constants of human emotion. The memory of past pain fades, allowing greed to supplant fear, which in turn leads to excesses that plant the seeds of the next downturn. As the historian John Kenneth Galbraith noted, the "extreme brevity of the financial memory" is a key reason why markets are able to move to such extremes of euphoria and panic. The most dangerous words in investing are "this time it's different."

The practical application of this pillar is to prepare, not predict. When the pendulum is at the extreme of fear and pessimism, when the news is uniformly bad and capital is scarce, assets are likely to be undervalued. This is the time to be aggressive and "move forward." Conversely, when the pendulum is at the extreme of greed and euphoria, when risk is ignored and capital is abundant, assets are likely to be overpriced. This is the time to be cautious and "play defense".

PILLAR 3: INVESTING DEFENSIVELY

The cornerstone of the entire approach is an unwavering focus on risk control, encapsulated by the principle of "investing defensively". This philosophy prioritizes the avoidance of loss over the pursuit of gain, operating on the conviction that over a full investment career, performance is more heavily influenced by the number and severity of losing investments than by the magnitude of the winners. It is a strategy built on achieving a high batting average, not a mix of brilliant successes and dismal failures.

A critical distinction in this philosophy is the definition of risk. The academic convention of equating risk with volatility is firmly rejected. For a long-term investor, price fluctuation is not the primary concern; it is often the source of opportunity. True risk is the probability of a *permanent loss of capital*. This reorientation is fundamental, as it dictates that analysis should prioritize deep, fundamental downside assessment—such as the recovery value of a bond in bankruptcy—over statistical measures of price behavior like beta or standard deviation.

The primary tool for implementing this defensive strategy is the insistence on a "margin of safety"—the practice of buying an asset for a price significantly below its conservatively estimated intrinsic value. This discount provides a crucial buffer against analytical error, unforeseen negative developments, or simple bad luck. In the realm of distressed debt, the margin of safety is calculated by purchasing a debt instrument at a price well below its estimated recovery value in a conservative bankruptcy scenario. This focus on the downside is what creates an asymmetric return profile: the potential for gain is preserved, while the risk of permanent loss is assiduously controlled.

PILLAR 4: PATIENT OPPORTUNISM

Patient opportunism is the behavioral discipline required to execute the philosophy successfully. It is grounded in the understanding that truly superior investment opportunities—those offering high potential returns with low risk—are inherently rare. The correct strategy, therefore, is to wait for these opportunities to present themselves, rather than actively chasing investments in a fully-priced market. This often means being willing to hold cash or remain relatively inactive when no compelling bargains are available, a stance that runs counter to the institutional pressure to always be fully invested.

The greatest challenge of this pillar is psychological. It requires resisting the powerful fear of missing out (FOMO) that pervades bull markets and withstanding the pressure to "do something" during periods of low opportunity. An investor must be comfortable looking wrong in the short term, holding cash while others are celebrating gains, in order to be right in the long term. As Marks has noted, to be a disciplined investor, you have to be willing to stand by and watch other people make money on investments you passed on.

This principle mandates that any robust investment framework must include an explicit "No-Trade" or "Hold Cash" path, triggered when the market environment does not offer opportunities that meet the stringent criteria for risk and value. This operationalizes patience, turning it from a mere virtue into a strategic imperative.

These four pillars are, in essence, a system for exploiting the behavioral failures of others. Second-level thinking is the antidote to herd mentality. Understanding cycles is the antidote to recency bias. Defensive investing is the antidote to greed and over-optimism. And patient opportunism is the antidote to FOMO and the compulsion to act. The entire framework is a behavioral and psychological defense mechanism as much as it is a financial one, designed to turn the market's emotional excesses from a source of risk into a source of opportunity.

The Macro View: Taking the Market's Temperature

Having established the philosophical foundation, we now turn to its practical, top-down application. The goal of this macro framework is to move beyond subjective "feel" and create a disciplined, evidence-based assessment of the present environment—to answer the crucial question, "Where are we in the cycle?". The objective is not to forecast the future but to create a probabilistic assessment of the present, translating the market's "temperature" into a clear decision to either "move forward" with aggression or "play defense" with caution.

THE CREDIT CYCLE THERMOMETER: A DASHBOARD FOR DISCIPLINE

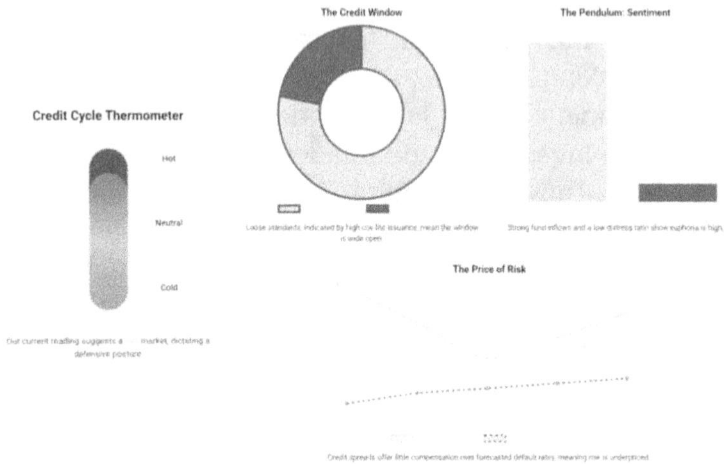

FIGURE 22 - THE CREDIT CYCLE THERMOMETER

To systematize this synthesis, we use a "Credit Cycle Thermometer." This dashboard provides a concise, at-a-glance summary of key macro indicators, mapping each to an intuitive temperature reading. This tool forces a disciplined, multi-faceted assessment and prevents over-reliance on any single metric or narrative. It combats the natural tendency of investors to be swayed by a single compelling story (e.g., "soft landing") by forcing a look at the cold, hard data across multiple, distinct categories. It provides historical context, making abstract data points meaningful. And it distills complexity into a single, actionable output, making the complex digestible without being simplistic.

The thermometer synthesizes data on capital availability, investor sentiment, and the market's pricing of risk. The core output is a classification of the market "temperature" on a spectrum from "Frigid" (characterized by maximum pessimism, closed capital markets, and wide spreads, thus maximum opportunity) to "Scorching" (characterized by maximum euphoria, wide-open capital markets, and tight spreads, thus maximum risk).

The following table illustrates the thermometer with hypothetical but realistic data for a "Hot" market environment:

TABLE 5 - THE THE CREDIT CYCLE THERMOMETER

Indicator Category	Indicator	Current Value	10yr Range (Min, 25%, Med, 75%, Max)	Implied Temperature
Credit Window	Net % of Banks Tightening (SLOOS)	-5%	(-50%, -10%, 5%, 25%, 60%)	Hot (Low is bad)
	% Covenant-Lite Issuance (YTD)	82%	(20%, 40%, 60%, 75%, 90%)	Scorching (High is bad)
Sentiment	HY Fund Flows (3mo rolling)	+$4.5B	(-$10B, -$2B, $0, +3B, +15B)	Hot (High is euphoric)
	Distress Ratio (%)	2.8%	(2%, 4%, 7%, 12%, 35%)	Cool (Low is euphoric)
Price of Risk	HY Spread (OAS in bps)	330	(300, 380, 500, 650, 1100)	Scorching (Low is expensive)

Indicator Category	Indicator	Current Value	10yr Range (Min, 25%, Med, 75%, Max)	Implied Temperature
	Forward 12m Default Rate Forecast	3.5%	(1.5%, 2.5%, 3.5%, 5%, 11%)	Neutral
OVERALL TEMP				**Hot**

COMPONENT 1: ASSESSING THE "CREDIT WINDOW" (CAPITAL AVAILABILITY)

The "Credit Window" is a powerful metaphor for the overall availability of capital in the market. When the window is "open," capital is abundant, lenders are eager, credit standards are loose, and even fundamentally weak deals can secure financing. When the window is "shut," capital becomes scarce, lenders are highly risk-averse, and only the most creditworthy borrowers can access funding. The swing from open to shut is often what precipitates a downturn and creates distressed debt opportunities.

We gauge its state through key indicators. The first is **Lending Standards**, measured directly by the Federal Reserve's quarterly Senior Loan Officer Opinion Survey (SLOOS). A net percentage of bankers reporting they are *easing* standards, as with the -5% reading in our example, signals an open and accommodating environment. The second is

Covenant Quality. Covenants are contractual protections for lenders. In periods of high capital availability, borrowers have more negotiating power, leading to a rise in "covenant-lite" loans, which lack traditional financial tests. A high percentage of new issuance being cov-lite—such as the 82% in the example—is a hallmark of a late-cycle, lender-unfriendly environment where risk is high.

COMPONENT 2: GAUGING "THE PENDULUM" (INVESTOR SENTIMENT)

This step maps the market's collective mood on the euphoria/despair spectrum of the Pendulum. In euphoric times, investors focus only on positive developments, ignore negatives, and willingly accept high prices and low prospective returns. In times of despair, they obsess over negatives, interpret all news unfavorably, and sell assets at prices far below intrinsic value.

We assess this sentiment through two primary quantitative measures. The first is **Fund Flows.** Data on investor flows into and out of high-yield bond funds provide a direct measure of sentiment. Sustained, strong inflows, like the +$4.5B in the example, suggest greed and high risk tolerance. The second, and perhaps most important, is the **Distress Ratio.** This key "fear gauge" measures the percentage of high-yield bonds trading at distressed levels (typically spreads over 1,000 basis points). A very low distress ratio, such as the 2.8% in our example, indicates widespread complacency and a lack of perceived risk—a classic sign that the pendulum is near the "greed" extreme.

COMPONENT 3: EVALUATING THE "PRICE OF RISK" (MARKET VALUATION)

This step moves from sentiment to price. The central question is not whether spreads are historically wide or narrow, but whether they are *sufficient* to offset the credit losses that will likely occur over the investment horizon.

The analysis centers on the relationship between credit spreads and default rates. First, we place the current **Credit Spread** in a historical context. An Option-Adjusted Spread (OAS) of 330 basis points, as in our example, may sound abstract. But knowing it falls in the 15th percentile of its 10-year range immediately tells us that risk is being priced very cheaply relative to the past.

Second, we perform the crucial second-level calculation: an **Implied vs. Forecasted Loss Analysis**. The spread is the market's "insurance premium" against default. We can estimate the expected annual credit loss with a simple formula:

$$\begin{aligned}\text{Expected Credit Loss (bps)} \\ &= \text{Forecasted Default Rate (\%)} \\ &\times \text{Expected Loss Given Default (\%)}\end{aligned}$$

Using the example data, with a forecasted default rate of 3.5% and an assumed historical Loss Given Default of 60%, the expected credit loss is 210 basis points ($3.5\% \times 60\%$). The current spread of 330 bps offers a risk premium of only 120 bps over this expected loss. While positive, this premium is historically thin and offers a minimal margin of safety against a worse-than-expected default environment. The market appears to be pricing in a benign economic outcome with a high degree of confidence.

SYNTHESIZING THE READING

The final step is to integrate these findings. In our example, the Credit Window is "Open," Sentiment is "Optimistic," and the Price of Risk is "Cheap" (meaning compensation is low). The collective weight of the evidence points to an overall "Hot" market environment. Such a reading demands a defensive posture. The appropriate action is to increase selectivity, demand a higher margin of safety on any new investments, and maintain a patient, opportunistic stance, holding capital in reserve for the day when the thermometer inevitably cools.

The Micro Playbook: A Forensic Dive into Distressed Debt

While the macro view tells us *when* the environment is favorable for investing, the micro playbook provides the rigorous, bottom-up process for identifying *what* to buy. It is a forensic guide to finding a "good company with a bad balance sheet"—an enterprise whose viable operating business is obscured by an unsustainable capital structure. The goal is not to find exciting growth stories, but rather to find assets with a defensible, tangible value that can be purchased at a significant discount to their conservatively estimated recovery value. This entire playbook is the practical application of second-level thinking. It forces the analyst to look past the prevailing narrative of distress—the first-level thought—and conduct a deep inquiry into the underlying reality of assets, cash flows, and legal structures to find a non-consensus view of value.

STEP 1: FORENSIC BALANCE SHEET ANALYSIS

The first step is to create a comprehensive map of the battlefield: the company's capital structure. This involves systematically listing all claims on the company's assets in a "waterfall," from the most senior secured debt down to the common equity.

This is more than an accounting exercise; it requires a deep legal review. The analyst must dissect the indentures and credit agreements that govern each debt instrument. The goal is to "read the fine print," understanding the key covenants that protect creditors. This includes searching for weaknesses, loopholes, or permissive "baskets" that could allow a desperate management team to transfer value away from creditors to shareholders or other junior stakeholders.

A primary goal of this analysis is to identify the "fulcrum security"—the most senior class of debt that is likely to be impaired in a restructuring and therefore converted into the equity of the reorganized company. For an investor pursuing a "loan-to-own" strategy, where the objective is to gain control of the company post-bankruptcy, identifying and accumulating a position in the fulcrum security is the central strategic objective.

STEP 2: DOWNTURN-RESILIENT CASH FLOW ANALYSIS

The core of any credit analysis is determining a company's ability to service its debt. In distressed situations, this analysis must be particularly rigorous, focusing not on a rosy base-case scenario but on the company's capacity to generate cash and survive through a prolonged downturn. The analysis prioritizes cash flow over accounting profits, as cash is what ultimately pays interest and principal.

The process is not about accepting management's projections but about modeling for survival. A multi-scenario financial model is constructed, including a "Base Case," a "Downside Case" reflecting a moderate recession, and, most importantly, a "Severe Downside Case" reflecting a deep, prolonged economic contraction. Within these scenarios, key assumptions are stress-tested to find the company's financial breaking points. Critical debt service coverage ratios, such as the Interest Coverage Ratio (EBITDA/InterestExpense), are calculated for each scenario. The analysis identifies the specific conditions under which these ratios would fall below 1.0x, signaling a likely payment default.

STEP 3: ASSET VALUATION AND RECOVERY ANALYSIS

This step is the crux of the bottom-up analysis and the heart of the defensive approach. Its purpose is to establish a conservative, defensible estimate of the intrinsic value of the target security in a default scenario. This "recovery value" is the anchor for the entire investment decision.

The recovery value is estimated using two primary, complementary methodologies that must be contrasted. The first is a **Liquidation Analysis**, which is the most conservative method. It assumes the company ceases to be a going concern and its assets are sold off piecemeal under forced-sale conditions. Each asset class is valued at a significant discount to its book value—for example, inventory might be valued at 30-60% and equipment at 20-50%.

The second is a **Going-Concern Enterprise Value Analysis**. This approach, typically used for businesses with a viable underlying operating model, assumes the company is successfully reorganized and continues to operate. A conservative, post-reorganization EBITDA (often based on the downturn cash flow scenario) is estimated and multiplied by a conservative valuation multiple, derived from comparable companies or transactions, to arrive at an enterprise value.

The estimated value from either analysis is then distributed down the capital structure waterfall according to the absolute priority rule. This determines how much value, if any, flows down to the specific debt instrument being analyzed, yielding a recovery estimate in cents on the dollar.

STEP 4: THE MARGIN OF SAFETY DECISION

This final step synthesizes all prior analysis into a single, unemotional investment decision. The decision is not based on the potential upside or yield, but on whether the current market price offers a sufficient margin of safety relative to the conservatively estimated recovery value.

The calculation is the quantitative embodiment of the defensive investing pillar:

$$Margin\ of\ Safety(\%) = 1 - \frac{Current\ Market\ Price}{Estimated\ Recovery\ Value}$$

A predefined, disciplined decision rule is then applied. An investment is initiated only if the calculated margin of safety exceeds a specified threshold, which might typically be 30% or more depending on the complexity of the situation. This quantitative hurdle enforces the principle of "buying things well" and prevents emotional biases from clouding judgment. The final output is a clear "Buy" or "No-Buy" recommendation, anchored in a rigorous, repeatable, and defensible process.

Case Study: The Anatomy of a Distressed Deal (ACME Corp)

To bring this framework to life, let us walk through a hypothetical but realistic case study of a distressed debt investment in ACME Corp. The company is a mature industrial manufacturer whose bonds are trading at deeply distressed levels. The market narrative—the first-level thought—is one of panic. Investors are focused on the company's high leverage and its vulnerability to an economic downturn, and they are selling indiscriminately. This is precisely the environment of fear where a second-level thinker begins their work.

Our forensic dive begins with the capital structure. We find that ACME has $500 million of senior secured debt sitting atop our target security: $750 million of Senior Unsecured Notes. The market is terrified of this subordination, believing little value will be left for the unsecured creditors. Our cash flow analysis confirms the market's fear of default is justified; in our "Severe Downside Scenario," we project that ACME will breach its interest coverage covenants within 12 months, making a restructuring highly probable.

Here, however, our path diverges from the market's. The crucial question is not *if* ACME will default, but *what the assets will be worth* when it does. The market is pricing the Senior Unsecured Notes at just **35 cents on the dollar**. This price implies a recovery consistent with a fire-sale liquidation, where our analysis suggests the notes would recover only about 20 cents.

But our deeper, second-level analysis of the business suggests a going-concern reorganization is the more probable outcome. ACME has a solid brand, a valuable distribution network, and a viable underlying business, despite its broken balance sheet. Using a conservative EBITDA projection from our downturn scenario and applying a discounted valuation multiple, we arrive at a reorganized enterprise value that would result in a recovery for our Senior Unsecured Notes of **55 cents on the dollar**.

This is the non-consensus insight upon which the investment thesis is built. The market's first-level panic has created a significant dislocation between price and our conservative estimate of intrinsic value. We can now apply the final filter—the margin of safety decision:

$$\text{Margin of Safety} = 1 - \left(\frac{\text{35 cents (Price)}}{\text{55 cents (Value)}}\right) = 1 - 0.636 = 36.4\%$$

With a margin of safety of 36.4%, comfortably exceeding our minimum threshold of 30%, the decision is a clear "BUY".[37]

1. Capital Structure Analysis

ACME Corp, a cyclical manufacturer, is over-leveraged. A forensic analysis of its balance sheet reveals four key tranches. We identify the Senior Notes as the "fulcrum security" because, in a downturn, the enterprise value is likely to be insufficient to cover them, making them the most probable candidate for conversion to equity.

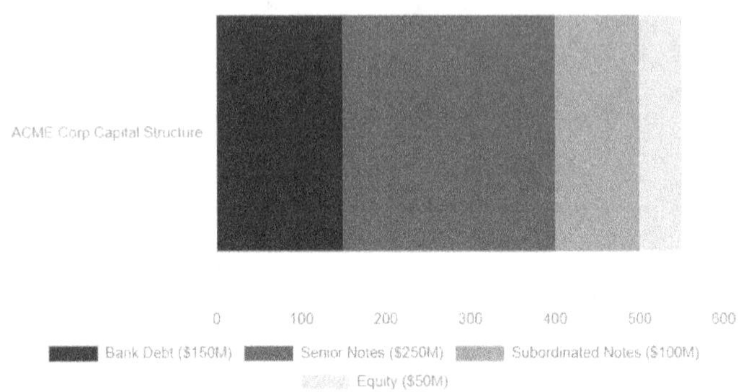

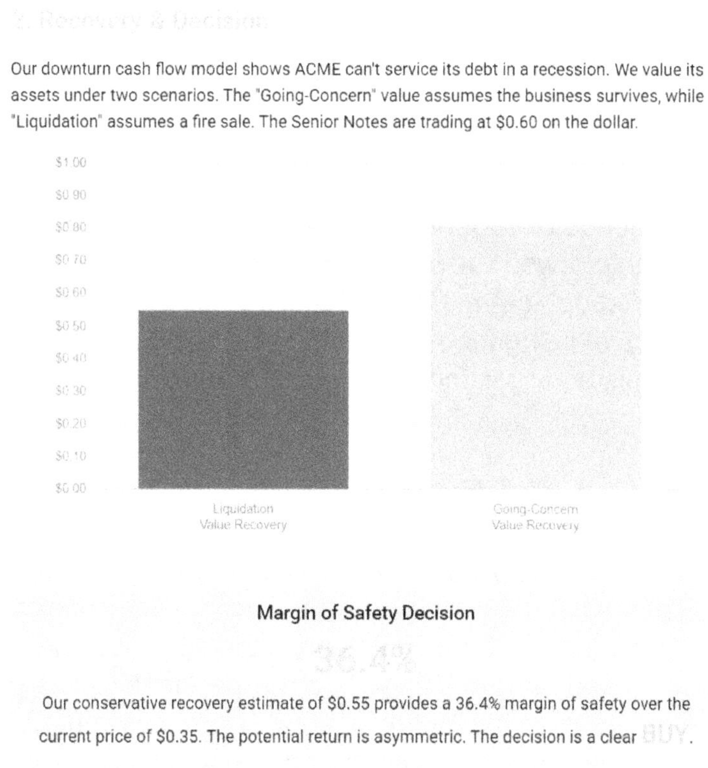

FIGURE 23 - MARGIN OF SAFETY DECISION

To ensure intellectual rigor, we formally challenge this thesis with a "Devil's Advocate" memo. This memo argues the consensus view: that ACME is not merely in a cyclical downturn but a secular decline, making it a classic "value trap" where a liquidation is more probable than we assume. This forces a rebuttal. We acknowledge the risk but conclude that our due diligence, including interviews with industry experts, supports the view that the decline is cyclical. The brand and distribution network retain significant value, and the large margin of safety is designed precisely to provide a cushion should the recovery be lower than our base case. The investment is approved, not because we are certain of the outcome, but because the odds are heavily skewed in our favor.

Key Takeaways: The Most Important Things

The practice of superior investing is not a science with immutable laws, but an art that requires a disciplined and philosophical mindset. Distilling the lessons from decades of navigating the credit cycle, a set of timeless principles emerges for the thoughtful investor.[38]

- Superior performance comes from correct, non-consensus forecasts, but superior *risk-adjusted* performance comes from superior risk control.[39]
- You can't predict, but you can prepare. The most crucial preparation is having a well-founded sense of where you stand in the current cycle.[40]
- Risk is not volatility; it is the permanent loss of capital. Your entire analytical process must be oriented around protecting the downside.
- It's not what you buy, it's what you pay. A high-quality asset can be a risky investment if bought at too high a price, and a low-quality asset can be a safe one if bought cheaply enough.
- The pendulum of investor psychology swings from "flawless" to "hopeless." It rarely rests at the happy medium. The greatest opportunities are found at the extremes.
- To outperform the market, you must think differently from the consensus. This requires deep, complex, and often contrarian second-level thinking.
- The most dangerous words in investing are "this time it's different." Cycles always prevail, driven

by the unchanging constants of human emotion.[41]

- Be fearful when others are greedy, and greedy when others are fearful. This is easy to say but requires immense behavioral discipline to execute.
- Patience is a strategic asset. The discipline to wait for the “fat pitch” is what separates the thoughtful investor from the speculator.
- If you avoid the losers, the winners will take care of themselves. A high batting average, built on a foundation of defensive investing, is the surest path to long-term success.[42]

Chapter 7: The Deep Value & Forensic Framework (Michael Burry)

The financial markets are not a polite debating society. They are a crime scene, perpetually shrouded in the fog of consensus. The evidence is often tampered with, the witnesses are unreliable, and the official narrative—broadcast daily by the well-credentialed experts on Wall Street—is designed to comfort, not to clarify. In this world of hidden risks and sanctioned illusions, the most valuable asset is not a complex algorithm or insider access. It is the eye of the detective.

And in the modern history of finance, no detective has been more relentless, more prescient, or more reclusive than Dr. Michael Burry. He is the investigator who arrives at the scene long before the yellow tape goes up, sifting through the evidence everyone else has dismissed as mundane. He reads the footnotes no one else bothers with, connects the clues no one else sees, and builds a case so airtight that when the crisis finally hits, he is the only one who isn't surprised. This is not a story about prophecy; it is a story about a process—a rigorous, repeatable framework for uncovering the hidden truths of the financial world.

The Doctor of Doom: A Portrait of the Investigator

To understand Michael Burry's method, one must first understand that his greatest strengths are born from his status as an outsider. His journey began not in an Ivy League business school but at Stanford Medical Center, where, as a neurology resident, he endured grueling 16-hour shifts. In the slivers of time that remained, he wasn't resting; he was conducting a second, more obsessive residency in the financial markets, sharing his meticulously researched findings on an investment blog. This origin story is the key to his entire philosophy. He arrived on the financial scene unburdened by its institutional biases, armed not with an MBA but with a physician's diagnostic rigor.

Burry doesn't invest like a financier; he invests like a diagnostician. His medical training instilled a systematic process that he ported directly to the world of capital: gather vast, often contradictory data (the patient's history); filter out the noise (the patient's anxiety vs. the lab results); identify the underlying pathology, not just the symptoms; and prescribe a precise, targeted intervention. This clinical mindset fosters a profound objectivity, a commitment to empirical evidence over sentiment.

This objectivity is amplified by a set of personal traits that function as strategic advantages. His self-diagnosed Asperger's Syndrome is not a colorful footnote to his story; it is central to his process. It fosters a capacity for intense, prolonged focus and insulates him from the social pressures and narrative-driven thinking that lead to herd behavior in markets. This intellectual isolation is not a preference; it is a functional requirement of his analytical engine. It creates a sterile environment, free from the contagion of consensus, allowing for the dispassionate, diagnostic work his method requires. His cognitive disposition necessitates a system based on verifiable, primary data because he is less influenced by the social cues and compelling stories that sway his peers. This forces him into a more rigorous, evidence-based process, turning what some might see as a social handicap into an unparalleled investigative edge.

The Contrarian's Mindset: The First Principles of Investigation

Every great detective operates by a code. Burry's code is built on a foundation of radical skepticism and an unwavering commitment to first principles.

His first principle is a profound and structural distrust of established authorities. This is not knee-jerk cynicism but a methodological demand for independent verification. The most potent example was his outright dismissal of assurances from Federal Reserve Chairman Alan Greenspan, who in 2003 claimed that "national bubbles in real estate simply do not happen". While the market accepted this pronouncement from the high priest of finance, Burry's own research into lending practices led him to the opposite conclusion. He treats the claims of regulators, ratings agencies, and Wall Street experts not as facts, but as hypotheses to be tested against primary evidence.

This leads to the core of his investigative technique: an obsessive focus on primary source documents. While other investors consume the polished summaries of sell-side reports, Burry goes to the source code. In the lead-up to the 2008 crisis, this meant personally reading thousands of pages of mind-numbing mortgage bond prospectuses and loan-level data. He was not merely reading; he was performing a forensic examination, scanning for anomalies. By analyzing the raw data, he could see the proliferation of toxic loan features like "teaser" rates and "stated income" options—a reality entirely obscured by the pristine AAA ratings assigned to the securities. This commitment to first-principles analysis allows him to build a proprietary understanding of reality, free from the biases and flawed assumptions embedded in all secondary analysis.

This entire framework rests on a bedrock of classic value investing. Burry is a devoted student of Benjamin Graham and David Dodd, stating, "All my stock picking is 100% based on the concept of a margin of safety". The Margin of Safety is the principle of buying an asset for significantly less than your conservative estimate of its intrinsic worth—in Graham's timeless words, buying "$1 assets for 50 cents". This discount provides a buffer against error and is the ultimate source of outsized returns.

To navigate the emotional chaos of the market, Burry internalizes Graham's allegory of "Mr. Market," a manic-depressive business partner who, each day, offers to buy your shares or sell you his at a wildly fluctuating price. Some days he is euphoric and quotes a ridiculous premium; other days he is despondent and offers his shares for pennies on the dollar. The intelligent investor is under no obligation to trade with him; Mr. Market is there to be exploited, not to be followed. Burry's ability to ignore his own panicked investors during the subprime crisis, as they begged him to sell, was a perfect real-world application of this principle. He trusted his own analysis of intrinsic value, not Mr. Market's daily hysteria.

This reveals a critical self-reinforcing loop at the heart of his success. The exhaustive, primary-source research builds an unshakable, data-driven conviction. This conviction, in turn, provides the psychological armor needed to withstand the "agony of waiting" when the market—and even his own investors—tells him he's wrong. One cannot exist without the other. His patience is not a passive virtue; it is *earned* through thousands of hours of investigative work.

The Telescope: A Framework for Hunting Bubbles

Burry's dual-track methodology begins with the telescope—a top-down process for identifying systemic risks and asset-class bubbles before they become obvious to the rest of the world. It is a systematic hunt for the market's largest and most dangerous delusions.

STEP 1: THE BUBBLE CHECKLIST

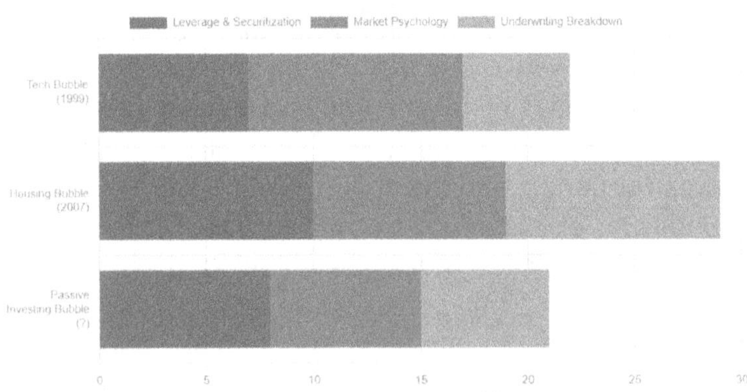

FIGURE 24 - BUBBLE IDENTIFICATION MATRIX SCORES

The investigation begins with a systematic evaluation against a checklist of historical bubble indicators. This transforms a subjective assessment into an objective, evidence-based process. The detective is looking for a specific profile, a signature that has appeared time and again throughout financial history.

TABLE 6 - BUBBLE INDICATOR

Bubble Indicator	Dot-com Bubble (1999-2000)	Housing Bubble (2005-2007)	Potential Passive Bubble (2019-2021)
Parabolic Price Action	Nasdaq Composite +200% in 2 years.	National home prices deviate sharply from long-term trend.	S&P 500 doubles from 2019 to 2021.
"New Era" **Narrative**	"Clicks over cash." "The internet changes everything."	"Housing prices never go down nationally." "Securitization has eliminated risk."	"Passive investing is always superior." "Don't fight the Fed."
Widespread Public Part.	Day trading becomes a national pastime. Taxi drivers giving stock tips.	Flipping houses becomes a popular TV genre. High homeownership rates.	Rise of commission-free trading apps. "Meme stock" phenomenon.

Bubble Indicator	Dot-com Bubble (1999-2000)	Housing Bubble (2005-2007)	Potential Passive Bubble (2019-2021)
Extreme Valuations	P/E ratios for tech stocks exceed 100x or are infinite.	Price-to-rent and price-to-income ratios at all-time highs.	Market cap-to-GDP (Buffett Indicator) at all-time highs.
Pernicious Leverage	High use of margin debt.	Proliferation of subprime, interest-only, and no-doc loans.	Implicit leverage in options markets; price-agnostic flows into index funds.
Financial Innovation	IPOs for companies with no revenue.	Collateralized Debt Obligations (CDOs), Synthetic CDOs.	Exchange-Traded Funds (ETFs), Special Purpose Acquisition Companies (SPACs).

Applying this matrix to the 1999 tech bubble or the 2007 housing bubble reveals a perfect match across all criteria. More recently, Burry used this same lens to identify what he called the "bubble in passive investing". He argued that the flood of price-agnostic capital into index funds, driven by the narrative that passive is always superior, has removed price discovery from the markets. This creates hidden fragilities and liquidity mismatches, particularly in small-cap indices, that are analogous to the flawed risk models that underpinned the subprime CDO market.

STEP 2: FINDING THE EPICENTER (FINANCIAL ARCHAEOLOGY)

Recognizing a bubble is not enough. The detective must find the precise point of failure—the faulty joint in the system's plumbing that will burst under pressure. Burry calls this process "financial archaeology". It is a painstaking deep dive into the primary source documents of the asset class in question.

In the housing crisis, this meant reading the SEC filings and prospectuses for mortgage-backed securities. Through this meticulous work, he discovered the epicenter of fragility was not just "subprime loans," but a hyper-specific segment: the **BBB-rated tranches of Residential Mortgage-Backed Securities (RMBS) from the 2005 vintage**. He saw that these bonds were packed with adjustable-rate mortgages whose low "teaser" rates were contractually designed to reset to unaffordable levels in 2007. The catalyst wasn't a guess; it was written into the fine print of the contracts. He had found the bomb and, more importantly, its timer.

STEP 3: THE ASYMMETRIC BET (STRUCTURING THE WEAPON)

Once the target is identified, the final step is to structure a trade with an asymmetric or convex payoff. The goal is to make a bet where the potential downside is known, capped, and small, while the potential upside is a massive multiple of the capital at risk.

For the housing short, Burry's weapon of choice was the Credit Default Swap (CDS). In simple terms, a CDS is an insurance policy on a bond. Burry paid a regular premium to investment banks, and in return, they agreed to pay him the full value of the bonds if they defaulted. The genius of this structure was twofold. First, it gave him direct exposure to the epicenter of fragility he had identified. Second, his maximum possible loss was limited to the sum of the premiums he paid. The potential gain, however, was enormous. He had engineered a trade with a capped downside and explosive upside.

For other macro theses, like a broad market decline, Burry often uses long-dated put options (LEAPs). A LEAP put gives him the right to sell an index or stock at a set price far in the future. This allows him to make a leveraged bearish bet while strictly limiting his risk to the premium paid for the option. This structure is crucial because it allows him to be early—a common trait of contrarians—without going broke. It transforms the unknowable risk of timing into a fixed, budgeted cost.

The Microscope: A Framework for Sifting Value

Parallel to his top-down macro hunting, Burry runs a bottom-up, company-specific analysis focused on uncovering deep, idiosyncratic value. This is the microscope, an evolved Graham-Dodd process designed to find treasure in the market's trash heap.

STEP 1: HUNTING FOR "ROADKILL"

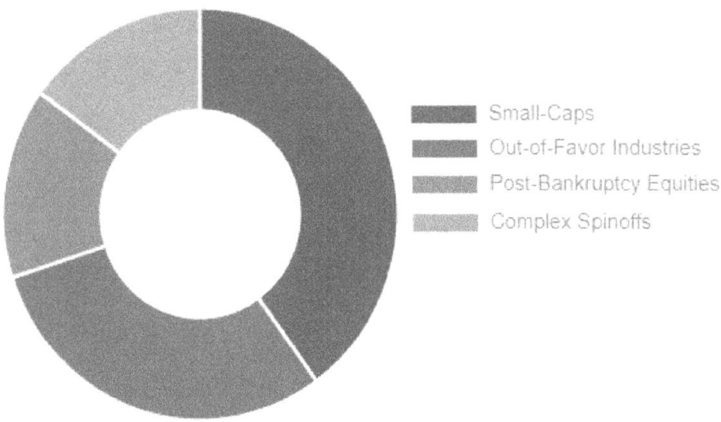

FIGURE 25 - BURRY'S HUNTING GROUNDS FOR VALUE

The search begins where most institutional investors refuse to look. Burry deliberately hunts for opportunities in the most inefficient and neglected corners of the market: small-cap and micro-cap companies, illiquid stocks, and what he terms "roadkill"—companies in out-of-favor industries that have been discarded and left for dead. This is the practical application of what he calls "ick investing": actively seeking out companies mired in litigation, scandal, or seemingly terminal decline that inspire a visceral "ick" reaction from the consensus.

A classic example was his investment in Avant! Corporation, a software company embroiled in a major lawsuit for allegedly stealing source code. Most investors fled. Burry, however, performed a dispassionate analysis. He looked past the scandal and discovered a company with $100 million in cash, generating $100 million in free cash flow, yet trading at a market capitalization of only $250 million. He recognized that the market had over-punished the stock for the legal risk and bought shares that were eventually acquired at a massive profit. He goes where inefficiency reigns because that is where the largest discrepancies between price and value are found.

STEP 2: THE FORENSIC GAUNTLET (THE INTERROGATION)

Every potential investment is subjected to a meticulous, skeptical review of its financial statements. The operating assumption is that financials are instruments of persuasion designed to obscure, not clarify. This is the forensic gauntlet—an interrogation of the numbers to find the truth.

TABLE 7 - THE FORENSIC GAUNTLET

Checklist Area	Key Questions and Red Flags
1. Earnings Quality	- **Accruals vs. Cash Flow:** Is Net Income consistently higher than Cash Flow from Operations? A high or rising accruals ratio is a major red flag for phantom earnings. - **Revenue Recognition:** Are policies aggressive? Is Days Sales Outstanding (DSO)

Checklist Area	Key Questions and Red Flags
	increasing faster than revenue, suggesting the company is struggling to collect cash? - **Non-GAAP Adjustments:** What recurring expenses are being deceptively labeled as "one-time" charges?
2. Balance Sheet Risks	- **Hidden Liabilities:** Scour footnotes for off-balance sheet entities, contingent liabilities (lawsuits), and underfunded pension obligations. - **Debt & Covenants:** Are there restrictive covenants that could be breached? Look for toxic instruments like "death spiral convertibles" that can destroy shareholder value. - **Asset Quality:** Is the balance sheet bloated with goodwill from overpriced acquisitions?
3. Management & Gov.	- **Incentive Alignment:** Does the executive compensation plan (in the proxy statement) reward long-term value creation (e.g., Return on Invested Capital) or short-term manipulation (e.g., adjusted EBITDA)? - **Capital Allocation:** Does management have a track record of value-destructive acquisitions or disciplined, value-creating buybacks? - **Insider Behavior:** Are insiders consistently selling shares? Are there

Checklist Area	Key Questions and Red Flags
	any undisclosed related-party transactions?

This checklist is not about finding fraud, but about achieving a more accurate understanding of a company's true economic reality than the market's consensus view.[43]

STEP 3: CREATING THE CATALYST (FORCING A CONFESSION)

A cheap stock can remain cheap indefinitely. A true value detective understands that a low price is not enough; there must be a plausible catalyst that will force the market to recognize the hidden value. Unlike passive investors who wait for a catalyst to appear, Burry is often willing to become the catalyst himself.

His primary tool for this is shareholder activism. This was most famously demonstrated in his investment in GameStop. After his forensic analysis revealed a fortress balance sheet, he didn't just wait. He wrote a series of public letters to the board in 2019, excoriating them for poor capital allocation and demanding they use the company's excess cash to execute a massive share repurchase. He argued this was the most accretive action possible for shareholders and the most direct way to close the gap between the stock price and its intrinsic value. He was not content to find the evidence; he was willing to take it to court and force a resolution.

Case Studies in Conviction

Theory is sterile without application. Burry's two most famous trades serve as the ultimate case studies, demonstrating the power of his dual-track framework in the wild.

THE BIG SHORT: A SYMPHONY OF THE TELESCOPE

The subprime mortgage trade was the perfect synthesis of his macro framework, the ultimate financial investigation. It began in 2005 by applying the Bubble Checklist to the U.S. housing market, which scored a perfect 10/10.[2] He then moved to "financial archaeology," digging through thousands of pages of prospectuses to pinpoint the epicenter of fragility: the BBB-rated tranches of 2005-vintage RMBS, which contained loans contractually set to explode in 2007. Finally, he structured the perfect asymmetric weapon—the Credit Default Swap—to make a targeted, defined-risk bet on their collapse.

The true test, however, was not analytical but psychological. From 2005 to early 2007, he endured the "agony of waiting." As the housing bubble inflated further, his positions lost value, and he was forced to pay millions in monthly premiums. He faced a full-blown investor revolt, with clients demanding their capital back from a trade they deemed insane. His ability to hold his ground, armed only with the conviction born from his own primary research, was a historic triumph of discipline over hysteria. It was not just an analytical victory; it was a testament to his extraordinary endurance.

THE GAMESTOP SAGA: A MASTERCLASS OF THE MICROSCOPE

FIGURE 26 - GAMESTOP CORPORATION COMMON STOCK 2019-01-01 TO 2021-01-27

If the Big Short was his macro masterpiece, his GameStop investment was the quintessential application of his micro framework. In 2019, he identified GameStop as classic "roadkill"—a hated, discarded business in terminal decline. His forensic deep dive, however, looked past the ugly income statement and found a fortress balance sheet: the company's market value was less than the net cash and inventory on its books. He then became the catalyst, writing public letters to the board demanding a share buyback to unlock this value.

The most crucial lesson came at the end. Scion Asset Management built its stake at an average cost of around $4 per share and exited the position in the fourth quarter of 2020, realizing a substantial profit after the company initiated the buyback and the thesis played out. He was out *before* the Reddit-fueled short squeeze sent the stock into the stratosphere in January 2021. This disciplined exit demonstrates the core of his philosophy: he is a value investor, not a speculator. The goal is to exit when a stock reaches a rational estimate of its intrinsic value, not to ride a speculative mania that has become detached from all fundamentals.

These two case studies appear to be different, but they are mirror images. "The Big Short" was a bet *on* a bubble bursting, requiring him to hold on through years of irrational optimism. The GameStop trade was a bet *against* irrational pessimism, but it required him to sell before irrational optimism took over again. This reveals a higher-order principle: Burry's entire strategy is a war against irrationality in both its manic and depressive forms. The discipline required to short a bubble is the same discipline required to sell into one.

Key Takeaways: Burry's Rules of Investigation

To invest like Michael Burry is to adopt the mindset of a financial detective. His entire philosophy can be distilled into a core set of investigative principles, a code for navigating the market's crime scene.[44]

- **Trust Only Primary Evidence.** Read the source documents yourself—the 10-Ks, the prospectuses, the credit agreements. The truth is in the primary data, not in the secondary summaries.
- **Maintain a Profound Skepticism of Authority.** Treat the pronouncements of CEOs, Wall Street analysts, and central bankers as self-serving narratives that must be rigorously tested, not as facts to be accepted.
- **Earn Your Conviction.** True conviction is not an emotion; it is the byproduct of thousands of hours of obsessive, independent research. It is the only thing that will allow you to stand your ground when the entire world tells you you're wrong.
- **Always Seek an Asymmetric Payoff.** Structure your investments so the potential loss is known, capped, and small, while the potential gain is a multiple of your risk. How you bet is as important as what you bet on.
- **Hunt Where No One Else Is Looking.** The greatest value is found in the market's most hated and neglected corners—the "roadkill" and the "ick investments" that institutions are structurally unable or unwilling to own.

- If a Catalyst Doesn't Exist, Create It. A cheap stock can stay cheap forever. Don't be a passive observer; use your position as a shareholder to force management to unlock the value you have uncovered.
- **Master the Psychology of the Trade.** Learn to endure the agony of waiting when you are early, but have the discipline to exit when your fundamental thesis is realized, regardless of market mania. Your temperament, not your intellect, will ultimately determine your success.
- **Know Your Boundaries.** Define your "circle of competence" with brutal honesty and operate ruthlessly within it. The biggest mistakes are made when you stray into investigations for which you are not equipped.

Chapter 8: The Shareholder Activism Framework (Carl Icahn & Bill Ackman)

The Activist's Playbook: Value Creation by Force

THE CORPORATE RAIDER'S MANDATE

In the ecosystem of modern finance, shareholder activists are the apex predators. They are not passive investors content to ride the market's currents; they are forces of nature who seek out underperformance, challenge entrenched power, and fundamentally alter the trajectory of the world's largest corporations. This is not value investing in the traditional sense; it is value creation by force. To understand this world is to understand the two archetypes who defined it: Carl Icahn, the original corporate raider, and Bill Ackman, the modern grand strategist.

Carl Icahn emerged from the bare-knuckled world of 1980s finance, a Queens-born philosophy major from Princeton who found his calling in the art of the hostile takeover. In his early days, he developed a reputation as a ruthless "corporate raider," using junk bonds to take large stakes in companies like TWA, forcing change, and often extracting "greenmail"—a premium paid by management to make him go away. His core philosophy, honed over decades, is a brutal and simple one: most chief executives are overpaid, insulated by compliant boards, and fundamentally misaligned with the shareholders they are meant to serve. Icahn's intervention became so predictably potent that it spawned a market phenomenon: the "Icahn Lift," a jump in a target company's stock price on the mere anticipation that he would, through sheer force of will, uncover and unlock shareholder value.

If Icahn is the brawling pioneer, Bill Ackman is the polished, modern face of shareholder activism. The founder of Pershing Square Capital Management, Ackman wages his campaigns not with blunt force alone, but with meticulous, research-intensive assaults. His method involves deep fundamental analysis, culminating in sprawling public presentations that are part investment thesis, part courtroom prosecution. He seeks to win not just the vote, but the hearts and minds of fellow shareholders, framing his interventions as crusades for superior strategy and operational excellence.

While their styles differ, their mandate is the same: to solve the principal-agent problem that plagues modern corporations. They operate on the premise that the greatest source of market-beating returns is not in finding undervalued companies, but in identifying *undermanaged* ones and forcing the changes necessary to close the value gap. To witness this playbook in action, one need look no further than Ackman's landmark campaign to remake a titan of North American industry.

SIGNATURE CAMPAIGN: THE BATTLE FOR CANADIAN PACIFIC RAILWAY

In 2011, Canadian Pacific Railway (CP) was a sleeping giant. One of North America's largest railroads, it was also a portrait of complacency, posting the worst operating ratio—a key measure of efficiency—in the entire industry. Its board, however, was content. The company had won awards for its governance practices and believed it was a model of corporate citizenship. This disconnect between self-perception and actual performance is precisely the vulnerability that attracts an activist. For years, portfolio managers had lamented the company's chronic underperformance, blaming a leadership team that consistently used excuses like harsh weather and difficult terrain to justify its laggard status.

Into this environment stepped Bill Ackman. In the fall of 2011, his fund, Pershing Square, began accumulating shares, ultimately disclosing a 14.2% stake that made it CP's largest shareholder. Ackman immediately sought a meeting with the board, not to make suggestions, but to demand a change in leadership. The board, led by Chairman John Cleghorn and CEO Fred Green, met his overture with defiance, declaring their unanimous support for the current strategy before even hearing Ackman's case in full.

This dismissal was a fatal miscalculation. Ackman's "Fix" was not an abstract plan; it was a person. He had identified and recruited Hunter Harrison, the legendary and recently retired CEO of CP's chief rival, Canadian National (CN), who was widely regarded as the best railroader of his generation. Harrison was the architect of "precision scheduled railroading," a revolutionary operating model that had transformed CN into the industry's most efficient player. Ackman's thesis was simple and powerful: install the industry's best operator at the industry's worst-performing asset.

The CP board fought back, commissioning a consultant's report which concluded that Harrison's methods wouldn't work at CP due to the network's steeper grades and track curvature. They dismissed Ackman and Harrison's target of lowering the operating ratio from over 81% to 65% as a "shot in the dark". But in doing so, they fell into Ackman's trap. The battle was no longer just about financial metrics; it was about the future versus the past. Ackman had seized control of the narrative, framing the conflict as one of progress and proven excellence against a stagnant, excuse-making status quo. He presented a clear, compelling vision for a revitalized railroad, led by a proven winner, while the incumbent board could only defend a record of failure.

The campaign reached its climax in the spring of 2012. Ackman launched a full proxy fight to replace a slate of directors and, by extension, the CEO. Just hours before the shareholder meeting, with defeat all but certain, the board capitulated. CEO Fred Green resigned, and five directors, including the chairman, announced they would not stand for re-election. Hunter Harrison was installed as CEO, and the turnaround was immediate and dramatic. Under his leadership, CP's operating ratio plummeted, its profits soared, and its stock price surged. By the time Pershing Square exited its investment in 2016, it had netted a profit of $2.6 billion. The campaign became the archetype of modern activism, a clear demonstration that a well-researched thesis, combined with a superior strategic narrative and the will to fight, could topple even the most entrenched corporate leadership.

The Activist's Mindset: Creating Your Own Catalyst

The fundamental principle that separates shareholder activism from every other form of investing is this: the passive value investor buys a stock and waits for a catalyst to unlock value. The activist *is* the catalyst. This is not a subtle distinction; it is the philosophical core of the entire strategy. Alpha is not discovered in the market; it is manufactured in the boardroom and on the battlefield of a proxy contest.

The process begins when an activist crosses the 5% ownership threshold in a company, triggering the legal requirement to file a Schedule 13D with the Securities and Exchange Commission. This filing is far more than a regulatory formality; it is a public declaration of intent, a shot across the bow of incumbent management. It announces to the world that a major shareholder believes the company is undermanaged and that the status quo is no longer acceptable. This act alone puts the company "in play," forcing every stakeholder—other investors, analysts, employees, and the media—to choose a side. The activist does not wait for the future; they create it by initiating a conflict that demands resolution. This mindset is executed through four key strategic pillars.

THE FOUR PILLARS OF THE ACTIVIST'S STRATEGY

1. "Sum-of-the-Parts (SOTP) Arbitrage" The activist views a diversified conglomerate not as a single, cohesive entity, but as an inefficiently managed portfolio of distinct

businesses. The SOTP analysis is the scalpel used to dissect this portfolio. The objective is to prove that the constituent parts are worth materially more if separated—through spinoffs, divestitures, or an outright sale—than they are when bundled together under a single corporate umbrella. This valuation discrepancy, known as the "conglomerate discount," arises because the market struggles to properly value disparate assets and penalizes a lack of strategic focus. The SOTP valuation becomes the central economic justification for the activist's campaign, a clear, quantifiable measure of the value being destroyed by management's empire-building or strategic paralysis.

2. "Hidden Asset Identification" This pillar involves a forensic examination of a company's balance sheet and business structure to find assets whose true economic value is either misstated under conventional accounting rules or obscured by a flawed corporate strategy. These assets can take many forms: a portfolio of undervalued real estate carried on the books at historical cost; a non-core division with suppressed profitability that could thrive as a standalone entity; valuable patents or intellectual property that are not being monetized; or an overfunded pension plan that represents a source of excess capital. The activist's job is to bring these assets into the light, present a clear plan for their monetization, and reveal to all shareholders the value that incumbent management has failed to realize.

3. "Proxy Fight as Corporate Warfare" The proxy contest is the activist's weapon of last resort, the ultimate tool of leverage. It is a direct battle for control of the corporation's primary decision-making body: the board of directors. A proxy fight is not merely a shareholder vote; it is an all-out campaign to oust the existing directors and install a new slate loyal to the activist's agenda. Winning is the equivalent of a hostile takeover of the boardroom, granting the activist the absolute power to implement their proposed "Fix" without negotiation or compromise. It is an expensive, time-consuming, and brutal process, but its power lies as much in its threat as its execution.
4. "Boardroom Negotiation as Strategic Diplomacy".

   While the proxy fight represents total war, many activist campaigns are won through strategic diplomacy. The power of an activist in the boardroom is directly proportional to the market's belief in their willingness and ability to win a proxy fight. Without a credible threat of war, diplomacy is merely a suggestion. A well-timed letter, a detailed "white paper" laying out the case for change, and the implicit threat of a costly and embarrassing public battle are often sufficient to force a complacent board to the negotiating table. A successful negotiation can achieve the activist's primary goals—typically one or more board seats and a commitment to explore strategic alternatives—without the expense and uncertainty of a full vote. It is boardroom negotiation backed by the credible threat of force.

The Hunting Ground: A Three-Step Guide to Finding Vulnerable Sectors

An activist campaign does not begin with a single company. It begins with a top-down analysis to identify entire sectors where undermanagement is systemic and vulnerabilities are widespread. This process is about finding fertile hunting grounds before selecting a specific target.

STEP 1: GAUGING THE CLIMATE FOR ACTIVISM

Before launching any campaign, the savvy activist must first act as a macro strategist, assessing the legal, regulatory, and political landscape to determine if conditions are favorable. This "regime identification" involves reading three key signals.

First are the rules of engagement. Shareholder-friendly regulations create powerful tailwinds. The adoption of the **universal proxy rule**, for instance, is a structural game-changer. By requiring companies to list all director nominees (both management's and the dissident's) on a single proxy card, it allows shareholders to "mix and match" candidates, making it significantly easier for a well-qualified dissident nominee to win a board seat.

Second is the state of the market. The cost and availability of capital are critical; rising interest rates, for example, increase the cost of borrowing to build the large stakes necessary to exert influence. Similarly, the M&A environment matters. An aggressive antitrust enforcement posture from regulators creates a significant headwind for campaigns where the ultimate "Fix" is the sale of the company or a major division. The current environment, with its combination of higher capital costs and tough antitrust scrutiny, favors campaigns focused on operational turnarounds and governance reforms over those reliant on M&A-driven exits.

Third is the political narrative. The prevailing political zeitgeist can be weaponized. An administration focused on deregulation may create opportunities for financial engineering, while a climate focused on environmental, social, and governance (ESG) issues can provide an alternative attack vector. Activists can leverage themes like sustainability or labor practices to attack a company on non-financial metrics, broadening their appeal to large institutional investors who have their own ESG mandates to fulfill.

STEP 2: FINDING BLOATED AND COMPLACENT INDUSTRIES

With a favorable macro climate confirmed, the next step is a broad, quantitative screen to find industries ripe for intervention. The goal is to identify sectors where undermanagement is not an isolated problem but a systemic one, signaled by four key characteristics:

- **Prevalence of Conglomerates:** Sectors with a high concentration of diversified, multi-division companies are prime hunting grounds. These complex structures often obscure the performance of individual units and are highly susceptible to the "conglomerate discount," making them ideal candidates for SOTP analysis and breakup campaigns.

- **Wide Performance Dispersion:** The analysis seeks sectors with a large gap between the top and bottom performers. This dispersion is a clear signal that a significant number of laggards are being fundamentally mismanaged relative to their peers, who have already proven a viable path to profitability.
- **Inefficient Capital Allocation:** The screen flags sectors where companies exhibit poor capital discipline. This includes hoarding excessive cash on the balance sheet with no clear plan for its use or, conversely, a history of value-destructive, empire-building acquisitions. Both are signs that management is not focused on maximizing shareholder returns.
- **Management Entrenchment:** The screen looks for sectors with a high average tenure for CEOs and board members. While experience is valuable, excessively long tenures often correlate with strategic inertia, a resistance to change, and a lack of accountability—the ideal conditions for an activist intervention.[45]

Based on these criteria, the current landscape reveals three priority sectors. **Diversified Industrials** exhibit a high prevalence of conglomerates with significant SOTP discounts. **Healthcare**, particularly biopharma, shows wide performance dispersion and inefficient R&D spending. Finally, **Consumer Discretionary**, especially retail, contains numerous companies with bloated balance sheets and entrenched management teams struggling to adapt to a changing world.

STEP 3: PINPOINTING THE NARRATIVE GAP

The final step in identifying a hunting ground is a qualitative deep dive to understand the underlying story of decay or opportunity. It is not enough to know a sector is underperforming; the activist must understand *why* and articulate a compelling story for how it can be fixed.

The most potent opportunities exist where there is a fundamental "narrative gap" between the story that incumbent management teams are telling and the new reality that the market is beginning to reward. The activist wins by identifying this disconnect, articulating a new and more compelling vision for the industry's future, and framing the target company as a relic that must be dragged into this new reality.

Within the Diversified Industrials sector, this narrative gap is profound. The core thesis is that legacy industrial conglomerates are strategically paralyzed, clinging to an outdated narrative of diversification and stability while the market demands pure-play focus and operational efficiency. Management teams believe their diversified model provides a defensive moat, but the market sees it as a source of capital misallocation and strategic confusion. This creates a powerful opportunity for activists to force breakups and unlock value.

This theme is powered by a self-reinforcing dynamic that can create a death spiral for complacent conglomerates. When an activist successfully breaks up one industrial conglomerate, the newly independent, pure-play entities often begin to trade at higher valuation multiples. This immediately makes the remaining conglomerates look even cheaper and more vulnerable by comparison, attracting more activists to the sector. The market's perception, altered by the first successful campaign, becomes a fundamental force that validates and accelerates the entire activist theme, turning a single victory into a sector-wide rout.

The Target: A Blueprint for Company Analysis

Once a fertile hunting ground has been identified, the focus shifts from the macro to the micro. The process becomes a bottom-up, forensic analysis to find the single most vulnerable and undervalued company within that sector. This requires a rigorous, six-step blueprint.

STEP 1: PINPOINTING THE WEAKEST LINK

This step applies a strict filter to the companies in a target sector to find the one with the most compelling combination of underperformance and a clear path to value creation. The ideal target will raise red flags across financial, operational, valuation, and governance metrics. The following checklist provides a practical tool for this screening process.

TABLE 8 - THE ACTIVIST'S TARGET CHECKLIST

Category	Metric/Flag	Threshold for Concern	Strategic Rationale
Financial	3-Year Total Shareholder Return (TSR) vs. Peer Median	< -20%	Clear evidence of long-term underperformance that shareholders will be frustrated with.
Financial	Cash / Market Capitalization	> 20%	Signals an inefficient "lazy" balance sheet and poor capital allocation by management.
Operational	Operating Margin vs. Peer Median	< -500 bps	Indicates operational inefficiency or a flawed business model relative to competitors.
Valuation	Sum-of-the-Parts (SOTP) Value vs. Market Cap	> 30% Discount	The core economic justification for a breakup or spinoff campaign.
Governance	CEO Pay vs. TSR Percentile	Top Quartile Pay, Bottom Quartile TSR	The most powerful evidence of misalignment between management and shareholders.

Category	Metric/Flag	Threshold for Concern	Strategic Rationale
Governance	Average Board Tenure	> 15 years	Suggests an entrenched, complacent board lacking fresh perspectives and susceptible to groupthink.
Governance	Percentage of Independent Directors	< 75%	Indicates a board potentially dominated by insiders or allies of the CEO, reducing oversight.
Governance	Insider Ownership	< 1%	Low "skin in the game" from management and the board makes them less aligned with shareholders.
Governance	Presence of a Staggered Board	Yes	A key defense mechanism that signals entrenchment and increases the difficulty of a proxy fight.

STEP 2: EXPOSING THE HIDDEN VALUE

This is the analytical core of the campaign, where the activist quantifies the value that management is destroying or leaving dormant. The SOTP valuation provides the economic justification for the activist's demands and serves as the central exhibit in the case presented to other shareholders. The process is systematic:

1. **Isolate the Segments:** Break the company down into its distinct operating divisions using the segment reporting section of its 10-K filing. For each segment, isolate or estimate key financial metrics like Revenue and EBITDA.
2. **Find Pure-Play Comps and Apply Multiples:** For each segment, identify a set of publicly traded "pure-play" comparable companies. Apply the median valuation multiples (e.g., Enterprise Value / EBITDA) from this peer group to the segment's financials to determine its standalone enterprise value.
3. **Value Corporate Overhead:** Treat unallocated corporate costs (e.g., headquarters staff, central marketing) as a standalone negative liability. Apply a conservative multiple to these costs to calculate their negative value.
4. **Aggregate and Calculate Per-Share Value:** Sum the enterprise values of the operating segments, subtract the negative value of corporate overhead, and adjust for the company's total net debt and other non-operating assets to arrive at the implied equity value. This final figure, divided by the number of shares outstanding, yields the SOTP per-share value. The fundamental formula is:

$$\text{Implied Equity Value} = \sum_{i=1}^{n} \text{EV}_{\text{Segment } i} - \text{EV}_{\text{Corp. Overhead}} - \text{Net Debt} + \text{Non-Operating Assets}$$

The goal is to produce a simple valuation bridge that clearly shows the current stock price on one side, the SOTP-derived "break-up" value on the other, and the massive "Value Gap" in between. This gap represents the value being destroyed by the current corporate structure.

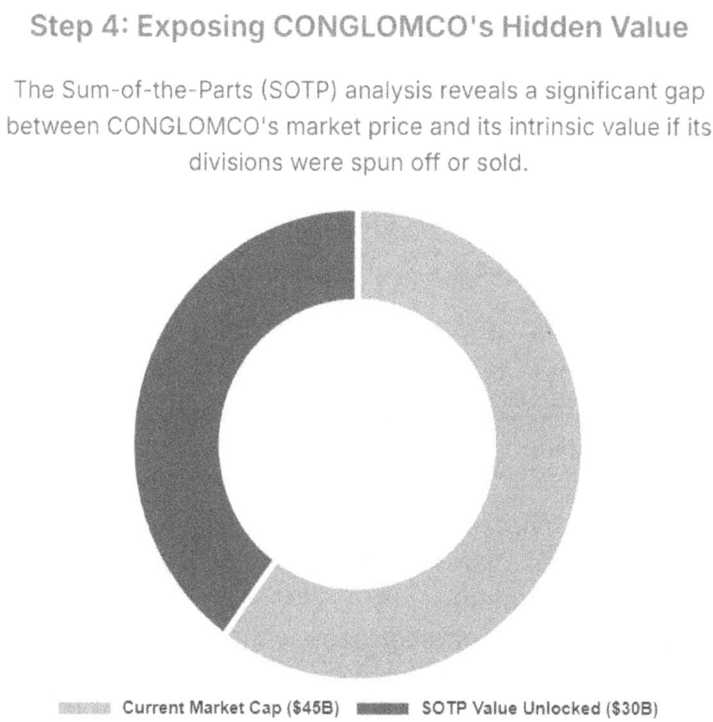

FIGURE 27 - EXPOSING CONGLOMCO'S HIDDEN VALUE

STEP 3: ASSESSING THE DEFENSES

A compelling valuation is useless without a viable path to force its realization. This step involves a cold-blooded assessment of the target's defenses and shareholder base to map the "Path to Victory".[46]

First, the activist must map the fortress walls by meticulously reviewing the company's corporate charter and bylaws to identify any "shark repellents" designed to thwart a hostile campaign. The most formidable of these is a[47]

staggered board, where directors are split into classes with only one class up for election each year. This forces an activist to win proxy contests in at least two consecutive years to gain majority control, dramatically increasing the time and cost of a campaign. Another key defense is a

poison pill, a shareholder rights plan that can be triggered by an activist crossing an ownership threshold, flooding the market with new shares and massively diluting the activist's stake.

Next, the activist must identify their allies by analyzing the company's shareholder base, typically found in the annual proxy statement (DEF 14A). The ideal target has a fragmented shareholder base with high ownership by large, passive institutional investors like Vanguard and BlackRock. These index funds have a fiduciary duty to maximize value but lack the resources to engage in activism themselves. They are the critical "swing voters" in a proxy contest and can be persuaded by a well-reasoned economic argument, especially when it is endorsed by influential proxy advisory firms like Institutional Shareholder Services (ISS) and Glass Lewis. Conversely, a company with a large, controlling founder or high insider ownership is often an impenetrable fortress.

STEP 4: ARCHITECTING THE PLAN

At this stage, the activist must move from diagnosis to prescription. The "Fix" is the specific, actionable plan that will unlock the value identified in the SOTP analysis. A vague demand to "maximize shareholder value" is useless; the plan must be concrete, credible, and directly address the root causes of the company's underperformance. The activist playbook contains a menu of solutions tailored to specific corporate ailments.

TABLE 9 - THE ACTIVIST'S MENU OF SOLUTIONS

If the Ailment Is...	**The Solution** Is...	**Economic Rationale**	**Classic Case Study**
Strategic Bloat (Unfocused Conglomerate)	**Spin-off / Divestiture**	Eliminates the "conglomerate discount" and creates focused pure-play companies that command higher valuation multiples.	Icahn pushes Manitowoc to separate its Cranes and Foodservice businesses.

If the Ailment Is...	The Solution Is...	Economic Rationale	Classic Case Study
Strategic Weakness (Lack of Scale / Inefficient Operator)	**Sale of Company**	Realizes an immediate and certain control premium for all shareholders; transfers assets to a more efficient operator.	Icahn pushes for Netflix to be sold to a larger tech company.
Operational Failure (Poor Leadership / Execution)	**New CEO / Board Seats**	Replaces failed leadership with a new team capable of executing a turnaround and restoring investor confidence.	Ackman replaces the CEO and board at Canadian Pacific Railway.
Financial Inefficiency ("Lazy" Balance Sheet)	**Share Buyback / Recapitalization**	Returns unproductive capital to shareholders, leverages the balance sheet to increase ROE, and signals the stock is cheap.	Icahn pressures Apple to dramatically increase its share repurchase program.

The chosen "Fix" becomes the central message of the campaign, the promise of a better future that the activist uses to rally support from other shareholders.

Case Study: The Campaign for CONGLOMCO (CGLO)

To bring this playbook to life, consider the hypothetical campaign for CONGLOMCO (ticker: CGLO), a company that represents the perfect activist target. The entire process, from identification to the final engagement strategy, illustrates the playbook in action.

The Hunt: The campaign begins with the macro screen, which flags the Diversified Industrials sector as a fertile hunting ground due to its high concentration of conglomerates and a persistent narrative gap between management's story of "diversification" and the market's demand for "focus". Applying the Activist's Target Checklist to companies in the sector, CONGLOMCO immediately stands out as the weakest link. Its 3-year total shareholder return is a dismal -25% against a peer median of +15%. Its operating margins are 800 basis points below the industry average. And its governance is a case study in entrenchment: the average board tenure is 18 years, and the CEO's compensation is in the 90th percentile while shareholder returns are in the 15th. CGLO is a company adrift, led by a misaligned and complacent board.

The Analysis: The next step is to quantify the opportunity. A detailed Sum-of-the-Parts analysis is conducted on CGLO's three disparate divisions: Aerospace, Consumer Goods, and Chemicals. By applying conservative, peer-based multiples to each segment, the hidden value is exposed. The analysis reveals an implied equity value of $60 per share. With CGLO currently trading at $40, this represents a staggering 50% upside. The market is applying a massive conglomerate discount, penalizing the company for its lack of strategic synergy and focus. The core hypothesis is formed: CGLO is worth at least 40% more broken apart than it is together, and its entrenched board is incapable of unlocking this value without external force.

The Battle Plan: With the economic case established, the focus shifts to the path to victory. The governance takedown reveals a formidable defense: a staggered board, which means a proxy fight for control will be a multi-year war of attrition. However, a critical vulnerability is also discovered: the company does not have a poison pill in place, leaving it exposed to a determined activist. The shareholder base analysis provides further encouragement. Ownership is 85% institutional, with the top five holders being large, passive index funds that control 40% of the shares. With insider ownership below 1%, this is a shareholder base that can be persuaded by a compelling economic argument.

The "Fix" is then architected as a clear, two-pronged attack. The primary demand is a tax-free spinoff of the Consumer Goods and Chemicals divisions into two separate public companies. This will eliminate the conglomerate discount and create three focused, pure-play entities that the market can value appropriately. The secondary demand is to replace two long-tenured directors on the board of the remaining Aerospace company with the activist's own nominees, ensuring the spinoffs are executed properly and a new culture of accountability is installed.

The War: The final engagement strategy is a patient, two-year campaign designed to overcome the staggered board defense.

FIGURE 28 - CASE STUDY: THE 2-YEAR CAMPAIGN FOR CONGLOMCO

- **Year 1:** The campaign will launch publicly with the filing of a 13D and the release of a detailed "white paper." This document will lay out the $60 per share SOTP valuation, critique management's long history of underperformance, and present the spinoff plan as the only logical path forward. The activist will nominate a slate of highly qualified directors for the one-third of board seats up for election. The goal is to win at least one seat and secure a high "withhold" vote against incumbent directors, demonstrating widespread shareholder dissatisfaction and building a foundation of momentum.
- **Year 2:** Leveraging the momentum and credibility gained in Year 1, the activist will return

> to nominate a second slate of directors. With a victory in the second year, the activist-backed directors will constitute a majority of the board, giving them the power to execute the spinoff plan and unlock the 50% valuation gap for all shareholders.

This entire campaign is engineered to become a self-fulfilling prophecy. The initial 13D filing is designed to force sell-side analysts to run their own SOTP models, which will validate the activist's thesis and lead to price target upgrades. The public white paper is crafted to win the support of proxy advisory firms. A strong showing in the first year's proxy vote will demonstrate momentum, making it easier to attract support from other institutions in the second year. Each tactical victory—a positive analyst report, a supportive statement from an institution, a favorable ISS recommendation—makes the next victory more likely, creating a snowball effect of credibility that makes the activist's plan feel not just possible, but inevitable.

Key Takeaways: The Activist's Code

Shareholder activism is one of the most intellectually demanding and combative disciplines in finance. Success requires a mastery of valuation, corporate law, and human psychology. The lessons learned from decades of campaigns, from the victories of Carl Icahn and Bill Ackman to their cautionary defeats, can be distilled into a core set of principles: The Activist's Code.

- **Be the Catalyst.** Alpha is not found; it is manufactured. Passive investors wait for change; activists create it. Your actions—the 13D filing, the public letter, the proxy fight—must be the force that compels the market and the company to recognize the value you have identified.
- The "Fix" is Everything. A campaign without a clear, credible, and actionable plan is just a complaint. Whether it's a strategic spinoff, a financial recapitalization, or an operational overhaul, the "Fix" must be a concrete prescription for the company's specific ailments. As the Canadian Pacific campaign proved, the most powerful "Fix" is often a world-class leader.
- **Win the Narrative.** The battle is fought with numbers, but it is won with a more compelling story about the future than the one management is telling. Frame the conflict as progress versus stagnation, focus versus bloat, and accountability versus entrenchment.
- **Know Your Battlefield.** A brilliant valuation is useless if you cannot overcome the company's defenses. Governance analysis is not optional; it is the map to victory. You must understand every "shark repellent" and chart a viable path to control before you invest a single dollar.
- **Build Your Coalition.** You cannot win alone. Your primary audience is the large, passive institutional investors who represent the critical swing vote. Your argument must be tailored to convince them and the proxy advisory firms that guide their decisions.
- **Ego is the Portfolio Killer.** As demonstrated by high-profile losses in campaigns like Herbalife

and Valeant, making a fight personal or falling in love with your own thesis is the fastest path to ruin. Never underestimate your opponent's will to fight, and be willing to admit when you are wrong.

- **Always Be Re-underwriting.** An activist campaign is a dynamic battle, not a static investment. The thesis must be constantly challenged and re-evaluated in the face of new information, whether it's a defensive move by the company or a fundamental change in the business. Hope is not a strategy.

The Global Macro Thinkers

In this section, we pivot from the microscope to the telescope. Where the value school taught us to be forensic accountants and business analysts, the global macro thinkers teach us to be historians, political scientists, and global detectives. Their focus is not on the intrinsic worth of a single company, but on the great tides of capital, politics, and human psychology that shape the destinies of entire markets.

Our guides on this global odyssey are the undisputed titans of the field, **George Soros and Stanley Druckenmiller**. They will introduce us to the powerful concepts of reflexivity and liquidity—the feedback loops and flows of money that are the true prime movers of asset prices. From their philosophical heights, we will descend into the specialized domains of masters who applied a top-down, global lens to specific asset classes. We will ride the commodity supercycles with the legendary adventurer **Jim Rogers**, navigate the boom-and-bust world of the oil patch with the wildcatter-turned-raider **T. Boone Pickens**, and explore the volatile but high-growth frontiers of developing nations with the pioneer **Mark Mobius**.

These chapters will challenge you to think bigger, to connect disparate global events, and to understand that sometimes the most important factor for your stock is not its earnings, but the policy decision of a central banker half a world away.

Chapter 9: The Reflexive Macro Framework (George Soros)

The Alchemist of Finance

To understand the investor who made a billion dollars in a single day, one must first understand the boy who survived the Nazi occupation of Hungary. George Soros was born György Schwartz in Budapest in 1930 to a prosperous Jewish family. His comfortable upbringing was shattered in 1944 when Nazi Germany occupied his homeland. That year, which Soros would later call the best of his life, was a crucible of survival. As over 500,000 Hungarian Jews were murdered, the Schwartz family survived by changing their name to Soros and securing false identity papers, living as Christians and helping others do the same. At just 14, Soros learned a lesson that would define his life and his financial career: the official version of reality is often a dangerous fiction, and survival depends on recognizing the chasm between perception and fact.

This profound skepticism of rigid, official ideologies was reinforced after the war. As the Communists consolidated power, Soros left for London in 1947, working as a railway porter and waiter to fund his studies at the London School of Economics. There, he encountered the philosopher Karl Popper, whose work on "open societies" gave Soros the formal language to articulate his intuitive understanding of the world. He learned that any system of thought that claims to have a monopoly on the truth, be it Nazism or communism, is fundamentally flawed. This worldview, forged in the fires of 20th-century European history, would become the intellectual foundation for one of the greatest financial trades in history.

The Trade of the Century: Breaking the Bank of England

By 1992, George Soros was a successful hedge fund manager, but not yet a household name. That would change on a single day: September 16, 1992, a day that would be immortalized in financial lore as "Black Wednesday".

The stage was set by a political project called the European Exchange Rate Mechanism (ERM). A precursor to the Euro, the ERM was designed to stabilize European currencies by pegging them to the powerful German Deutsche Mark. In 1990, Britain, under Prime Minister John Major, joined the ERM at a rate of roughly 2.95 Deutsche Marks to the pound—a rate many economists believed was too high and made British exports uncompetitive. This was a political act of faith, an attempt to import Germany's low-inflation credibility, but it created a fatal structural weakness.

By 1992, that weakness had become a crisis. Germany, grappling with the inflationary costs of reunification, was raising its interest rates, making the Deutsche Mark even stronger. Meanwhile, Britain was mired in a deep recession, a situation that desperately called for *lower* interest rates to stimulate the economy. The British government was caught in an impossible bind: defending the pound's peg within the ERM required raising interest rates, which would strangle the domestic economy, while saving the economy required cutting rates, which would shatter the peg.

Soros, along with his brilliant lead portfolio manager Stanley Druckenmiller, identified this fundamental contradiction. They saw that the British government's commitment to the ERM was a flawed perception at war with a brutal economic reality. They began to build a massive short position, borrowing billions of pounds and selling them for other currencies, betting that the pound would have to be devalued.

The pressure mounted. On the morning of Black Wednesday, the Bank of England began a desperate defense, buying up pounds on the open market. When that failed, the government announced it would raise interest rates from an already high 10% to 12%. The market didn't flinch; the selling continued. In a final, panicked move, the government promised to raise rates to a crippling 15% the next day. But the traders, led by Soros, knew this was an empty threat. No government could sustain such high rates during a severe recession. By 7:00 pm that evening, the British government capitulated. Britain crashed out of the ERM, and the pound plummeted. Soros's Quantum Fund netted a profit of over $1 billion, and he was forever branded "The Man Who Broke the Bank of England".

This legendary trade was not merely a shrewd currency speculation; it was the physical manifestation of a philosophical argument. Soros was not just betting against the pound. He was betting against the fallibility of politicians who believed they could defy economic gravity. He was betting that a rigid, flawed belief system—the ERM—would ultimately collapse under the weight of its own contradictions. It was the ultimate proof of his core theory: that flawed human perceptions actively shape reality, but only until reality can no longer sustain the fiction.

The Flaw in the Machine: Understanding Reflexivity

At the heart of George Soros's investment philosophy are two powerful, interconnected concepts he adapted from his mentor, Karl Popper: Fallibility and Reflexivity. These are not complex financial metrics but fundamental ideas about the human condition and how it interacts with the world.[48]

The Twin Pillars of Soros's Thought

The first pillar is the **Principle of Fallibility**. This idea posits that our understanding of the world, especially complex systems with thinking participants like financial markets, is always incomplete and distorted. This isn't just about making mistakes or having cognitive biases; it's a fundamental condition. Because we are *inside* the system we are trying to analyze, we can never be purely objective observers. Our very participation changes the system we are studying. This guarantees a persistent gap between our perception of reality and the actual state of affairs. For most economic theories, this gap is random "noise" that is quickly arbitraged away. For Soros, this gap is the fertile ground where all market opportunities are born.

The second pillar, **Reflexivity**, is the engine that fallibility drives. It describes the two-way feedback loop where our flawed perceptions don't just interpret reality, they actively *change* it. This is the radical departure from standard economic theory, which assumes that market prices passively reflect an independent reality. Soros argues that reality itself is not independent; it is being constantly shaped by the beliefs and actions of market participants.

The Two-Way Street: Cognitive vs. Manipulative Functions

To understand how this feedback loop works, Soros breaks it down into two functions that are always operating and interfering with each other.

1. The Cognitive Function (World → Mind): This is the familiar, one-way street of traditional analysis. We act as observers, trying to understand the world. We see rising corporate profits (reality) and form a belief that the company is a good investment (perception). In this function, reality is the independent variable that shapes our thoughts.
2. The Manipulative Function (Mind → World): This is Soros's key insight, the other side of the street. Our beliefs lead to actions that influence the course of events. Our belief that a company is a good investment leads us to buy its stock (action). If enough people share this belief, the stock price goes up, which might allow the company to raise capital more cheaply or attract better talent (new reality). Here, our perception becomes the independent variable that shapes the world.

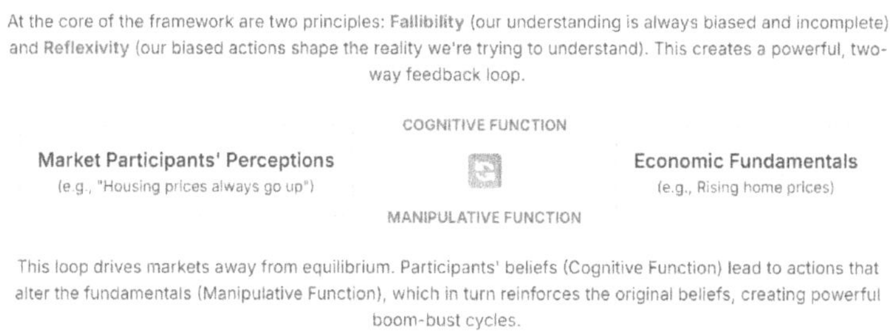

FIGURE 29 - THE FLAW IN THE MACHINE: UNDERSTANDING REFLEXIVITY

The core of reflexivity is that these two functions are locked in a perpetual dance. The 2008 housing crisis is a perfect, tragic example of this loop in action. First, the *cognitive function*: people observed rising home prices and formed the belief that "housing is a risk-free, can't-lose investment." Then, the *manipulative function* took over: this widespread belief led banks to dramatically ease lending standards, offering mortgages to almost anyone. This action created a new reality: a flood of cheap credit fueled a frenzy of buying, which drove home prices to astronomical levels. This new reality then powerfully reinforced the original belief, creating a massive, self-sustaining bubble that was destined to collapse when reality could no longer support the flawed perception.

This concept is the absolute antithesis of the Efficient Market Hypothesis (EMH), the bedrock of modern finance. The EMH assumes markets are passive and rational price-discovery machines, where prices simply reflect fundamentals. Reflexivity argues that markets are active, chaotic, and self-influencing social systems, where prices *create* fundamentals. An EMH proponent sees a high stock price as a reflection of a company's bright future. A reflexive investor understands that the high stock price may be the very thing *creating* that bright future, by giving the company access to cheap capital, the ability to acquire rivals with its stock, and the prestige to attract top talent. This is why Soros hunts for the disequilibrium of boom-bust cycles, while traditional finance assumes equilibrium is the natural state of affairs.

Riding the Wave: The Anatomy of a Boom-Bust Cycle

When a flawed idea takes root in the market and begins a reflexive feedback loop, it doesn't move randomly. It follows a predictable, albeit asymmetric, lifecycle. This is the boom-bust cycle, and for a reflexive investor, it is the fundamental pattern of market behavior. Understanding this pattern is not about predicting the future with certainty; it is about diagnosing the present with clarity. It is the story of how a market misconception is born, grows to dominate all thinking, and ultimately collapses under its own weight.

The following table serves as a field guide to this process. It breaks down the cycle into eight distinct phases, mapping how price action, the dominant narrative, underlying fundamentals, and participant behavior evolve at each stage. It is the single most valuable tool for transforming the abstract theory of reflexivity into a practical diagnostic checklist.

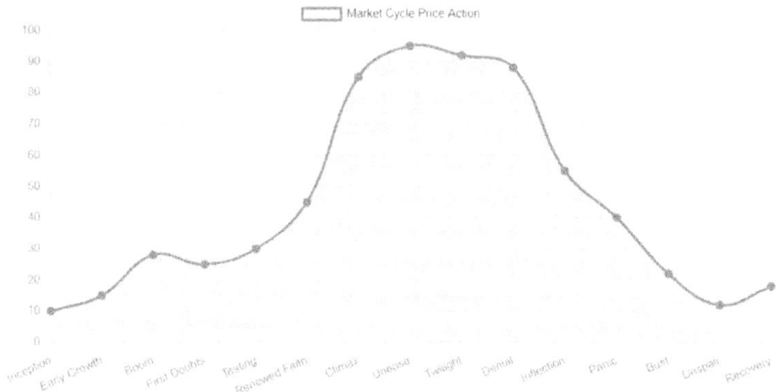

FIGURE 30 - RIDING THE WAVE: ANATOMY OF A BOOM-BUST CYCLE

TABLE 10 - THE ANATOMY OF A BOOM-BUST CYCLE

Phase	Price Action	Narrative & Sentiment	Fundamentals	Participant Behavior
Inception	Gradual, tentative uptrend. Low volatility.	Niche interest, skepticism from mainstream.	Underlying trend improves, but data is nascent.	Early adopters accumulate positions quietly.
Boom	Accelerating uptrend. Momentum increases.	Narrative gains traction. "This time is different."	Fundamentals improve, partly due to reflexive effects.	Trend-followers enter. Media coverage increases.
Testing	Sharp but short-lived correction.	Doubts surface, but are quickly dismissed. "Buy the dip."	A minor setback in data, quickly explained away.	Weak hands are shaken out; conviction of bulls is

Phase	Price Action	Narrative & Sentiment	Fundamentals	Participant Behavior
				reinforced.
Climax	Parabolic advance. High volume and volatility.	Euphoria. Narrative is accepted as fact. Dissent is ridiculed.	Fundamentals are good but cannot justify valuations.	Retail investors pile in. FOMO is rampant. Leverage peaks.
Twilight	Price action stalls, becomes choppy. "Distribution."	Cracks appear in the narrative. Insiders grow quiet.	Fundamental momentum begins to slow.	Insiders distribute positions to the public.
Inflection	Sharp, violent reversal. Break of key support levels.	Panic. Narrative shatters. Fear dominates.	A key catalyst confirms the flaw in the misconception.	Forced liquidation of leveraged positions. "Sell at any price."
Bust	Accelerating downtrend. Overshooting to the downside.	Despair. Recrimination. The asset is "un-investable."	Fundamentals deteriorate sharply.	Capitulation. Retail investors exit at the bottom.

Phase	Price Action	Narrative & Sentiment	Fundamentals	Participant Behavior
Recovery	Panic subsides, forced selling is exhausted, prices stabilize.	Indifference. Lingering fear.	Fundamentals bottom out and begin to stabilize.	Value investors begin to accumulate.

Let's walk through this lifecycle. It begins at **Inception**, where a new fundamental trend starts to develop but is largely unnoticed. Early adopters begin to buy, but the mood is skeptical. Then comes the **Boom**, or acceleration phase. The market recognizes the trend, and a powerful, positive narrative forms around it. The reflexive loop ignites: rising prices attract more buyers, which reinforces the belief and drives prices even higher. Credit often expands, adding fuel to the fire.

Inevitably, the trend faces a **Testing** phase. A negative news story or a market correction challenges the narrative. This is a critical juncture. If the trend survives, the conviction of its believers is strengthened, and the "buy the dip" mentality takes hold, propelling the trend forward with even greater force. This leads to the **Climax**. Here, the gap between perception and reality becomes a chasm. The narrative is accepted as undeniable truth. Valuations become detached from any historical precedent, euphoria is rampant, and leverage peaks as retail investors pile in, driven by a fear of missing out (FOMO).

This is the point of maximum risk. The **Twilight** phase arrives when reality can no longer sustain the exaggerated expectations. Insiders sense the change and begin to quietly sell their positions to the eager public. The price action becomes choppy and stalls. Then comes the **Inflection** point—the crash. The trend violently reverses as a catalyst shatters the narrative. The positive feedback loop flips into a negative one, amplified by the forced liquidation of leveraged positions, which causes a catastrophic price decline.

The **Bust** is the mirror image of the boom. Falling prices reinforce pessimistic beliefs, leading to more selling. The despair becomes as overdone as the initial optimism was. Finally, after the panic subsides and the forced selling is exhausted, the cycle enters **Recovery**, where prices stabilize at deeply undervalued levels, setting the stage for the next cycle to begin.

This cycle is inherently asymmetric. The boom is a long, drawn-out process, while the bust is short, sharp, and violent. This reflects the asymmetry of both human emotion and financial mechanics. Greed, fueled by gradually expanding credit, is a slow-burning fire. Fear, however, is an explosion triggered by the sudden panic of margin calls and forced liquidations. Understanding this asymmetry is crucial to appreciating why reversals are so violent and why the points of maximum opportunity—and danger—lie at the inflection points.

The Soros Playbook: A Practical Guide

Understanding the philosophy of reflexivity and the anatomy of a boom-bust cycle is one thing; translating it into an actionable investment process is another. The Soros framework provides a systematic, four-step playbook for identifying and exploiting these powerful market dynamics. It is a process designed to move from broad observation to a specific, disciplined trade idea.

Step 1: Scan the Horizon for a Flawed Story

The process begins not with a spreadsheet, but with a wide-angle lens. The goal is to identify the dominant market narrative—the story that everyone believes to be true. This involves consuming a vast array of information: high-level economic data, central bank communications, geopolitical news, and major media narratives. You are not looking for what is happening, but for what the market *thinks* is happening. The objective is to formulate a preliminary, testable hypothesis about where this consensus view might be fundamentally wrong. For example, in late 2023, the dominant narrative was that a "soft landing" was assured, meaning inflation would fall without a recession, allowing the Federal Reserve to cut interest rates deeply. A reflexive hypothesis might have been: "The market's belief in a painless disinflation is a misconception. Persistent wage pressures will force the Fed to hold rates higher for longer, triggering a hard landing".

Step 2: Find the "Fertile Fallacy"

A flawed story is not enough. To be tradable, it must be a "fertile fallacy"—a misconception so powerful that it is actively shaping reality. This is the heart of the analysis. Here, you must rigorously map the mechanics of the self-reinforcing feedback loop. How, precisely, does the flawed belief influence behavior? And how does that behavior then reinforce the original belief?

Using the "higher for longer" example, the feedback loop could be mapped as follows: The belief in future rate cuts (the misconception) leads to rallies in stocks and bonds. This, in turn, eases financial conditions, which supports economic growth and inflation. Initially, this stronger growth appears to validate the "soft landing" narrative. However, it ultimately forces the Federal Reserve to remain more hawkish, which eventually breaks the loop by causing bond yields to rise sharply. Identifying this causal chain is what separates a vague opinion from a robust reflexive thesis.

Step 3: Diagnose the Cycle's Phase

Once you have identified a fertile fallacy and its feedback loop, you must determine where it is in its lifecycle. Using the "Anatomy of a Boom-Bust Cycle" table as your guide, you analyze quantitative data to make an objective assessment. Are credit spreads tight and volatility low, suggesting the complacency of a mature **Boom** or **Climax** phase? Is investor positioning at an extreme, as measured by futures data or fund flows? Is leverage, such as margin debt, at a record high?16

The goal is to assess the asymmetry of the potential trade. The most favorable risk/reward opportunities exist at the very beginning of the **Boom** (to ride the trend) or at the **Inflection** point (to bet on the reversal). Trying to short a market in the midst of a euphoric **Climax** phase, even if you know it's a bubble, is exceptionally dangerous because the trend can remain irrational longer than you can remain solvent.

Step 4: Define Your Triggers and Escape Routes

This final step is what instills discipline and separates professional speculation from amateur gambling. A reflexive thesis should not be a passive, open-ended bet; it must be a time-bound and event-driven strategy. You must pre-define the specific, observable events that will act as your triggers.

- **Catalysts:** These are the future events that you believe will confirm your thesis and trigger the inflection point. A catalyst must be specific. For the "higher for longer" thesis, a catalyst might be: "An upside surprise in the next two Consumer Price Index (CPI) reports". This is your pre-defined signal to enter the trade.
- **Invalidators:** These are just as important. They are the pre-defined conditions that, if met, prove your thesis is wrong and signal that you must exit the position immediately, without emotion or hesitation. An invalidator might be: "Core inflation prints below 0.2% month-over-month for two consecutive months, which would validate the market's dovish view".

By defining these tripwires in advance, you subordinate your emotions to a pre-agreed plan. It is the ultimate tool for managing the intense psychological pressure that comes with making large, contrarian bets.

Key Questions to Ask

To distill this playbook into a set of core questions, an investor looking to apply this framework should constantly ask themselves:

- What is the dominant market narrative that everyone accepts as truth? Where is the most significant contradiction between this narrative and the underlying data?
- What is the core market misconception? How does this belief shape actions that, in turn, create a reality that reinforces the original belief?
- Looking at sentiment, positioning, and leverage, what phase of the boom-bust cycle are we in? Is the trade crowded and complacent, or fearful and capitulating?
- What specific, future event could act as the catalyst to shatter the prevailing narrative? And, just as importantly, what specific event would prove my own thesis wrong and force me to get out?

Case Studies in Reflexivity

Theory is best understood through practice. By examining historical trades through the lens of the reflexive framework, we can see how these principles play out in the real world, leading to both spectacular successes and humbling failures.

Case Study 1: The Pound Trade Deconstructed (1992)

Let's revisit Soros's most famous trade, but this time, analyze it using the four-step playbook to see the systematic thinking behind the legendary intuition.

- **Step 1 (Flawed Story):** The dominant narrative was the British government's absolute and unwavering political commitment to maintaining the pound's value within the ERM. The market, for a time, took politicians at their word.
- **Step 2 (Fertile Fallacy):** The fertile fallacy was the belief that a political construct (the ERM peg) could indefinitely suppress economic reality (a deep UK recession). The reflexive mechanism was viciously elegant: the more the Bank of England was forced to intervene by hiking interest rates and spending foreign reserves to defend the peg, the more pain it inflicted on the British economy. This worsening recession, in turn, made the peg even less credible, which invited even more aggressive selling from speculators. The defense of the peg was actively destroying the conditions necessary for the peg to survive.
- **Step 3 (Phase):** By late summer 1992, the process was clearly entering the **Twilight** and **Inflection** phase. The flaw in the narrative was becoming apparent to sophisticated observers as the UK's economic pain intensified and political rhetoric grew more desperate.[49]
- **Step 4 (Catalyst):** The ultimate catalyst was a series of public remarks from Germany's Bundesbank president, Helmut Schlesinger, which were interpreted by the market as a clear signal that Germany would not lower its own interest rates to help Britain defend the pound. This comment shattered the narrative of unified European support and was the final trigger that unleashed the full force of the speculative attack.

Case Study 2: A Lesson in Timing - The Tech Bubble Failure (1999-2000)

If the pound trade represents the framework's power, Soros's experience in the dot-com bubble illustrates its primary peril: timing. It is a powerful lesson in humility and the danger of fighting a euphoric trend.

Soros correctly diagnosed the bubble. He identified the "New Paradigm" narrative—the idea that for internet companies, profits didn't matter, only growth and "eyeballs"—as a classic fertile fallacy. He saw the reflexive loop with perfect clarity: soaring stock prices allowed unprofitable tech companies to raise billions in cheap capital, fund their losses, attract the best engineering talent with stock options, and use their inflated stock as a currency to acquire other companies. These actions created real business growth, which appeared to validate the initial narrative and fueled the bubble even higher.

His diagnosis was flawless, but his timing was fatal. He began to heavily short tech stocks in 1999, believing the **Climax** phase was ending. He was too early. The positive feedback loop was still incredibly powerful, and the market's euphoria had not yet broken. As the NASDAQ continued its parabolic ascent into early 2000, his fund suffered massive losses, reportedly in the hundreds of millions of dollars. He was eventually forced to cover his shorts near the top, just before the bubble finally burst.

The post-mortem of this failure is perhaps the single most important lesson in the entire framework: Correctly identifying a misconception and a reflexive bubble is insufficient. The timing of the inflection point is paramount. One must not short a bubble simply because it appears irrational; you must wait for clear, tangible evidence that the self-reinforcing feedback loop itself is breaking before committing significant capital to a reversal trade. Being too early is functionally indistinguishable from being wrong.

Key Takeaways: The Alchemist's Rules

Distilling this powerful and nuanced framework into a set of core principles provides a guide for any investor seeking to look beyond the market's surface noise and understand the deeper forces at play. These are the rules of the alchemist.

- **Embrace Fallibility.** Start from the premise that all market views, including and especially your own, are inherently biased and incomplete. The consensus view is not a source of safety; it is the source of the greatest potential misconception.
- **Hunt for Fertile Fallacies.** Do not just look for assets that are over or undervalued. Look for powerful, widely-held beliefs that are actively shaping economic reality. The most profitable opportunities lie in identifying a trend that is creating its own fundamentals.
- **Think in Cycles, Not in Straight Lines.** Markets do not move from one equilibrium to another. They are in a constant state of flux, moving through the phases of a boom-bust cycle. Your primary analytical task is to diagnose which phase of the cycle a given asset or theme is in.

- **Seek Asymmetric Payoffs.** The goal is not to be right more often than you are wrong. The goal is to structure your trades so that the amount of money you make when you are right is multiples greater than the amount you lose when you are wrong. The points of maximum asymmetry are typically at the beginning of a boom and at the final inflection point.[50]
- **Marry Conviction with Humility.** When you have identified a high-conviction, asymmetric opportunity, you must have the courage to make a large, concentrated bet. As Stanley Druckenmiller learned from Soros, "you have to go for the jugular". However, this aggression must be paired with the radical humility to recognize instantly when your thesis is wrong and cut the position without hesitation or emotion.
- **Wait for the Inflection.** This is the painful lesson of the tech bubble. Do not short a powerful, self-reinforcing trend simply because it seems irrational or overvalued. A bubble can always get bigger. Wait for concrete evidence—a clear catalyst—that proves the feedback loop is breaking and the narrative is shattering. In the game of reflexivity, timing is not just important; it is everything.

Chapter 10: The Liquidity & Reflexivity Framework (Stanley Druckenmiller)

In the unforgiving savannah of the global markets, there are grazers, there are predators, and then there is the apex predator. This is an investor whose vision, courage, and discipline are so profound that they don't just participate in the market—they shape it. For over three decades, Stanley Druckenmiller has been that apex predator. His track record is the stuff of legend: a multi-decade run of staggering compound annual returns without a single down year, a feat of consistency and aggression that places him in the pantheon of the greatest investors of all time. To understand his method is to understand a powerful and repeatable engine for navigating the complexities of the financial world.

The Apex Predator: The Man Who Broke the Bank of England

To grasp the power of the Druckenmiller doctrine, we must begin not with a theory, but with a story—a trade so audacious it became a legend. The year is 1992. The United Kingdom has tethered its currency, the British Pound, to the German Deutsche Mark through the European Exchange Rate Mechanism (ERM). This political arrangement, however, was a flagrant violation of economic reality. Germany, grappling with the costs of reunification, was forced to keep its interest rates sky-high to fight inflation. To maintain the pound's peg, the Bank of England had to match these punishing rates, strangling an already weak British economy in the process.

The market's consensus was that the Bank of England, backed by the full faith and credit of the UK government, would defend the peg at all costs. Druckenmiller saw something different. He saw an artificial policy construct stretched to its breaking point. He understood that politicians and central bankers have a pain threshold, and the economic agony inflicted on the British people was becoming unbearable. This was his core thesis: the peg was doomed.

He began building a massive short position against the pound. The trade was a masterclass in asymmetry. The downside was minimal—the cost to hold the position and the narrow band within which the pound was allowed to trade. The upside was a catastrophic devaluation. As he built his position, his mentor, George Soros, recognized the once-in-a-decade nature of the opportunity. He pushed Druckenmiller to do more, to size the bet for the history books. They did, leveraging their fund to build a gigantic position.

The pressure mounted. The act of selling the pound forced the Bank of England to intervene, buying sterling and, in a desperate final act, hiking interest rates even further. This was the reflexive loop—the trade itself was tightening the economic vise, making the original thesis more powerful with every passing moment. On September 16, 1992, "Black Wednesday," the breaking point came. The UK government capitulated, withdrawing from the ERM and allowing the pound to crash. Druckenmiller and Soros walked away with a profit exceeding $1 billion. This was not a lucky bet; it was the inevitable outcome of a superior process, a system of thought we will now deconstruct.

The Druckenmiller Doctrine: The "Why"

Stanley Druckenmiller's success is not a series of disconnected, brilliant trades. It is the result of a cohesive and deeply ingrained intellectual operating system, a doctrine built on a few powerful mental models that govern every decision. To invest like him, you must first learn to think like him.[51]

LIQUIDITY PRIMACY: "IT'S THE FED"

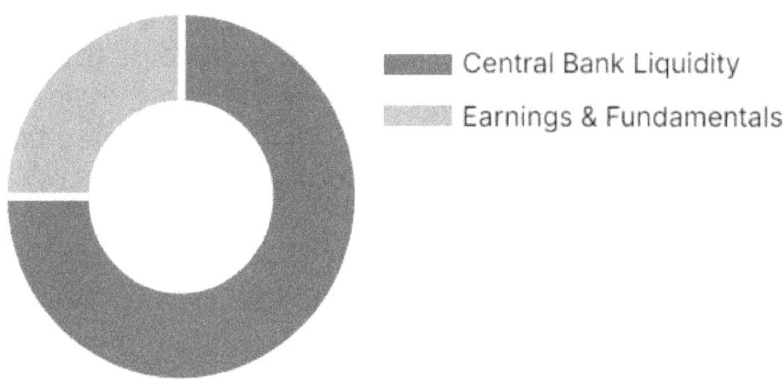

FIGURE 31 - LIQUIDITY PRIMACY

The central axiom of the Druckenmiller framework is that liquidity, not corporate earnings or economic growth, is the prime mover of markets. To understand this, imagine the global financial system is a giant bathtub. The assets—stocks, bonds, real estate, crypto—are all just rubber ducks floating in the water. The water level is liquidity, the sheer volume of money and credit sloshing around the system. The faucet that controls this water level is operated by the world's central banks, with the U.S. Federal Reserve holding the master valve.

When the Fed turns on the faucet by cutting interest rates or buying bonds (quantitative easing), the water level rises. As it does, all the rubber ducks—the good ones and the bad ones—are lifted higher. This is the "wall of money" that pushes asset prices up, often irrespective of their underlying fundamentals. Conversely, when the Fed opens the drain by hiking rates and shrinking its balance sheet (quantitative tightening), the water level falls, and all the ducks sink together.

This is why the first and most important question is never "Is this a good company?" but "What is the Fed doing, and what is it likely to do next?". Liquidity is not just another indicator; it is the primary causal force that creates the bull and bear markets in which all other activity takes place.[52]

THE 18-MONTH TELESCOPE: "NEVER INVEST IN THE PRESENT"

The second tenet of the doctrine is to "never, ever invest in the present". Today's economic data, last quarter's earnings reports, the current mood of the market—all of it is already reflected in asset prices. The information is known, and therefore, useless for generating true outperformance.

The opportunity, Druckenmiller argues, lies in identifying a significant gap between the consensus view of the future and a more accurate, variant perception. His tool for this is the "18-Month Telescope." He is constantly trying to visualize the economic landscape 18 to 24 months from now, based on the liquidity conditions of today. If the Fed is aggressively tightening the monetary screws today, he is thinking through the chain of consequences: how that will impact housing in six months, corporate capital spending in nine months, and finally, unemployment in 12 to 18 months.

This creates a powerful "time-horizon arbitrage." Most institutional investors are structurally trapped in the present, constrained by quarterly reporting cycles and the pressure to show short-term performance. They are looking at their feet. The 18-month telescope allows you to see the storm clouds gathering on the horizon long before others feel the first drop of rain, giving you time to position your portfolio accordingly. The goal is to build your position when the future is still murky to the consensus and exit when your 18-month-forward view becomes the market's obvious present.

THE CAPITAL PRESERVATION PARADOX: HOW TO "BE A PIG" AND SURVIVE

These first two principles lead to the third, and perhaps most radical: the rejection of diversification in favor of hyper-concentration. Druckenmiller has famously called diversification "probably the most misguided concept everywhere". The path to extraordinary, multi-decade returns is not by owning a little bit of everything, but by waiting patiently for that one perfect opportunity—the "fat pitch"—and then betting the ranch. When conviction is at its absolute peak, you must "be a pig" and "go for the jugular".

This philosophy of extreme aggression seems to contradict his flawless record of zero down years. This is resolved by the Capital Preservation Paradox: relentless, ironclad conservatism is the prerequisite for selective, hyper-aggression. You cannot "go for the jugular" if your capital has been bled dry by a series of small to medium losses from low-conviction trades. By preserving capital 90% of the time—cutting losses ruthlessly, staying out of choppy markets, and avoiding dangerous environments—you earn the right to be hyper-aggressive 10% of the time.

These principles form a powerful, sequential chain of logic. The analysis of liquidity informs the 18-month projection. The conviction generated by that non-consensus projection identifies the "fat pitch." And the capital that has been diligently preserved provides the firepower to act on that conviction with overwhelming force. It is a complete system where disciplined defense enables devastating offense.

The "Home Run" Playbook: The "How"

Philosophy is essential, but it is useless without a practical playbook for execution. The Druckenmiller framework translates these abstract ideas into a concrete, five-step process for developing and executing a high-conviction macro trade.

STEP 1: READING THE MONETARY TIDE

All analysis begins and ends with liquidity. This step is a quantitative and qualitative assessment of the global monetary environment to determine the direction and velocity of the primary force driving markets. To do this like Druckenmiller, you must ask a few key questions:

- What is the *rate of change* of the Fed's balance sheet? Is the faucet being turned on or off, and how fast?
- Are other major central banks—the European Central Bank (ECB), Bank of Japan (BOJ), and People's Bank of China (PBOC)—in sync with the Fed, or are they diverging? Divergences are where powerful cross-market and currency opportunities are born.[53]
- What is the "price" of money? Are real yields and credit spreads rising (a sign of tightening) or falling (a sign of easing)?

A proprietary way to synthesize this is by calculating a Net Liquidity Indicator for the US market, defined as:

$$Net\ Liquidity = Fed\ Balance\ Sheet - Treasury\ General\ Account - Reverse\ Repo\ Facility$$ [54]

The rate of change of this indicator is the primary signal of the underlying monetary tide.[55]

STEP 2: PROJECTING THE ECONOMIC FUTURE

With the liquidity environment defined, the next step is to use the 18-month telescope to project its second- and third-order impacts on the real economy. This is where you map the causal chain from monetary policy to economic activity, using leading indicators like building permits, freight indexes, and the yield curve. For example, if your liquidity analysis in Step 1 points to a sustained "Tightening" regime, you project forward. This implies higher borrowing costs, which will eventually cool the housing market, then squeeze corporate profit margins, and finally, lead to rising unemployment. While the consensus forecast might be for a "soft landing," your projection, rooted in the primacy of liquidity, points to a deeper, more prolonged recession beginning in 9-12 months.

STEP 3: FINDING THE ASYMMETRIC EDGE

This step translates your abstract macro projection into a concrete, tradable theme. The exclusive focus is on finding opportunities with an asymmetric risk/reward profile, where the potential gain is a multiple of the potential loss. This involves identifying the prevailing market misconception and, crucially, a potential reflexive feedback loop that could ignite the trade.

For instance, consider a theme of shorting long-duration U.S. Treasuries. The core of this trade is a variant perception. The hypothesis is that persistent inflation and massive government deficits will force long-term interest rates higher, steepening the yield curve. This challenges the market's prevailing misconception that the Fed will pivot and cut rates pre-emptively, saving the economy and allowing long-term rates to fall. The reflexive loop is the ignition switch: as long-term rates rise, financial conditions tighten, slowing the economy further. This, in turn, increases the budget deficit, requiring even more Treasury issuance, which puts further upward pressure on long-term rates. The trade itself helps create the conditions for its own success.

STEP 4: TIMING THE ENTRY WITH PRECISION

While the macro thesis is the *reason* for the trade, technical analysis dictates the *timing* of execution and the parameters for risk management. The idea is to enter with the market's momentum at your back, not to fight the tape. Your macro thesis tells you *what* to sell; the charts tell you *when*. You wait for the price action to confirm your thesis—a breakdown below a key multi-month support level, for example. Most importantly, you define your "uncle point"—a hard stop-loss level—before you ever enter the trade. This quantifies your risk to the penny. A "time-stop" is also critical: if the trade doesn't start moving in your favor within a set period, you cut it. Capital must not be held hostage by a stagnant idea.

STEP 5: SCORING CONVICTION AND SIZING THE BET

A "Home Run" trade scores high across all dimensions, while a low conviction idea should be avoided. This radar chart visualizes the difference.

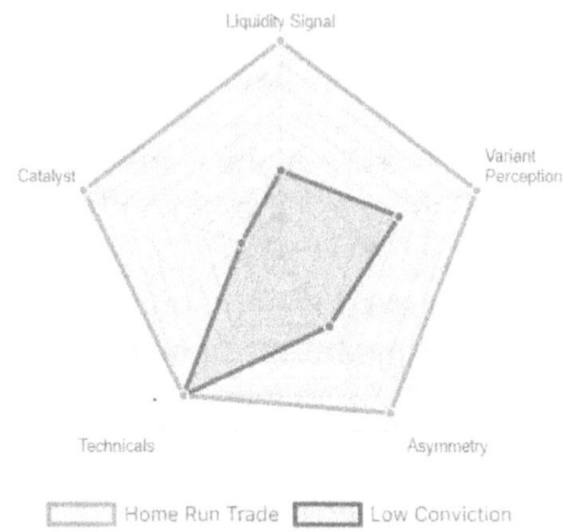

FIGURE 32 - THE CONVICTION CHECKLIST

This is the final step where analysis meets action. All prior work is synthesized into a single conviction score, which directly informs the most critical decision: position size. You formally score your idea against a weighted matrix. Is the macro thesis crystal clear? Is the risk/reward wildly asymmetric (e.g., 5:1 or greater)? Is the view highly non-consensus? Is the technical timing ripe? A low score might warrant a small "starter" position. But a score of 8 or higher out of 10? That is the green light to "go for the jugular".

The Analyst's Toolkit

To put this framework into practice, you need the right tools. This isn't about complex algorithms, but about focusing on a handful of high-signal, real-time indicators and a disciplined checklist to guide your judgment.

KEY DATA TO WATCH

The universe of economic data is infinite, but only a few points truly matter for tracking the monetary tide. This dashboard is your starting point.

TABLE 11 - THE DRUCKENMILLER DASHBOARD: KEY LIQUIDITY INDICATORS

Indicator	FRED Ticker	What It Tells You	Why It Matters
Fed Balance Sheet	WALCL	The size of the central bank's assets.	Its rate of change is the primary signal of liquidity injection or withdrawal.
Treasury General Acct.	WTREGEN	The U.S. government's checking account at the Fed.	A large drawdown injects cash into the banking system, boosting liquidity.
Reverse Repo Facility	RRPONTSYD	A financial drain absorbing excess cash from the system.	A rising balance indicates the Fed is pulling money out of the market.

Indicator	FRED Ticker	What It Tells You	Why It Matters
10-Year Real Yield	DFII10	The 10-year Treasury yield minus inflation expectations.	The true "risk-free" cost of capital; rising real yields are a headwind for assets.
High Yield Spread	BAMLH0A0HYM2	The extra yield investors demand to own junk bonds.	A widening spread is a classic sign of rising fear and tightening credit conditions.
U.S. Dollar Index	DXY	The value of the dollar versus a basket of currencies.	A rising dollar often signals global risk aversion and tightens financial conditions.

THE CONVICTION CHECKLIST

Before placing any significant trade, run it through this checklist. This transforms the "be a pig" philosophy from a reckless gamble into a calculated, disciplined act of aggression. Score each criterion from 1-10, calculate your weighted score, and let the result guide your sizing.

1. **Macro Thesis Clarity (Weight: 40%):** On a scale of 1-10, how simple and powerful is my core thesis? Can I explain it in two sentences?
2. **Risk/Reward Asymmetry (Weight: 30%):** Is my potential upside at least 5x my defined downside?
3. **Technical Confirmation (Weight: 15%):** Is the price action confirming my thesis, or am I fighting the tape?
4. **Non-Consensus Delta (Weight: 10%):** How much does my view differ from the prevailing market narrative? Am I betting on a story everyone already knows?
5. **Reflexive Loop (Weight: 5%):** Have I identified a potential self-reinforcing feedback loop that could amplify the trade?

A final weighted score above 8.0 is "home run" territory, justifying a maximum allocation. A score below 7.0 suggests a smaller position or waiting for a better setup.

Case Studies in Triumph and Tribulation

The framework is best understood by seeing it in action—in both a perfect victory and a humbling defeat. These two stories reveal that the system is designed not just to structure analysis, but to manage the psychological frailties that derail even the most brilliant investors.

THE PERFECT TRADE: THE 1992 POUND SHORT DECONSTRUCTED

Let's revisit the legendary pound trade, but this time through the lens of the five-step playbook.

- **Step 1 (Liquidity):** The analysis identified a stark divergence in monetary policy. Germany's central bank was tightening aggressively, while the UK economy desperately needed easing.
- **Step 2 (Projection):** The 18-month projection was clear: the economic pain of maintaining the ERM peg was politically and economically unsustainable. A breaking point was inevitable.
- **Step 3 (Asymmetry):** The trade was beautifully asymmetric. The downside was capped by the ERM's narrow trading band, while the upside was a massive devaluation. The reflexive loop was powerful: selling the pound would force the UK to raise rates, which would further weaken the economy and strengthen the case against the peg.
- **Step 4 (Timing):** The entry was timed as market pressure began to build, confirming the thesis was gaining traction.[56]
- **Step 5 (Sizing):** The conviction score was a 10/10. It was a generational opportunity, justifying a "gigantic" position size that would make history.

THE HUMBLING LESSON: THE 2000 TECH BUBBLE FAILURE

The pound trade shows the framework working to perfection. The tech bubble shows what happens when its most important component—the investor's emotional discipline—breaks down. It was a two-part failure.

First, in early 1999, convinced of a bubble, Druckenmiller went short on internet stocks and promptly lost $600 million as the mania intensified. The lesson was brutal: never fight a tidal wave of liquidity, no matter how insane valuations seem. The market can remain irrational far longer than you can remain solvent.

The second part was the true "emotional doozy." By January 2000, his analysis was spot-on. He saw the peak, sold all his tech holdings, and went to cash. He had won. But then, he watched for two months as the market screamed higher, and the young "gunslingers" he had hired continued to make fortunes. The fear of missing out (FOMO) became unbearable. In March 2000, at almost the exact top of the market, he abandoned his own correct analysis, threw his framework out the window, and bought $6 billion worth of tech stocks. The subsequent crash vaporized $3 billion of his fund's capital in six weeks.

In late 1999, despite his framework screaming caution, he got caught in the mania and bought tech stocks near the top, leading to massive losses. A powerful lesson: never abandon your discipline.

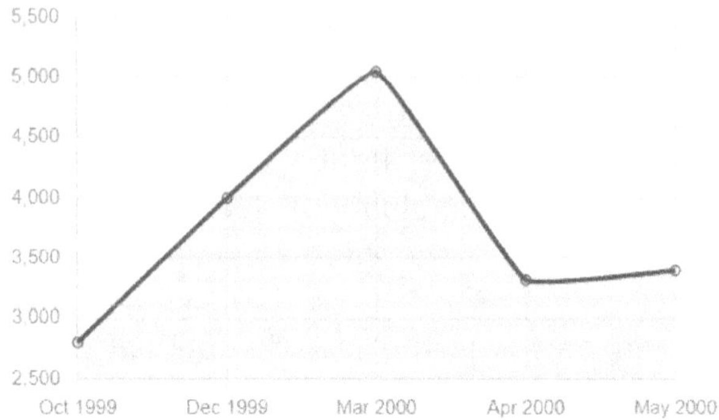

FIGURE 33 - THE HUMBLING LESSON: TECH BUBBLE

His own post-mortem was unflinching: "I didn't learn anything. I already knew that I wasn't supposed to do that. I was just an emotional basket case and couldn't help myself". This is the ultimate lesson. The framework is a guardrail designed to protect you from your own worst instincts. The greatest risk is not being wrong, but knowing you're right and acting wrongly anyway due to psychological pressure.

Key Takeaways: Druckenmiller's Rules for the Game

Distilling this powerful doctrine down to its essence leaves us with a set of actionable rules. These are the core principles for anyone aspiring to move beyond conventional investing and adopt the mindset of a market master.

- **Follow the Central Banks:** Liquidity moves markets. Your first and last question should always be: "What is the Fed doing?".
- **Invest in the Future:** The present is already priced in. Build your positions based on where you believe the world will be in 18 months, not where it is today.
- **Preserve Capital to Enable Aggression:** Stay conservative most of the time. This earns you the right to be hyper-aggressive when a truly asymmetric, high-conviction opportunity arises.
- **Forget Diversification; Concentrate on Conviction:** The path to exceptional returns is through a few, large, concentrated bets. When you see a "fat pitch," swing for the fences.
- **Asymmetry is Everything:** Only take trades where the potential reward is a significant multiple of the potential loss. A 5:1 ratio should be your target.
- **Use Charts for Risk, Not for Ideas:** Let your macro view form the thesis. Use technical analysis only to define your entry, your exit, and your risk.
- **Master Your Emotions:** The best analytical framework in the world is useless if you abandon it due to fear or greed. Emotional discipline is the ultimate edge.
- **Be Intellectually Flexible:** The goal is to make money, not to be right. If the facts change or the market tells you you're wrong, get out immediately. There is no room for ego in this game.

Chapter 11: The Commodity Supercycle Framework (Jim Rogers)

The Indiana Jones of Finance: A Biography of Conviction

To understand the investment philosophy of Jim Rogers is to first understand the man himself—not as a creature of Wall Street, but as a pioneer of the open road. While his contemporaries were tethered to ticker tapes and terminals, Rogers was kicking up dust on a motorcycle, treating the entire globe as his primary research document. He is, in essence, the Indiana Jones of Finance, a man for whom the greatest analytical tool has always been a passport, and the most valuable data is gathered not from a screen, but from the seat of a bike.

His legendary, record-setting motorcycle and road trips across 116 countries were not mere holidays; they were the ultimate expression of a deeply held conviction. They were expeditions designed to gather unfiltered, primary-source information, a physical manifestation of his belief that the truth of a market is found on the ground, not in a boardroom. Rogers famously quipped that one can "learn more about a country from speaking to the madam of a brothel or a black marketeer than from meeting a foreign minister". This is not a flippant remark but the core of a serious research methodology. It is about systematically seeking out the qualitative, anecdotal evidence that either confirms or, more importantly, disconfirms the sanitized official data peddled by governments and Wall Street analysts. While an economist in New York might analyze GDP figures, Rogers would be in a provincial town observing a different set of metrics: Are the shops busy? Are people optimistic? Is that new infrastructure actually being built and used?.

This approach reveals a profound understanding of the nature of knowledge in finance. In an age drowning in big data, Rogers makes a compelling case for the primacy of small, tangible data. The quantitative reports that drive Wall Street are universally available, making them a weak source of any real informational edge. Rogers's travels, by contrast, provide him with a stream of unique, qualitative data that cannot be replicated by a competitor. This isn't just about adding color to an investment thesis. The visceral, on-the-ground experience forges a depth of conviction that is impossible to achieve by looking at a spreadsheet alone. It is this hard-won conviction that provides the psychological fortitude necessary to take a large, concentrated, contrarian position and hold it for years, weathering the storms of volatility that would terrify an investor whose belief is built on a less solid foundation. The biker's edge, therefore, is not just an information advantage; it is a psychological one. The journey itself builds the courage required to execute the strategy.

The Investor's Compass: Core Philosophies

To invest like Jim Rogers, one must first learn to see the world through his eyes. His analytical process is not a black box of complex formulas but the disciplined application of a few powerful, interconnected mental models. These principles form the compass by which all investment decisions are navigated. Understanding them is not an academic exercise; it is the essential prerequisite for applying the framework that follows.

1. THE RHYTHM OF SCARCITY: THE COMMODITY SUPERCYCLE

The bedrock of the Rogers worldview is the Commodity Supercycle theory. This is the belief that commodities do not move in short-term business cycles but in great, multi-decade waves of boom and bust. These are not random fluctuations; they are the predictable, long-term consequences of the collision between transformative shifts in global demand and the stubbornly slow-moving nature of supply.

An upswing in a supercycle is a prolonged, powerful bull market, typically lasting 15 to 20 years, driven by a fundamental realignment of the global economy. Think of the industrialization of the United States in the early 1900s, the post-World War II reconstruction of Europe and Japan, or, most recently, the unprecedented urbanization of China that began around 1999. These events create a voracious, multi-decade appetite for the raw materials of progress.

The true engine of this cycle is a simple, unyielding fact of the physical world: supply is inelastic. It can take a decade or more to approve, finance, and build a new copper mine. It takes years to clear and develop new farmland or to construct the vast rail and port infrastructure needed to bring resources to market. This inherent lag between a price signal—surging demand—and the supply response is the crucial mechanism. When a new demand driver like China emerges, it quickly consumes existing surpluses. Prices rise, but new supply cannot come online to meet it. This structural deficit can persist for years, fueling a long and powerful bull market.

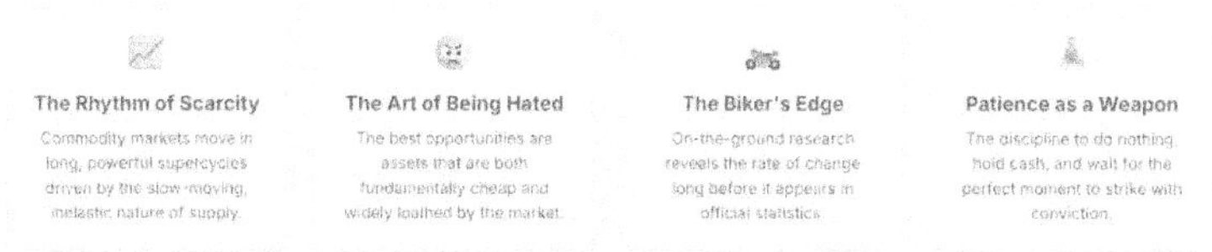

FIGURE 34 - THE INVESTOR'S COMPASS: CORE PHILOSOPHIES

This reveals a fundamental conflict between the financial world and the physical world. Financial markets can react to a new demand shock in microseconds, bidding up prices instantly. But the physical economy of mining, farming, and drilling moves at a geological pace. This temporal mismatch is the ultimate source of durable, multi-year trends. Investors who only analyze financial data will be perpetually surprised by the persistence of these commodity bull markets, while those who understand the physical constraints can anticipate them.

Eventually, attracted by years of high prices and exuberant media coverage, a flood of capital pours into the sector, financing a wave of new production. But by the time these massive projects finally come online, the initial demand surge may have already matured. The result is a supply glut that overwhelms the market, leading to a price collapse and the start of a long, grinding bear market that can also last for 15 to 20 years. The supercycle, therefore, is not merely a price phenomenon but a *capital cycle*. The most reliable signal for a generational bottom is not just a low price, but a multi-year period of industry-wide underinvestment, capital starvation, and widespread bankruptcies. Conversely, the signal for a top is a frenzy of capital expenditure and a universal consensus that "this time is different".

Rogers's deep study of history is his primary analytical tool. He believes fervently that history repeats, or at least rhymes, and uses past cycles as a map for the future. It is this historical perspective that provides the conviction to make bold, long-term calls, and it is the source of one of his most important observations: "Bottoms in the investment world don't end with four-year lows; they end with 10- or 15-year lows".

TABLE 12 - HISTORICAL COMMODITY SUPERCYCLES ANALOGUE

Cycle Period	Primary Demand Driver	Primary Supply Constraint	Peak GSCI/S&P 500 Ratio (Approx.)	Key Geopolitical Catalyst	Duration (Years)
~1890s-1917	U.S. Industrialization & Electrification	Slow development of new mining/extraction tech	> 8.0	WWI	~20
~1945 - 1970s	Post-WWII Reconstruction (Europe, Japan)	Wartime destruction of capacity	> 6.0	Korean War, Vietnam War, 1973 Oil Crisis	~25-30

Cycle Period	Primary Demand Driver	Primary Supply Constraint	Peak GSCI/S&P 500 Ratio (Approx.)	Key Geopolitical Catalyst	Duration (Years)
~1999-2011	China's Industrialization & Urbanization	20 years of underinvestment post-1980s bust	~5.5	9/11, Iraq War, 2008 GFC	~12

2. THE ART OF BEING HATED: DEEP CONTRARIANISM

The second pillar of the Rogers philosophy is a rugged, deeply ingrained contrarianism. It is founded on the simple but powerful premise that the consensus is almost always wrong, especially at major turning points. As he puts it, "If everyone thinks one way, it will likely be wrong. If you can figure out that it is wrong, you are likely to make a lot of money". This involves systematically buying assets that are unloved, ignored, and discarded by the mainstream, and selling them years later when they have become the darlings of Wall Street.

Rogers understands that markets are driven by human emotion. The final leg of a bull market ends in hysteria, and the final leg of a bear market ends in panic. The contrarian's job is to act as a clear-eyed rationalist amidst this emotional storm, buying the panic and selling the hysteria. This requires the psychological fortitude to go against the herd, a trait Rogers views as essential for superior returns. The classic anecdote of financier Bernard Baruch selling all his stocks in 1929 after receiving stock tips from his shoeshine boy perfectly encapsulates this mindset: when an investment idea becomes common knowledge, the opportunity is likely over. Rogers actively seeks out ideas that are met with laughter, viewing it as a "sign of potential success".

However, a critical challenge for any contrarian is the risk of being too early. An asset can be cheap and stay cheap for years. Rogers's contrarianism is not blind; he does not simply buy what is unpopular. He buys what is unpopular just as a fundamental catalyst for change is emerging on the horizon. An asset can be cheap for a very good reason. The Rogers method requires finding a cheap and hated asset where the structural reason for its unpopularity is about to reverse. He explicitly states that investors should "insist on waiting for the emergence of catalytic factors that can change the direction of the market before making decisions".

This creates a powerful two-factor entry signal that transforms contrarianism from a vague philosophy into a specific, actionable strategy:

- The asset must be at a point of maximum pessimism—it must be "cheap and hated".
- A **structural improvement in its supply/demand balance** must be on the horizon as a fundamental catalyst for change.

This dual-trigger mechanism is what separates a true Rogers-style opportunity from a simple value trap. It forces the investor to look forward to a catalyst for growth, not just backward at historical valuation. This synthesis of deep value investing (buying what is cheap) and growth investing (identifying a catalyst for change) is the source of its power and what makes the approach so distinct.

3. THE BIKER'S EDGE: THE SECOND DERIVATIVE

Data and charts are necessary, but for Jim Rogers, they are insufficient. The third pillar of his philosophy is the unshakable belief that the most valuable insights are found on the dusty roads of the real world. His methodology is not aimless tourism; it is a targeted inquiry designed to assess the *rate and direction of change*.

The key is not to observe the current state of a place (e.g., "this country is poor") but to gauge its momentum (e.g., "this country is poor, but developing rapidly, and its people are incredibly motivated and hardworking"). This focus on the second derivative—the acceleration of change—is what allows an investor to get in early, before the transformation is obvious to everyone.

His early investments in Austria and China serve as perfect examples. In the 1980s, Austria was a forgotten, tiny market. Rogers visited the country and met with government officials, learning that they had realized the importance of capital markets and were planning to roll out policies to encourage investment. Crucially, he sought disconfirming evidence and found that "none of the political parties or interest groups opposed foreign investment". The on-the-ground evidence confirmed the macro thesis, giving Rogers the conviction to invest heavily in a market that Wall Street had completely ignored. His deep conviction in China was forged in the same way. His travels, beginning in 1984, allowed him to witness the country's dynamism and nascent capitalist spirit firsthand, long before it became a consensus view. This boots-on-the-ground intelligence provided the confidence to invest heavily and repeatedly when others were skeptical.

4. PATIENCE AS A WEAPON: THE POWER OF DOING NOTHING

The final pillar, and perhaps the most difficult to practice, is patience. In an industry that prizes constant action and abhors cash, Jim Rogers champions the strategic value of doing nothing. His philosophy is encapsulated in his famous statement: "I just wait until there is money lying in the corner, and all I have to do is go over there and pick it up. I do nothing in the meantime".

For Rogers, patience is not passive waiting; it is an active, disciplined strategy. It requires resisting the siren song of the market and the immense institutional pressure to always be "doing something". Most successful investors, he argues, do nothing most of the time. They wait, sometimes for years, for the perfect confluence of a hated asset, a compelling valuation, and a fundamental catalyst for change.

This discipline means being comfortable holding large amounts of cash for long periods. For Rogers, cash is not a sign of fear or indecision. It is an offensive weapon held in reserve. It ensures survival during the inevitable bear markets and, more importantly, provides the firepower to act decisively and in size when a true "fat pitch" opportunity finally presents itself. This approach is inextricably linked to his preference for a highly concentrated portfolio. Rogers is a critic of wide diversification, which he believes is “only required when investors do not understand what they are doing”. He seeks to make a few, large, high-conviction bets over his lifetime. Such a concentrated strategy is only viable if one is extraordinarily selective, and selectivity requires immense patience.

The Playbook: From Global Odyssey to Specific Bet

Philosophy is the compass, but a playbook is the map. This section translates the Rogers worldview into a repeatable, step-by-step process, guiding the investor from the grand sweep of history to the specifics of a single trade.

1. THE MACRO VIEW: SPOTTING THE NEXT SUPERCYCLE

The first task is to identify a broad, multi-decade structural bull market in a commodity sector. This requires a contrarian’s eye and a historian’s perspective.[57]

A primary tool for this is the ratio of a broad commodity index to a broad equity index, such as the S&P GSCI to the S&P 500 ratio. Charted over decades, this ratio provides a powerful visual of the great cycles of under- and over-valuation between real assets and financial assets. When this ratio hits multi-decade lows—as it did in the late 1990s before the China boom and again in the late 2010s—it signals that commodities are at a point of generational cheapness relative to stocks, presenting a compelling entry point for a new supercycle.

Rogers uses the GSCI/S&P 500 ratio as a key valuation tool. When the ratio is at historic lows, it signals that hard assets (commodities) are fundamentally undervalued relative to financial assets (stocks).

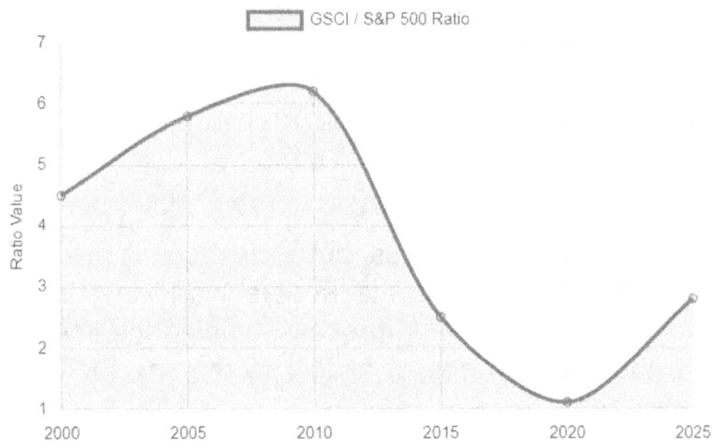

FIGURE 35 - SIGNAL 1: IS IT CHEAP?

But cheapness alone is not enough. The asset class must also be hated. This is where a systematic checklist can translate the qualitative art of contrarianism into a quantitative process. By scoring an asset class on metrics ranging from its weight in major indices to the sentiment on magazine covers, an investor can build a data-driven case for whether it has reached a point of maximum pessimism.[58]

TABLE 13 - THE "CHEAP AND HATED" INDICATOR CHECKLIST

Indicator	Current Value	Historical 10th Percentile	Historical 90th Percentile	Score (-2 to +2)	Notes
GSCI/SPX Ratio	1.2	1.0	6.5	+2	Near generational lows, indicating extreme relative cheapness.
Sector Weight in S&P 500	4.5%	4.0%	15.0%	+2	Energy & Materials sectors are a fraction of their historical weight.
CFTC Net Spec Positioning (Agg.)	-1.2 Z-score	-2.0	+2.0	+1	Speculators are net short, but not at an extreme washout level yet.
Major Magazine Covers (Last 12m)	Bearish (3) / Neutral (5) / Bullish (0)	N/A	N/A	+2	Narrative is dominated by "end of oil" and recession fears.
Analyst Consensus (Top 10 Producers)	25% Buy / 60% Hold / 15% Sell	N/A	N/A	+1	General apathy and caution, few strong advocates.
MBA Graduates	<1%	<1%	>5%	+2	Talent is flowing to

Indicator	Current Value	Historical 10th Percentile	Historical 90th Percentile	Score (-2 to +2)	Notes
Entering Sector					tech and AI, not mining or agriculture.
Composite Contrarian Score				**+10 / 12**	

2. THE MICRO STRATEGY: RIDING THE WAVE

Having identified a favorable macro tide, the focus now shifts to the individual waves. This step involves a granular analysis of the specific commodity chosen to express the theme. A bullish thesis on industrial metals is abstract; a thesis on copper is actionable. This requires a deep understanding of its unique supply chain, the concentration of its production, and its vulnerability to idiosyncratic shocks. Geopolitical risk analysis is paramount here. A view on oil is incomplete without an analysis of OPEC+ policy; a view on wheat requires understanding Black Sea port logistics and weather patterns in Ukraine.

After analyzing the long-term flow of supply and demand, the next step is to assess the short-term stock. This involves a rigorous analysis of visible warehouse inventories at major global exchanges like the London Metal Exchange (LME), COMEX, and the Shanghai Futures Exchange (SHFE). The key metric is not the absolute level of inventory, but the level relative to consumption, often measured in "days of supply." Critically low inventories are a powerful bullish catalyst.

They indicate immediate physical market tightness, increase the market's vulnerability to supply shocks, and can force the futures curve into a state of backwardation—a condition highly profitable for long investors.

3. CHOOSING YOUR VEHICLE: FROM THESIS TO TRADE

The final step is to select the most effective instrument to execute the trade. This is a critical decision, as the wrong vehicle can lead to poor returns even if the underlying thesis is correct. The choice of vehicle is not merely a tactical decision; it is a strategic one that reflects the nature of the bet itself.

A multi-year supercycle thesis is poorly served by futures contracts, which can suffer from the slow bleed of "roll decay" (contango) over long holding periods. Producer equities, like shares in a mining company, offer the powerful benefit of operational leverage: a 10% rise in the underlying commodity price can lead to a much greater than 10% rise in profits and, consequently, the stock price. However, investing in a single company introduces idiosyncratic risks—a mine collapse, a political expropriation—that are unrelated to the core commodity thesis.

For a high-conviction *thematic* bet, an ETF of producers often represents the optimal vehicle. It captures the desirable operational leverage of the sector while diversifying away the undesirable single-company risks. It is an explicit decision to bet on the theme's tailwind rather than the execution of a single management team.

TABLE 14 - INVESTMENT VEHICLE SELECTION MATRIX

Vehicle	Purity of Expo-sure	Levera-ge	Liquidi-ty	Holding Cost (Annuali-zed)	Counter-party Risk	Suitabi-lity Horizon
Futures (HG)	High	High	Very High	~ -1.5% (Avg. Roll Yield)	Medium (Exchange)	Short-Term (<1 Year)
Producer Equity (FCX)	Medium	High	High	N/A (Potential Dividend)	Low	Medium-Term (1-5 Years)
Miners ETF (COPX)	Medium	Medium	High	0.65% (Expense Ratio)	Low	Medium-Term (1-5 Years)
Physical ETF (CPER)	High	Low	Medium	~0.88% (Expense Ratio)	Low	Long-Term (>3 Years)

Case Study: The Electrification Supercycle

Let us now walk through the entire framework with a powerful, contemporary example: the Electrification Supercycle. This is the story of how an investor, thinking like Rogers, would identify and build a position in the industrial metals complex, a generational opportunity unfolding before our eyes.

The journey begins with the macro view. The historical analogue is the late 1990s. After a decade-long bear market from 2011 to 2020, the commodity sector was left for dead, hated by investors and starved of capital. The GSCI/S&P 500 ratio hit rock bottom. The sector was both cheap and hated. Then, the catalyst: a once-in-a-century demand shock from the global energy transition. The policy-mandated, legally-binding shift to electric vehicles and renewable energy creates a non-negotiable, inelastic source of new demand for industrial metals that will persist for the next two decades. This is not a cyclical story; it is a structural collision course between anemic supply and explosive demand.

Next, we drill down to the micro story, selecting copper as the purest expression of this theme. The supply side is exceptionally fragile. Chile and Peru, which account for nearly 40% of global supply, face a perfect storm of headwinds: political instability, rising resource nationalism, and recurring labor strikes. Major producers are struggling with declining ore grades and project delays. The "boots-on-the-ground" check confirms the data. Local news reports from Chile are filled with stories of escalating tensions between mining unions and corporate management. Trade journals highlight the severe, ongoing drought in the Atacama Desert, which threatens production. This qualitative "scuttlebutt" strongly suggests that official production forecasts are overly optimistic.

Simultaneously, we check the inventories. Global visible copper stocks are at critically low levels, representing just 2.5 days of global consumption—more than two standard deviations below the five-year average. The physical market is screaming tightness, a condition that provides a powerful catalyst and a significant margin of safety, as the market has no buffer to absorb even minor supply disruptions.

Finally, we choose our vehicle. For this multi-year thematic bet, futures are suboptimal. A single mining stock carries too much idiosyncratic risk. The logical choice is a diversified basket of producers that captures the sector's operational leverage while mitigating single-stock risk. The **Global X Copper Miners ETF (COPX)** emerges as the preferred vehicle. It provides a powerful, liquid, and diversified way to express the long-term bullish thesis on copper, making a convicted bet on the supercycle tide that will lift all boats in its path.

Key Takeaways: Rogers's Rules for the Road

The wisdom of Jim Rogers, honed over a lifetime of adventure and investing, can be distilled into a set of timeless rules. They are not complex algorithms but principles of thought and action—a compass for the independent investor navigating the often-treacherous currents of the global market.

- See the world for yourself; the best research is not found on a screen but on the open road.[59]
- Think like a historian; the patterns of boom and bust, of scarcity and abundance, are as old as human ambition.[60]
- Buy when there is blood in the streets, even if some of it is your own. The point of maximum pessimism is the point of maximum opportunity.

- Wait for a catalyst; being cheap is not enough. An asset needs a reason to stop being cheap.[61]
- The most profitable action is often inaction. Have the courage to do nothing until money is lying in the corner.[62]
- If an idea becomes common knowledge, from the taxi driver to the shoeshine boy, it is time to sell.[63]
- Concentrate your bets on your best ideas; wide diversification is often a confession of ignorance.[64]
- Never follow a model, especially your own. The world is always changing, and you must change with it.

Chapter 12: The Energy Framework (T. Boone Pickens)

The Wildcatter's Edge

To understand how to make money in the oil patch, you first have to understand that it's not Wall Street. It's not a collection of numbers on a screen or a series of charts. It's a physical business. It's about geology, pressure, and machinery. It's about having mud on your boots. Most people in the stock market have never set foot on a drilling rig, and that's where their disadvantage begins and your advantage is born.

My own story didn't start in a Manhattan skyscraper. It started in the flatlands of Oklahoma and Texas, with a degree in geology from Oklahoma State University. My first language was rocks, not stock tickers. I was a wildcatter—an explorer who drills for oil in unproven territory. It's a high-risk, high-reward business that teaches you two things very quickly: how to read the earth and how to stomach calculated risk. That background, that visceral understanding of the physical asset, is the "Wildcatter's Edge."

When a typical financial analyst looks at an energy company, they see a spreadsheet. They see a line item for "Property, Plant & Equipment." They look at quarterly earnings, price-to-earnings ratios, and dividend yields. They are analyzing a representation of the business, a financial shadow cast by the real thing. When I look at an energy company, I see what's in the ground. I see rock formations, reservoir pressures, decline curves, and the quality of the acreage. The analysis starts from the ground up, with the intrinsic worth of the reserves. This is a fundamentally different way of seeing the world. Wall Street analyzes the past performance of the management team, which is reflected in historical financial statements. The wildcatter analyzes the future potential of the assets.

This creates a persistent opportunity. When a company has great assets but is run by a management team with a poor track record, Wall Street's backward-looking models will assign it a low price. The stock will look cheap, and for good reason—the people in charge are squandering the potential. But the wildcatter sees the disconnect between the high value of the assets and the low performance of the management. The edge comes from recognizing that management is a variable that can be changed. You can buy the company based on the enduring value of its physical assets and then execute a plan to fix the temporary problem of the people running it. That's the synthesis of geological insight and financial action. It's an edge that can't be replicated by someone who has only ever lived in the world of spreadsheets.

The Booneisms: A Philosophy of Simplicity and Action

Over the years, people have tried to make the energy business complicated. They build complex models and write dense reports. But the truth is, this business, like most things in life, is governed by a few simple, powerful rules. These aren't just folksy sayings; they are the operational mandates that should guide every dollar you invest.

"SUPPLY AND DEMAND ARE KING": THE PRIMACY OF PHYSICAL MARKETS

This is the central, non-negotiable tenet. It's the law of gravity for commodities. In the long run, the price of oil, natural gas, or anything else that comes out of the ground is determined by one simple thing: the physical balance of how much is being produced versus how much is being consumed. Everything else is noise. Geopolitical headlines, Wall Street sentiment, complex derivatives—it's all a distraction from the fundamental arithmetic of physical barrels.

This principle demands a relentless focus on tangible data. You have to track OPEC production quotas, watch the Baker Hughes rig count like a hawk, and tear apart the weekly EIA inventory reports. In 2007, when oil was trading around $70 a barrel, I said it was going to $100. People thought I was crazy. But I wasn't looking at charts; I was looking at the simple math. Global demand was rising steadily, and the world's spare production capacity was shrinking to dangerously low levels. The physical market was tight as a drum. It was a simple case of more buyers than sellers for the physical product, and the price had to go up to balance the market. It did. Anchoring your analysis in the physical reality of supply and demand is the only way to tune out the noise and see the market for what it truly is.

"PEAK OIL" AND PRAGMATISM: CONVICTION TEMPERED BY REALITY

For a long time, I was a big believer in the "Peak Oil" theory—the idea that global oil production was at or near an irreversible peak. With demand from places like China and India set to explode, it was a simple and powerful thesis: if supply is capped and demand is rising, the price has only one way to go. That view formed the basis of a strong, secular bullish outlook for much of the 2000s.

But then, the facts changed. A couple of wildcatters in Texas figured out how to combine horizontal drilling with hydraulic fracturing, and the shale revolution was born. This new technology upended the entire theory by unlocking vast new reserves of oil and gas that were previously unreachable. Suddenly, the narrative of scarcity was replaced by a new reality of abundance. When the facts change, you have to change your mind. Stubbornness is not a strategy. What this demonstrates is a critical meta-principle: you must have a strong, simple thesis, but you must not become dogmatically attached to it. The framework must be built on core beliefs, but it must have a mechanism to incorporate game-changing technological shifts that fundamentally alter the supply and demand equation. Intellectual honesty is paramount. Your job is to see the world as it is, not as you wish it were.

"A FOOL WITH A PLAN CAN BEAT A GENIUS WITH NO PLAN": A BIAS FOR ACTION

My father taught me this one, and it's the most important rule for execution. The world is full of geniuses who suffer from "analysis paralysis." They can study a problem from every angle, build the most elegant models, and write the most brilliant reports, but they never pull the trigger. They get stuck in the "ready-aim-

aim-aim-aim" syndrome that plagues big corporate bureaucracies.

A plan, even an imperfect one, is useless without execution. This philosophy translates directly into an investment style. First, you hunt for elephants, not rabbits. You concentrate your energy and your capital on a small number of high-conviction ideas where the supply-demand imbalance is obvious and the valuation disconnect is significant. Second, you must have a clear, simple, and executable plan *before* you invest. What is your thesis? What is the catalyst that will unlock the value? What is your exit strategy? Answering these questions forces clarity and discipline. In the oil patch and on Wall Street, a bold, decisive plan is everything.

These three principles work together as a complete system. "Supply and demand" tells you what to analyze—the objective, physical reality of the market. The principle of "pragmatism" tells you how to think—form a strong thesis but be ruthlessly willing to invalidate it when the facts change. And "a fool with a plan" tells you how to act—decisively, with focus and conviction. It's a system for moving from data to analysis to conviction to action, and it's designed to avoid the most common investor mistakes: getting lost in the noise, falling in love with a bad idea, and failing to act when a true opportunity presents itself.

Take #1: The Top-Down View (Reading the Global Energy Map)

Before you can even think about buying a stock, you have to have a view on the commodity itself. You need a map of the global energy landscape. Is there a tailwind or a headwind at your back? The process of building this map is systematic. It's about gathering the right data and putting it together in a simple framework to get a clear, directional forecast.

STEP 1: ANALYZING GLOBAL SUPPLY

The supply side of the equation is a function of geology, technology, and politics. You have to break it down into its three key components.[65]

- **OPEC:** Start with the cartel. The Organization of the Petroleum Exporting Countries should be viewed as a business whose goal is to manage supply to maximize revenue for its members. The first thing to check is their production versus their stated quotas. This is a measure of their discipline. But the single most critical variable is **spare capacity**—the amount of oil production that can be brought online quickly (within 30 days) and sustained. This is OPEC's lever of power. When spare capacity is high, the market has a comfortable buffer against disruptions. When it's low, the market is vulnerable, and any small outage can cause prices to spike.
- **U.S. Shale:** This is the most dynamic and technology-driven piece of the supply puzzle. The best leading indicator for future U.S. production is the **Baker Hughes Rig Count**, released every week. A rising rig count means more investment and more oil is coming. But you can't just look at the raw number. You have to adjust for rig productivity—how much oil each rig can produce—which has increased dramatically

with better technology. You also have to watch the financial health of the shale producers. When oil prices are low, their access to capital dries up, forcing them to cut back on drilling regardless of the geology.

- **Non-OPEC Conventional:** This category includes everyone else—major producers like Russia, Canada, and Brazil. Here, the analysis focuses on tracking production from existing fields, monitoring the pipeline of new projects, and, most importantly, assessing geopolitical risk. Supply from these regions is often subject to disruptions from sanctions, civil unrest, or infrastructure attacks. You have to apply a risk discount to production forecasts from unstable regions.

STEP 2: ANALYZING GLOBAL DEMAND

Demand for energy is fundamentally tied to economic activity. A growing global economy needs more fuel to power its factories, trucks, and planes.[66]

- **Economic Drivers:** The primary driver is global GDP growth. You need to focus on the big consumers. For mature OECD countries, the key is transportation fuels like gasoline and diesel. But the real engine of demand growth is the non-OECD world, particularly China and India, where industrial activity and a rising middle class are creating immense new appetite for energy. Real-time indicators like Purchasing Managers' Indexes (PMIs) can give you a more current read on economic health than official GDP forecasts.

- **Weather:** For natural gas and heating oil, weather is the dominant short-term demand driver. A colder-than-average winter in the Northern Hemisphere can cause a massive draw on natural gas storage for heating. A hotter-than-average summer can drive huge demand for gas-fired power plants to meet air conditioning load. You have to monitor seasonal forecasts and track metrics like Heating Degree Days (HDDs) and Cooling Degree Days (CDDs).
- **Efficiency & Substitution:** Over the long term, technology and policy can create structural shifts in demand. Rising vehicle fuel economy standards can dampen gasoline demand growth even if the economy is expanding. My own "Pickens Plan" was a thesis on substitution—arguing for the replacement of imported diesel with cheaper, cleaner, domestic natural gas in America's trucking fleet. You have to account for these long-term trends in your model.

STEP 3: MONITORING INVENTORIES - THE MARKET'S TRUE CONFESSION

Inventories, or storage, are the shock absorber for the entire system. They are the buffer between the volatile swings of daily supply and demand. While the absolute level of inventory is important, the most powerful signal is the **rate of change**. The change in inventory levels is the market's true confession; it is the irrefutable, high-frequency signal of the real-time market balance. A market that is consistently drawing down its inventories is in a deficit, meaning demand is outstripping supply.

That is bullish. A market that is building inventories is in a surplus. That is bearish.

The single most important data release for this analysis is the **EIA Weekly Petroleum Status Report**, which comes out every Wednesday morning. When you look at that report, you need to check four things:[67]

1. The headline change in commercial crude oil inventories.
2. How current inventory levels compare to the seasonal five-year average. A large deficit to the average is a strong bullish signal.
3. The inventory level at Cushing, Oklahoma, which is the delivery point for the WTI crude oil futures contract and a key barometer of physical tightness in North America.
4. The inventories of refined products like gasoline and diesel, which tell you about end-user demand.

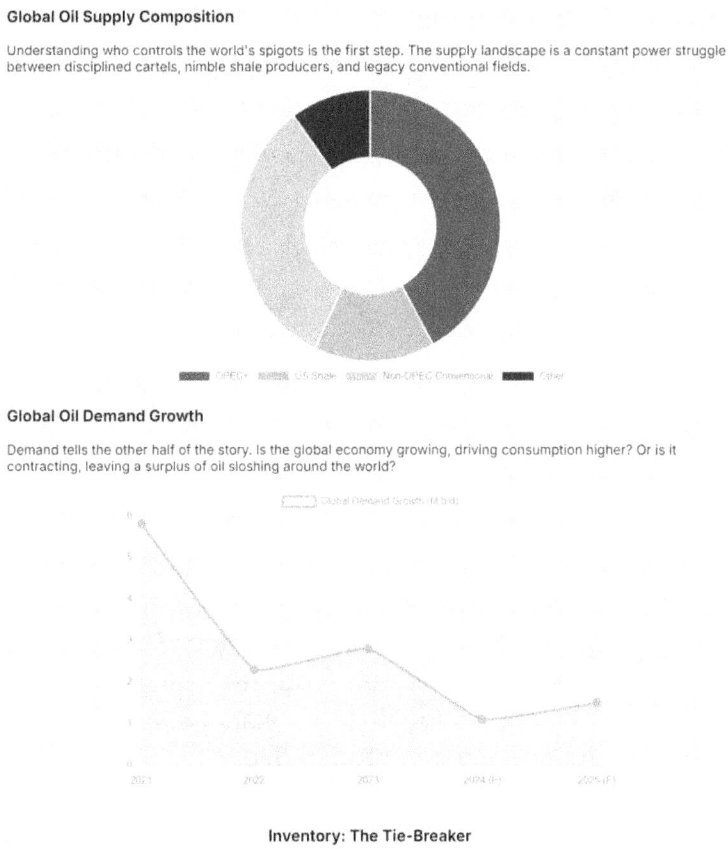

FIGURE 36 - READING THE GLOBAL ENERGY MAP

Inventory: The Tie-Breaker

Inventories are the market's shock absorber. When they are low (measured in "days of supply"), prices are sensitive to any disruption. When high, they cushion supply shocks.

60.5

OECD Days of Supply

▲ Above 5-Year Average

The S&D Balance Sheet

The final step is to combine these elements into a simple forecast. A deficit (demand > supply) pulls oil from inventories and pushes prices up. A surplus does the opposite.

-0.5 M b/d

Forecasted 2025 Market Balance

(Slight Deficit)

STEP 4: THE COMMODITY S&D BALANCE SHEET - THE FINAL VERDICT

The final step is to bring all this analysis together into a single, coherent framework. The tool for this is the Commodity Supply & Demand Balance Sheet. It's a simple table that forces you to quantify your assumptions and shows the relationship between supply, demand, and inventories over time.

The final line item—the **Implied Stock Change**—is the ultimate output of your entire macro analysis. It is the verdict. If your forecast shows a sustained period of negative numbers (inventory draws), your price forecast is **UP**. If it shows a sustained period of positive numbers (inventory builds), your forecast is **DOWN**. And if supply and demand look to be roughly in balance, leading to stable inventories, your forecast is **NEUTRAL**. A neutral forecast is a command to stay on the sidelines and preserve your capital. This framework demands a clear signal; in its absence, the best action is no action.

TABLE 15 - THE COMMODITY S&D BALANCE SHEET

Category	Q1 (Actual)	Q2 (Actual)	Q3 (Estimate)	Q4 (Forecast)	FY Forecast
SUPPLY					
OPEC Production	26.5	26.8	27.0	27.2	26.9
Non-OPEC Production	45.2	45.4	45.5	45.6	45.4
US Production	13.1	13.2	13.3	13.4	13.3
Total Supply	**84.8**	**85.4**	**85.8**	**86.2**	**85.6**
DEMAND					
OECD Demand	46.0	46.5	47.0	46.8	46.6
Non-OECD Demand	55.0	55.5	56.2	56.5	55.8
Total Demand	**101.0**	**102.0**	**103.2**	**103.3**	**102.4**
BALANCE (Supply-Demand)	**-1.2**	**-1.6**	**-1.4**	**-1.1**	**-1.3**
INVENTORY					
Implied Stock Change	-1.2	-1.6	-1.4	-1.1	-1.3
Days of Forward Cover	59.5	58.0	56.8	56.0	56.0

Note: Table values are illustrative, in millions of barrels per day (MMbpd), and would be populated using the data gathered in the preceding steps.

Take #2: The Bottom-Up View (Finding the Undervalued Asset)

Once you've established a macro tailwind—a clear forecast that the price of the commodity is going up—the hunt begins for the right company to express that view. This is where the Wildcatter's Edge meets the activist's mindset. The goal is not to find a "good company" in the conventional sense. The goal is to find undervalued assets. The core question is always: "Are this company's assets worth more than its stock price, and can I force the market to recognize it?"

STEP 1: THE WILDCATTER'S VALUATION - WHAT ARE THE ASSETS WORTH?

Valuation doesn't start with earnings multiples; it starts with the ground. You have to figure out the intrinsic, tangible value of the company's oil and gas reserves. The key metric for this is **PV-10**. You'll find it in a company's annual 10-K filing. PV-10 is the present value of the estimated future revenue from a company's proved reserves, net of direct costs, discounted at 10%. It is a standardized, pre-tax measure that provides a common yardstick for comparing the "in-the-ground" value of different companies.

PV-10 may be considered the bedrock of intrinsic value. The most compelling opportunities arise when a company's total enterprise value (its stock market capitalization plus its net debt) is trading at a significant discount to its PV-10 value. Think about what that means: the public market is valuing the company's audited, engineer-certified reserves at less than their calculated worth. You are essentially buying assets for cents on the dollar.

But the numbers are only the start. The Wildcatter's Edge requires a qualitative assessment of the asset base. Are the reserves located in a premier, low-cost basin like the Permian, or a mature, high-cost region? Is the acreage position concentrated in large, contiguous blocks that allow for more efficient development? And what is the upside potential? Beyond the Proved (1P) reserves that go into the PV-10 calculation, what is the potential for converting Probable (2P) and Possible (3P) reserves into the proved category? A company with a deep inventory of undeveloped, high-quality acreage has enormous growth potential that isn't captured in the official PV-10 number.

Pickens ignored earnings and focused on PV-10: the value of a company's proven reserves if they were produced and sold at current prices, then discounted back to today. If the PV-10 was higher than the stock market value, he'd found a potential bargain.

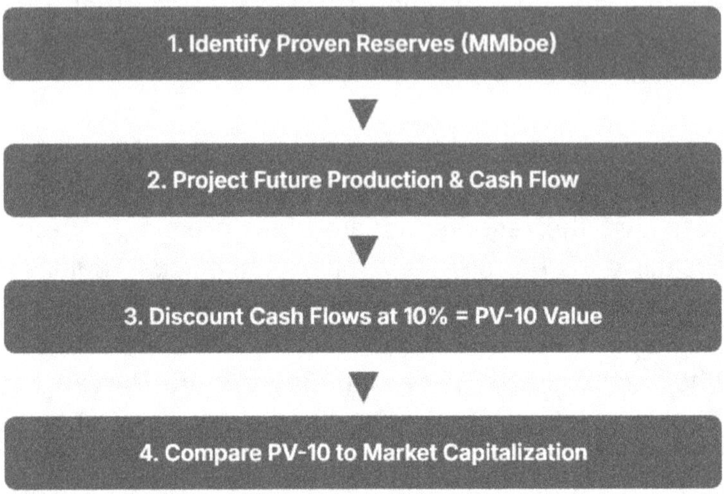

FIGURE 37 - THE WILDCATTER'S VALUATION (PV-10)

STEP 2: SEPARATING THE DRILLERS FROM THE DUDS - COST STRUCTURE ANALYSIS

You can have the best geology in the world, but it can all be ruined by an inefficient operator. This step is about identifying waste and mismanagement by analyzing a company's cost structure and benchmarking it against its peers operating in the same basin. There are two key metrics.

- **Finding & Development (F&D) Costs:** This is the all-in capital cost to add one new barrel of oil equivalent (BOE) to a company's reserve base. It's the ultimate measure of capital efficiency. A company with a consistently low F&D cost is a hallmark of an efficient explorer with high-quality geology. A high or rising F&D cost is a major red flag that management is either drilling in the wrong places or is simply bad at deploying capital.

- **Lease Operating Expenses (LOE):** This is the direct cash cost of lifting a barrel of oil out of the ground—things like labor, maintenance, and power. LOE is a pure measure of operational efficiency. A company with a high LOE per BOE relative to its peers is a classic sign of a bloated, inefficient operation. It's a prime target for an activist campaign focused on cutting the fat.

STEP 3: FIRING THE MANAGEMENT - THE ACTIVIST ANGLE

Let's be blunt. Corporate managers are employees. Shareholders are the owners. If the employees are doing a poor job of managing the owners' assets, they should be fired. This was the simple, revolutionary idea behind my activist campaigns in the 1980s, and it's just as true today.

The entire bottom-up process is a search for a specific type of arbitrage: a *management-quality arbitrage*. The stock market is often very efficient at pricing a company based on the demonstrated ability of its current management team. If the team has a history of missing targets and destroying capital, the stock will trade at a discount. The market is correct about the management. But the market is often *inefficient* at pricing the underlying assets in a scenario where that management is replaced. The activist's job is to exploit this inefficiency. You buy the stock at the discounted "bad management" price and then act as the catalyst to force a corporate action—like a sale of the company—that realizes the higher intrinsic asset price.

The ideal target is what I call an "undermanaged" company. It has a specific profile:

1. **High-Quality Assets:** Confirmed by a low EV/PV-10 ratio and a strong geological assessment.
2. **Poor Operations:** Evidenced by a high cost structure (high F&D and LOE) and poor capital allocation (low returns).
3. **Misaligned Management:** A team with a poor track record, low insider stock ownership (no skin in the game), and compensation tied to the wrong metrics, like growth instead of returns.

When you find a company that fits this profile, you have a prime target. The activist plan isn't a complex operational turnaround; it's a set of simple, decisive actions designed to close the value gap. The most common plans are to sell the company to a more competent operator, divest non-core assets, or force a large return of capital to shareholders. The following scorecard is the tool to systematize this diagnosis.

TABLE 16 - ACTIVIST SCORECARD

Metric	Company X Value	Peer Average	Score (1-5, 5=Best)	Rationale
Valuation				

Metric	Company X Value	Peer Average	Score (1-5, 5=Best)	Rationale
Enterprise Value / PV-10	0.67x	1.1x	5	Trading at a deep discount to intrinsic asset value.
Costs				
LOE per BOE	$12.00	$9.50	1	Significantly higher costs suggest operational bloat.
F&D per BOE (3-yr avg)	$18.00	$14.00	2	Inefficient at replacing reserves.
Capital Allocation				
3-Yr ROCE	6%	11%	1	Consistently destroying value relative to peers.
Governance				
CEO Tenure	15 years	7 years	2	Entrenched management may be resistant to change.
Insider Ownership	0.8%	3.5%	1	Management has little skin in the game.
Strategy				

[68]

Metric	Company X Value	Peer Average	Score (1-5, 5=Best)	Rationale
Non-Core Assets	Yes (Midstream)	No	2	Distraction from core E&P, potential for value-unlocking sale.
Balance Sheet				
Net Debt / EBITDA	2.8x	1.5x	2	High leverage limits financial flexibility.
OVERALL SCORE			**2.0 / 5.0**	**Conclusion: PRIME ACTIVIST TARGET**

Note: The scorecard operationalizes the search for an undermanaged company, turning a qualitative concept into a data-driven process.

Case Study: The Hunt for Company X

Let's walk through how this all comes together in a real-world hunt.

The Setup (Macro): Our top-down analysis is complete. The Commodity S&D Balance Sheet is forecasting a global crude oil deficit of 1.3 million barrels per day for the full year. Inventory draws are accelerating, and stocks are already 5% below the five-year average. The physical market is tight, and our forecast is clear: the price of oil is going up. It's time to find a company with high-quality assets that will benefit from this tailwind.

The Discovery (Valuation): We run a screen of U.S. E&P companies, looking for those with two characteristics: a primary focus on the low-cost Permian Basin and an enterprise value trading below their PV-10. One name immediately stands out: Company X. The numbers are compelling. The company's enterprise value is $10 billion. But when we dig into its latest 10-K, we find its PV-10 value is $15 billion. The EV/PV-10 ratio is just 0.67x. The market is offering us the company's audited, proved reserves for 67 cents on the dollar. The asset quality is rated as high, with an estimated five years of additional drilling inventory in probable locations not yet reflected in the PV-10 value.

The Diagnosis (Costs & Management): A 33% discount to intrinsic value is a huge red flag. We need to know why. So, we start digging into the operations. The diagnosis becomes clear very quickly. Company X's 3-year average F&D cost is $18 per BOE, a full 30% higher than its direct peers drilling in the same basin, whose average is $14/BOE. Their Lease Operating Expense is $12 per BOE, 25% higher than the peer average of $9.50.[1] This is a bloated, inefficient operation.

Then we look at the management team. They have missed their own production guidance in five of the last eight quarters. Their 5-year average Return on Capital Employed is a dismal 6%, while their peers are averaging 11%. We pull the proxy statement and find the smoking gun: the CEO's bonus is primarily tied to production growth, not returns, and insider ownership is less than 1% of the company. They have no skin in the game. The market isn't wrong about the management; it's just failing to separate the value of the assets from the incompetence of the people running them.

The Plan (Activism): The Activist Target Scorecard lights up like a Christmas tree. Company X is a prime target. The value gap is clear, the cause is obvious, and the solution is simple. The plan is not to go in and run the company ourselves. The plan is to act as the catalyst to unlock the value that is already there. We will launch a proxy contest to replace a majority of the board of directors. The new board's mandate will be simple and singular: immediately hire an investment bank and explore a sale of the entire company to a larger, more efficient operator. A strategic buyer could easily cut the cost bloat and would be willing to pay a price close to the PV-10 value to acquire these high-quality Permian assets. That is how you close the gap between the $10 billion market price and the $15 billion asset value.

Key Takeaways: Pickens's Rules for the Oil Patch

This entire framework boils down to a set of simple, hard-won rules. If you follow them, you'll have a fighting chance. If you don't, the market will eat you alive.

- **Supply and demand are the only laws that matter.** Ignore them at your peril.
- **Have a plan or get run over.** Know your thesis, your catalyst, and your exit before you invest a dime.
- **Keep it simple.** If you can't explain your investment idea on the back of a napkin, it's a bad idea.

- **Value starts in the ground.** Know the physical assets better than anyone else on Wall Street.
- **Hunt for good assets run by bad management.** That is the sweet spot where deep value is found.
- **Management works for you.** If they aren't maximizing value for you, the owner, fire them.
- **The best catalyst is one you create yourself.** Don't wait for the market to recognize value; force it to.
- **When the facts change, change your mind.** Dogma is the enemy of profit.
- **When you find an elephant, bet big.** Don't waste your bullets chasing rabbits.
- **Learn from your mistakes.** Every dry hole and every bad trade teaches you something, but only if you're willing to listen.

Chapter 13: The Mobius Map: A Disciplined Journey into Emerging Markets (Mark Mobius)

The Cartographer of Emerging Markets

To understand the world of emerging market investing is to understand the career of Mark Mobius. The story begins not in a sterile trading room, but perhaps on a bone-jolting ride along a mountain road in rural China, or at a dinner table sampling scorpions on toast in Thailand. For Mobius, investing was never a remote-control activity; it was a full-contact sport, an adventure into the world's most dynamic, misunderstood, and often chaotic economies. He is, in essence, the Indiana Jones of emerging market finance, a pioneer who charted the territory that many now take for granted.

The scale of this endeavor is staggering. Over a career spanning more than three decades, Mobius traveled over a million miles, visited 112 countries, and personally vetted thousands of the more than 5,000 companies his funds invested in. In an era before the internet made global data ubiquitous, he was the original search engine for opportunity, powered by jet fuel and shoe leather. This relentless travel was not tourism; it was a systematic quest to build a global information network, to gain an edge by seeing, touching, and understanding the realities on the ground.

His path to becoming a global investor was as unconventional as his methods. With a PhD in economics from MIT and degrees in communications from Boston University, his early career saw him marketing Snoopy merchandise across Asia and working as a political consultant. This eclectic background, far from being a detour, was the ideal training ground. To successfully market a beloved cartoon character in diverse Asian cultures required a deep, nuanced understanding of local tastes, distribution networks, and consumer psychology—the very qualitative factors he would later prioritize in his investment analysis. His academic work in communications provided the tools to build relationships and extract subtle, crucial information from management teams across cultural divides. This was not a series of disconnected jobs, but an unconventional apprenticeship that forged the core skills that would become his durable competitive advantage.

The pivotal moment arrived in 1987. Sir John Templeton, the legendary titan of value investing, personally recruited Mobius to run one of the world's first dedicated emerging market funds. This appointment established Mobius's intellectual lineage, grounding his adventurous spirit in the disciplined, contrarian, value-oriented philosophy of his mentor. It was the fusion of Templeton's timeless principles with Mobius's on-the-ground grit that would create a new map for navigating the world's economic frontiers.

The Mobius Doctrine: A Philosophy for Growth and Value

The enduring success of the Mobius approach is not rooted in a secret formula or a black-box algorithm. It is built on a disciplined, repeatable philosophy resting on three foundational pillars. These principles are not independent ideas but form a reinforcing, interconnected system for decision-making under pressure.

PILLAR 1: THE FUTURE IS IN EMERGING MARKETS

The central, unwavering thesis of the Mobius doctrine is a multi-decade, secular conviction in the superior growth trajectory of emerging and frontier markets. This is not a tactical trade but a strategic, long-term allocation. While developed economies often contend with mature growth rates, emerging nations are in a phase of rapid transformation. This dynamism is powered by a confluence of powerful, structural tailwinds that are set to reshape the global economy for decades to come:

- **Favorable Demographics:** These nations are characterized by young, growing populations, creating both a vast, productive workforce and a new generation of consumers.[69]
- **Rapid Urbanization and Industrialization:** The historic shift from rural to urban life is the engine of economic transformation, unlocking massive productivity gains and creating demand for infrastructure, housing, and services.[70]
- **A Burgeoning Middle Class:** With rising disposable incomes, hundreds of millions of people are entering the consumer economy for the first time, fueling demand for everything from banking services to brand-name goods.[71]

The quantitative evidence for this belief is compelling. On average, emerging markets have historically grown at double the rate of their developed counterparts. This macroeconomic velocity provides a powerful tailwind for corporate performance, as a country's stock market will often grow at a multiple of its GDP. This core belief necessitates a strategic investment horizon of 5 to 15 years, or even longer, providing the essential patience required to withstand the inevitable bouts of volatility and capture the profound, underlying growth trend.

PILLAR 2: BOOTS-ON-THE-GROUND RESEARCH

In the informationally opaque and inefficient environments that characterize many emerging markets, relying solely on financial statements is necessary but dangerously insufficient. The Mobius framework asserts that a durable competitive edge is gained only through direct, primary, on-the-ground research. This principle is the very embodiment of his career.

The method is a systematic process of intelligence gathering designed to uncover truths that never appear in an annual report. It involves factory tours to assess operational efficiency, face-to-face meetings with management to gauge their character and competence, and candid conversations with local employees, suppliers, customers, and even competitors. The ultimate objective is to understand the

people and the culture behind the balance sheet. As Mobius has long maintained, investors often become too fixated on numbers and forget that it is people who run companies. This qualitative data provides crucial context, serving to either validate or invalidate the story the numbers are telling. It is this deep, local knowledge that can uncover hidden risks—such as the discovery of pipes secretly siphoning refined product from a Romanian refinery—that would be utterly invisible to an analyst sitting thousands of miles away behind a screen.

PILLAR 3: CONTRARIAN VALUE & THE POINT OF MAXIMUM PESSIMISM

Inherited directly from his mentor, Sir John Templeton, the principle of contrarian value is the core entry signal for the entire framework. The strategy is not merely to buy cheap stocks. It is to buy good companies when they have become cheap for reasons of widespread fear, crisis, or political turmoil. Templeton's guiding question was not "Where is the outlook good?" but rather, "Where is the outlook the most miserable?". This is because a true bargain price only occurs for one reason: others are selling, often despondently and emotionally.

This principle is supercharged in emerging markets, where political and economic crises are more frequent and often more severe. The Mobius doctrine posits that country-level risk is systematically mispriced during these episodes. The market's panic creates a window of opportunity to acquire high-quality assets at prices far below their intrinsic worth. This approach reframes the concept of political risk. Instead of a threat to be universally avoided, it is seen as a primary source of market mispricing and, therefore, opportunity. The market consistently overreacts to short-term chaos, extrapolating temporary instability indefinitely into the future. This creates the "point of maximum pessimism"—the ideal entry point for the disciplined, long-term investor.

These three pillars are not a simple checklist; they form a powerful, causal loop. The secular belief in the long-term growth of emerging markets provides the psychological fortitude and conviction necessary to execute a contrarian strategy. It is this unwavering belief that allows an investor to act when every emotional instinct screams "flee." However, conviction alone is not enough. The "boots-on-the-ground" research provides the critical verification needed to distinguish a temporary crisis from a permanent impairment of capital. It is this deep, local intelligence that confirms whether a country's long-term fabric remains intact and its best companies are fundamentally sound, giving the investor the analytical confidence to step in and buy when others are consumed by panic.

The Top-Down Lens: A Framework for Country Analysis

Before a single stock is analyzed, the Mobius framework begins with a panoramic view of the world. The top-down process is a rational, sequential filtering system designed to narrow the vast universe of over 100 emerging and frontier markets down to a handful of the most promising opportunities. It is a disciplined approach that prioritizes risk management above all else.

STEP 1: THE GO/NO-GO POLITICAL RISK FILTER

The first and most important stage is not about potential returns, but about the preservation of capital. This initial screen serves as a hard, qualitative filter designed to answer two critical questions: "Can we get our money in?" and, more importantly, "Will we be able to get our money out?".

This step acts as an absolute veto. It screens for non-negotiable risks that could lead to the permanent loss of capital, regardless of a company's quality or valuation. Triggers for a "No-Go" decision include active warfare, a high and credible probability of asset expropriation or forced nationalization, or an existing capital control regime that makes the repatriation of funds practically impossible. This is not a theoretical exercise. The framework's disciplined application of this filter dictated a complete exit from Venezuela when the government's rhetoric of nationalization became a credible threat to invested capital, demonstrating that this tool is used for both entry and exit decisions.

STEP 2: MACROECONOMIC FUNDAMENTALS ANALYSIS

For countries that pass the initial "Go" filter, the analysis shifts to the underlying health and long-term growth trajectory of the economy. The core premise is that a robust and rapidly growing economy provides a powerful tailwind for corporate earnings and, by extension, equity market returns.[72]

The assessment is a comprehensive check-up of the nation's economic vitals. Key metrics include real GDP growth rates (both historical and forecast), consumer price inflation trends, government debt-to-GDP ratios, the current account balance, and, crucially, the level of foreign exchange reserves, which indicates a country's ability to withstand external shocks. A positive demographic profile, characterized by a young and growing populace, is also a key long-term driver of consumption and labor force expansion. An ideal candidate exhibits high growth, stable inflation, a strong fiscal position, and positive demographics.

STEP 3: THE CONTRARIAN FILTER (MARKET SENTIMENT & VALUATION)

The final step in the top-down process is designed to operationalize the "point of maximum pessimism" principle. It systematically searches for markets that are not just cheap, but "cheap and hated," as this is where the greatest potential for a significant valuation re-rating exists.[73]

The analyst seeks a confluence of indicators pointing to extreme negative sentiment. These include:

- **Valuation:** Aggregate market price-to-earnings (P/E) and price-to-book (P/B) ratios trading at multi-year or even decadal lows compared to their own history and to other markets.[74]
- **Fund Flows:** Evidence of sustained and large-scale capital outflows from foreign investors, indicating that international capital has abandoned the market.[75]
- **Narrative:** A qualitative assessment of the dominant story in the international financial

press. The goal is to find a pervasive narrative of crisis, decline, or hopelessness.

SYNTHESIS: THE COUNTRY SCORING MATRIX

The outputs from these three distinct steps are then synthesized into a unified country attractiveness score. A weighted model combines the scores, reflecting the philosophy's priorities: identifying undervalued opportunities in fundamentally sound economies that meet a minimum threshold of investability. The table below provides an illustrative example.[76]

TABLE 17 - THE COUNTRY SCORING MATRIX

Country	Political Risk Score (1-10)	Macro Score (1-10)	Pessimism Score (1-10)	Weighted Final Score
Brazil	6.0	6.0	8.5	7.0
India	7.0	8.5	4.0	6.6
Turkey	5.0	5.0	9.0	6.6

This matrix makes the synthesis tangible and reveals the framework's priorities. Notice how Brazil, with mediocre political and macro scores but an extremely high "Pessimism Score," can rank higher than India, which boasts excellent macroeconomic fundamentals but is viewed more favorably by the market. This visually and intuitively teaches the essence of the contrarian approach: an investor is compensated for taking on perceived risk when fundamentals are adequate and sentiment is at rock bottom.

The rigid, sequential structure of this top-down process is more than just an analytical tool; it is a powerful defense against behavioral biases. By forcing the "Go/No-Go" political check *first*, the framework erects a crucial psychological guardrail. It prevents the investor from being seduced by a cheap valuation (Step 3) in a country where the rule of law is so weak that they could lose their entire investment (Step 1). This disciplined sequence prioritizes the return *of* capital before considering the return *on* capital, a principle that is the bedrock of long-term success in volatile markets.

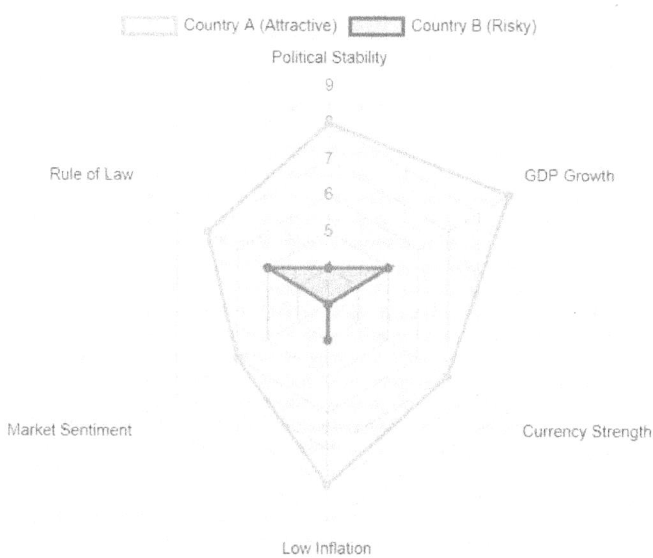

FIGURE 38 - COUNTRY SCORING MATRIX

The Bottom-Up Lens: Finding Local Champions

Once an attractive country has been identified, the analytical lens zooms in from the satellite view to the microscopic. The bottom-up process is a deep-dive investigation designed to find the highest-quality, best-managed, and most attractively valued companies within those target markets.[77]

STEP 1: SCREENING FOR LOCAL CHAMPIONS

The search begins by filtering the entire universe of stocks in a target country for "Local Champions." These are high-quality, fundamentally strong companies that are poised to dominate their domestic markets and benefit directly from the country's growth. They are typically "price makers" with deep competitive moats, not commodity "price takers" subject to global price swings.

To identify these candidates, a strict quantitative screen is applied, creating a shortlist of companies that exhibit superior financial discipline and profitability. The key hurdles are:

- **Profitability:** A consistent Return on Equity (ROE) of over 20%.
- **Solvency:** A conservative Debt-to-Equity ratio below 50%.
- **Growth:** A proven track record of consistent earnings growth, typically above 10% per year.
- **Liquidity:** A minimum average daily trading volume (e.g., $1-2 million) to ensure a position can be built and exited efficiently.[78]

STEP 2: RISK-ADJUSTED VALUATION

A quality company is only a good investment if purchased at the right price. The valuation process must explicitly account for the unique political and economic risks associated with the country of domicile.[79]

While standard methodologies like Discounted Cash Flow (DCF) analysis are used, they are modified for the emerging market context. The key adjustment is to the discount rate. A specific **Country Risk Premium (CRP)**, derived from the top-down analysis, is added to the Weighted Average Cost of Capital (WACC). This systematically and conservatively increases the discount rate, thereby lowering the calculated intrinsic value of the company. This process builds in a crucial margin of safety to compensate for the higher uncertainty. The ultimate goal is to purchase the stock at a significant discount to this risk-adjusted intrinsic value, providing a buffer against unforeseen negative events.

STEP 3: THE CORPORATE GOVERNANCE DEEP DIVE: THE ULTIMATE VETO

This is arguably the most critical and nuanced step in the entire process. In emerging markets, the greatest danger is often not market volatility but the permanent loss of capital due to poor stewardship, opaque related-party transactions, or outright fraud. For this reason, an unacceptable score on corporate governance acts as a **final and absolute veto**, regardless of how compelling the growth story or how cheap the valuation may appear.[80]

The analysis is structured around a comprehensive checklist designed to identify common governance risks. The goal is to assess the quality and integrity of the people stewarding the capital. The following table provides a practical tool for investors to conduct their own due diligence.

TABLE 18 - GOVERNANCE RISKS CHECKLIST

Category	Checklist Item	Assessment (Low/Med/High Risk)	Notes
Ownership & Control	Is ownership highly concentrated in one family?	High	60% owned by founding family. Risk of family interests > others.
Board Structure	What percentage of the board is independent?	Med	40% independent, but some have long tenures.
Minority Rights	Are dividends paid consistently?	Low	Consistent dividend payer for 10+ years.
Transparency	Are related-party transactions clearly disclosed?	High	Opaque transactions with other family-owned entities. Major red flag. [81]

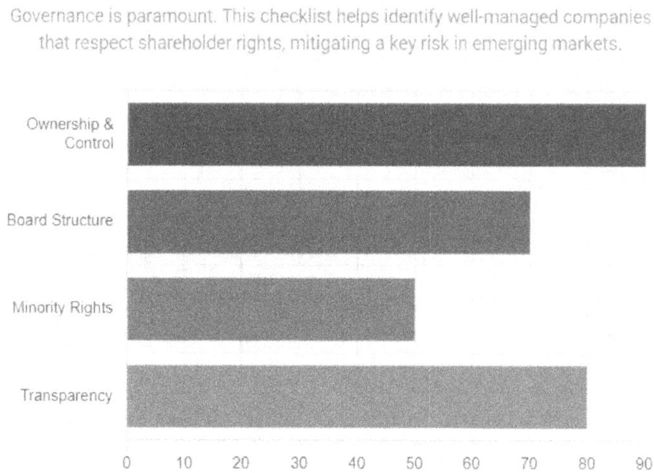

FIGURE 39 - EM CORPORATE GOVERNANCE CHECKLIST

This checklist transforms the abstract concept of "good governance" into a concrete, investigable roadmap. It empowers the investor to identify clear warning signs, such as opaque transactions with entities controlled by the founding family, which represent a major red flag for potential value extraction at the expense of minority shareholders.

The framework's intense focus on low debt (Debt/Equity < 50%) and strong corporate governance is a direct reflection of the unique dangers of emerging markets. These are not just generic "quality" factors; they are targeted defenses against the two most common causes of permanent capital loss during a crisis. When a country's currency collapses, highly indebted companies are often pushed into bankruptcy. During the chaos of a crisis, managers of poorly governed companies have the greatest incentive and opportunity to siphon value away from minority shareholders. These two filters are designed to ensure that a chosen "Local Champion" is a financial fortress, capable of surviving the storm long enough for the contrarian investment thesis to play out.

Case Studies from the Frontier

Theory is best understood through the lens of history. The following case studies illustrate how the Mobius framework is applied in the real world, providing a disciplined map to navigate both crisis and opportunity.

CASE STUDY 1: THE EYE OF THE STORM - NAVIGATING THE 1997 ASIAN FINANCIAL CRISIS

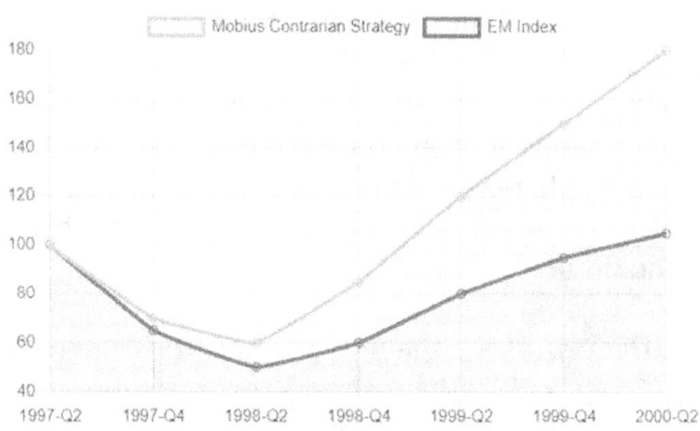

FIGURE 40 - CONTRARIAN STRATEGY PERFORMANCE

The Scene: In the mid-1990s, the "Asian Tiger" economies of Southeast Asia were the darlings of the global economy, lauded as economic miracles with years of seemingly unstoppable growth. The crisis, which began with the devaluation of the Thai baht on July 2, 1997, caught the world almost completely by surprise. What followed was a terrifying contagion. Currencies plunged, stock markets collapsed, foreign capital fled, and a deep crisis of confidence swept across the region, threatening a global meltdown.

Applying the Framework: This was a classic "point of maximum pessimism" event.

- **Top-Down:** The Contrarian Filter would have been lighting up across the region. Countries like Thailand, Indonesia, and South Korea, once praised, were now international pariahs. The prevailing narrative was one of complete and irreversible collapse. Their "Pessimism Scores" would have been at a perfect 10.
- **Bottom-Up:** The key to navigating the crisis was to differentiate between companies that were fundamentally broken and those that were merely caught in the indiscriminate panic selling. Many banks and over-leveraged corporations with huge dollar-denominated debts were indeed insolvent. However, the panic also dragged down high-quality "Local Champions" with strong balance sheets (low debt), dominant market positions, and honest management.[82]
- **The Mobius Action:** With the discipline provided by his framework, Mobius did exactly what his philosophy dictated: he went bargain hunting. He famously "snapped up bargains during the Asian financial crisis after Thailand floated its currency in 1997". This was the doctrine in action: having the conviction, backed by on-the-ground research, to buy quality assets at the moment of maximum fear.

CASE STUDY 2: OPPORTUNITY AND PERIL - THE RUSSIAN PRIVATIZATIONS OF THE 1990S

The Scene: The collapse of the Soviet Union in 1991 ushered in a "chaotic and turbulent" decade for Russia. The new government embarked on a massive and rapid privatization program, using a voucher system to transfer thousands of state-owned enterprises into private hands. This created what many called the "firesale of the century," an unprecedented opportunity to acquire world-class assets at pennies on the dollar.

Applying the Framework: This environment was the ultimate test of the framework's risk filters.

- **Political Risk & Governance:** This was not a macroeconomic crisis like Asia's; it was a crisis of institutions and governance. The "Go/No-Go" filter would have signaled extreme caution. The core risk was not a currency collapse, but the fundamental question of property rights in a legal vacuum. The voucher system often resulted in "insiders"—company managers—gaining control, and many auctions were rigged, leading to the rise of a new class of powerful "oligarchs". The EM Corporate Governance Checklist would have been the most critical tool. For any potential investment, the key questions were: Who *really* controls this company? Are the rights of minority shareholders respected? In many cases, the answer was a clear "No," triggering an immediate investment veto.[83]
- **Finding the Gems:** Despite the peril, generational opportunities existed. The natural gas monopoly

> Gazprom, for instance, was sold for roughly $250 million in vouchers in 1994; just two years later, its market valuation was nearly $37 billion. The framework's job was to sift through the hundreds of corrupt, insider-controlled firms to find the rare few with plausible governance and world-class assets. True to form, Mobius was an active investor, buying Russian stocks during the panic of 1998, demonstrating his contrarian nerve in one of the world's most challenging markets.

These two case studies serve as perfect foils, illustrating the adaptability of the Mobius framework. The Asian Crisis was primarily a macroeconomic and sentiment-driven event, making the Contrarian Filter and balance sheet analysis the key tools. The Russian Privatization was fundamentally a political and governance crisis, making the Political Risk and Corporate Governance filters the most critical lines of defense. The framework is not a monolithic tool; it is a complete toolkit, equipping the investor to identify the primary risk in any given situation and apply the right analytical lens.

Key Takeaways: The EM Investor's Creed

The lessons from a lifetime of navigating the world's most dynamic markets can be distilled into a clear and actionable creed. For any investor, novice or experienced, who wishes to follow this disciplined path, these principles are the essential guideposts.

- **Believe in the Long-Term Story:** The future of superior growth is in emerging markets. Anchor your strategy in their secular tailwinds of demographics and development.
- **Walk the Ground:** Information is your greatest edge. Go beyond the screen to understand the people, culture, and reality of the businesses you own.
- **Run Towards the Fire:** The greatest opportunities are found at the "point of maximum pessimism." Cultivate the discipline to buy quality assets when others are panic-selling.
- **Put Governance First:** The quality and integrity of management are paramount. Never compromise on corporate governance; it is your best defense against the permanent loss of capital. A cheap stock with bad governance is a trap, not a bargain.
- **Analyze Countries, Then Companies:** Follow a disciplined dual-lens process. Ensure the country is a safe and fertile ground for investment before you plant capital in a specific company.
- **Demand a Margin of Safety:** Account for the inherent risks of emerging markets by systematically adjusting your valuations and buying only at a significant discount to intrinsic worth.
- **Be Patient:** Think in terms of years and decades, not quarters. Long-term compounding is the prize for which you are aiming; volatility is merely the price of admission.
- **Diversify Broadly:** The future is inherently uncertain. Protect your portfolio from the

inevitable shocks by diversifying across at least 20 countries and 100 individual stocks.

- **Avoid Leverage:** Volatility is a given in emerging markets. Leverage turns manageable drawdowns into catastrophic, portfolio-ending losses. Never use it.

Chapter 14: The Venture Framework: Secrets & Monopolies (Peter Thiel)

The Contrarian's Question: A Worldview Apart

To understand the architecture of modern value creation, one must first understand Peter Thiel. He is not merely a venture capitalist of legendary success—a co-founder of PayPal and Palantir, the first outside investor in Facebook—but a philosopher of technology whose life's work is a direct confrontation with the future. His methodology is born from a profound dissatisfaction with the incrementalism of the present, a belief that we have been lulled into a state of technological stagnation disguised as progress. At the heart of this worldview is a single, deceptively simple question that serves as the key to his entire framework:

"What important truth do few people agree with you on?".

This is not a clever interview tactic; it is the foundational query of a system designed to unearth generational companies. It functions on multiple levels. Intellectually, it is a filter for original thought, a demand for an idea that cannot be found in a textbook or a newspaper headline. Psychologically, it is a test of courage, a measure of one's ability to stand alone against the tide of consensus. A good answer is not a prediction about the future but a declaration about the present, taking the form: "Most people believe X, but the truth is the opposite of X". Before Airbnb, the consensus was that no sane person would let a stranger sleep in their home; the contrarian truth was that they would, given a platform of sufficient trust and simplicity. That truth, that "secret," unlocked a global market.

This question is more than a starting point; it is the engine of a causal chain that defines the entire process of value creation. Each principle in the Thielian worldview is a necessary link in this chain, flowing logically from the one before it. A correct and courageous answer to the contrarian question reveals a *Secret*. This Secret—this non-obvious truth about the world—is the only possible foundation for a *Zero to One* innovation. A sufficiently powerful Zero to One innovation creates an entirely new market, which is the only way to build a *Durable Monopoly*. And a durable monopoly is the only business structure capable of generating the exponential cash flows required to produce a *Power Law* return. To understand this chain is to understand the blueprint for building the future.

The Monopoly Thesis: Why Competition is for Losers

The modern world, particularly in the West, is built on the intellectual bedrock of competition. Economists idealize it as "perfect competition," a state of equilibrium where no single company makes an economic profit. For a business, however, this state is not equilibrium; it is a death sentence. Competition is a destructive force, a war of attrition fought over diminishing margins. It forces companies into a myopic, short-term struggle for survival, where the focus is on today's sales and this quarter's earnings. In a competitive market, you are defined by your rivals, forced to copy their features and match their prices until all distinction, and therefore all profit, erodes to zero. Thiel's axiom is as blunt as it is profound: "Competition is for losers".

The alternative to this destructive cycle is not collusion or predatory pricing, but the creation of something so new and valuable that it has no competitors. This is the fundamental distinction between two modes of progress: Zero to One versus 1 to N.[84]

- **1 to N (Globalization):** This is horizontal or extensive progress. It means copying things that work—taking a successful model and replicating it across the globe. When a Chinese company builds a smartphone that looks and feels like an iPhone, it is moving from 1 to n. This is the world of competition, of imitation, of globalization.
- **Zero to One (Technology):** This is vertical or intensive progress. It means doing something entirely new—creating a new category of abundance for the world. Taking a typewriter and building a word processor is going from 0 to 1. The next Bill Gates will not build an operating system, and the next Mark Zuckerberg will not create a social network. Copying them is an act of 1 to n. True innovation, the creation of all durable value, happens in these "Zero to One" moments.

The reward for a successful Zero to One creation is a monopoly. In a static world, a monopolist is a rent-seeker, like the owner of a utility company. But in the dynamic world of technology, a creative monopolist gives customers more choices by adding entirely new categories of products to the world. Google's monopoly in search did not preclude other search engines; it was the reward for creating a product so superior that it rendered them irrelevant. This state of monopoly is not a social ill; it is the necessary condition for progress. A company free from the daily struggle of competition can afford to think long-term. It can pay its employees well, invest in ambitious research that may not pay off for decades, and care deeply about its impact on the world. The goal of every startup, therefore, should be to become a monopoly.

This is not achieved by accident. A durable monopoly is built upon a combination of four key pillars 1:

1. **Proprietary Technology:** This is the most substantive advantage a company can have. The technology must be at least 10 times better than its closest substitute on some critical dimension. A mere 2x improvement is insufficient to overcome customer inertia and switching costs; the leap must be a quantum one. Amazon's ability to offer 10 times as many books as any physical bookstore, or PayPal's ability to make payments 10 times faster than mailing a check, are prime examples. This 10x advantage makes competition effectively impossible.
2. **Network Effects:** A business benefits from network effects when its product becomes more valuable as more people use it. Facebook is the canonical example: its value to any single user is a direct function of how many of their friends are also on the platform. Network effects create powerful barriers to entry, but they are notoriously difficult to build. They require solving the "cold start" problem: the product must be

valuable to its very first users, even when the network is small, before it can grow into a self-reinforcing loop.

3. **Economies of Scale:** A business with strong economies of scale has high fixed costs to create its product but very low (or zero) marginal costs to produce additional units. Software businesses are the perfect example. The cost to develop a complex AI model can be hundreds of millions of dollars, but the marginal cost of serving one more API call is effectively zero. This allows a monopoly to serve a massive market and achieve enormous profit margins, while a new entrant would have to replicate the massive upfront investment just to compete.
4. **Branding:** A strong brand is a powerful and subtle form of monopoly. Apple has built a brand that is synonymous with minimalist design, quality, and a seamless user experience, allowing it to command premium prices and intense customer loyalty. A brand is not a logo or an advertising campaign; it is the culmination of a company's substance, technology, and culture, projected outward to create a unique and defensible identity in the minds of consumers.

The intellectual core of this entire endeavor is the **Search for Secrets**. A secret is an important, undiscovered truth about the world. Secrets can be about nature (the laws of physics, the structure of DNA) or about people (unrecognized market needs, hidden psychological desires). Every great business is built around a secret it was the first to discover. The consensus view is that there are no secrets left—that all the great discoveries have been made. This is the dogma of a stagnant world. The contrarian believes that there are countless secrets left to find, hidden in plain sight, waiting for someone with the courage to look where no one else is looking and question what everyone else takes for granted.

This entire philosophy is underwritten by the unforgiving mathematics of the **Power Law**. Venture capital returns do not follow a normal distribution or a bell curve; they are governed by a Power Law, where a tiny fraction of events accounts for the majority of the outcomes. This leads to what Thiel calls "the biggest secret in venture capital": **the best investment in a successful fund will equal or outperform the entire rest of the fund combined.**

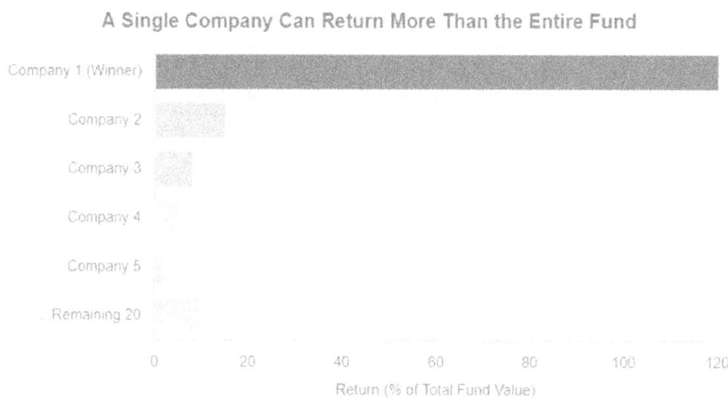

FIGURE 41 - THE POWER LAW IN VENTURE

This single observation fundamentally reshapes investment strategy. It renders traditional diversification not just suboptimal, but irrational. If one company's success can eclipse the performance of dozens of others, then the only rational strategy is to focus exclusively on finding that one company. This imposes two iron laws of investing:

- **Rule 1: Only invest in companies that have the potential to return the value of the entire fund.** This is an incredibly restrictive filter. It eliminates the vast majority of opportunities, including many that might become good, profitable businesses on a more humble scale. It forces the investor to think in terms of exponential, not incremental, outcomes.
- **Rule 2: Because Rule 1 is so restrictive, there can be no other rules.** An investor hunting for these rare, fund-returning outliers cannot afford to be constrained by conventional heuristics about what a "good" investment looks like. They must be open to strange ideas, unconventional founders, and unproven markets that other investors dismiss.

The Power Law completely inverts the conventional definition of risk. In a traditional portfolio, risk is the potential for loss of capital. In a Power Law world, the greatest risk is not the money lost on failed investments; that is an expected and manageable cost of doing business. The greatest risk—the only one that truly matters—is the **opportunity cost of *missing* the one investment that becomes a generational company**. Therefore, the entire framework is optimized not to minimize downside, but to maximize the probability of finding and capturing an outlier return. It is a rational response to the unforgiving mathematics that govern the future.

The Macro Framework: A Guide to Finding the Future

The "Search for Secrets" is a compelling philosophical mandate, but it requires a practical methodology. The Macro Framework provides this, transforming the abstract hunt for non-obvious truths into a systematic, four-step process for identifying the secular trends that will shape the next decade. This top-down analysis acts as an idea-refining funnel, designed to filter the noise of the present into a high-conviction, proprietary thesis about the future.

Step 1: Mapping the Present Consensus[85]

Before one can be a contrarian, one must have a precise understanding of what the consensus view actually is. It is not enough to have a vague sense of popular opinion. This step requires the systematic documentation of the "official future"—the dominant narratives, prevailing dogmas, and widely held beliefs within a specific domain. This is achieved by a comprehensive review of mainstream technology journalism, reports from major industry analysts, influential academic papers, and the public statements of established market leaders. The output is a clear map of conventional wisdom, a set of declarative "Consensus Statements." For example, in the domain of artificial intelligence, a consensus statement might be: "Progress in AI is a continuous, incremental process of scaling existing model architectures".

Step 2: The Search for Secrets (Contrarian Questioning)[86]

This is the creative heart of the process. With the map of consensus in hand, the analyst systematically inverts each belief, asking, "What important truth emerges if the opposite of this is true?". This is not a simple negation but a creative exploration of an alternative future. If the consensus is that AI will automate existing white-collar jobs, the contrarian hypothesis might be: "The most significant impact of AI will be the creation of an entirely new class of artisans and creators, super-powering individual human capabilities rather than replacing them". This step generates a wide set of plausible, non-obvious "Contrarian Hypotheses" that are, by definition, differentiated from the market's current expectations.

Step 3: Identifying Paradigm Shifts (Weak Signal Analysis)[87]

A contrarian hypothesis is just an idea; an investment thesis requires evidence. A true paradigm shift rarely announces itself through mainstream channels. It begins with weak signals on the periphery. This step involves a systematic hunt for these signals in sources that lie outside the consensus bubble: pre-print academic archives like arXiv for novel breakthroughs, patent filings for clusters of new inventions, and niche technical communities where early adopters congregate. The goal is to find early, quantifiable evidence of an exponential trend—a rapid acceleration in publications, open-source contributors, or early-stage funding that suggests the contrarian hypothesis is moving from inception to a rapid growth phase. This provides the first layer of empirical support, narrowing the field of hypotheses to those with nascent traction.

Step 4: Thesis Validation (The "Bad Contrarian" **Check)**[88]

This is the final and most critical guardrail. Being contrarian is not an end in itself; one must be contrarian and right. Many ideas are unpopular simply because they are wrong. This step is a rigorous stress test designed to separate genuine insight from flawed speculation. It involves several checks:

- **First-Principles Analysis:** The thesis is deconstructed to its most fundamental assumptions. Do these assumptions align with the laws of physics, mathematics, or well-established principles of human psychology? A thesis predicated on a perpetual motion machine would fail immediately.
- **The Pain Test:** A true secret solves a problem that is both significant and often poorly articulated by the market itself. The analysis must confirm that the problem the new paradigm addresses is a genuine "painkiller" (a must-have), not merely a "vitamin" (a nice-to-have).
- **Defining Falsification Conditions:** A strong investment thesis, like a scientific hypothesis, must be falsifiable. The analyst must explicitly state: "This thesis would be proven wrong if X, Y, or Z were to happen." This prevents confirmation bias and provides a clear basis for re-evaluation if the underlying reality changes.

Only a thesis that survives this intellectual gauntlet graduates from a "Contrarian Hypothesis" to a high-conviction "Secret." It is the final, most rigorous filter in the funnel, ensuring that the output is not just a collection of interesting ideas, but an actionable, battle-tested worldview upon which capital can be deployed.

The Micro Framework: The Seven Questions of a Monopoly Blueprint

Once the Macro Framework has identified a promising secret—a new secular trend that the world is overlooking—the focus shifts to the micro level. The challenge is now to find the specific company that will be the chosen vehicle to monopolize the future created by that secret. The Micro Framework operationalizes this bottom-up analysis through a seven-question checklist. A company must have a compelling answer to all seven to be considered a potential Power Law investment.

1. **The Engineering Question:** Do you have a breakthrough technology? The foundational requirement is proprietary technology that is at least 10 times better than its closest substitute. This is the source of a monopoly's initial, overwhelming advantage.
2. **The Timing Question:** Is now the right time to start this particular business? This question links directly to the Macro Framework. A great idea can fail if the technological or cultural preconditions for its success are not yet in place. One must be riding a secular wave of change.
3. **The Monopoly Question:** Are you starting with a big share of a small market? This is Thiel's unique and counter-intuitive approach to market analysis. He rejects the "1% of a $100 billion market" fallacy, as this is the hallmark of a

competitive strategy. The correct approach is to identify a small, specific niche market—a "beachhead"—that is small enough to be dominated quickly. Once that niche is monopolized, the company can strategically expand into adjacent, progressively larger markets. Amazon's path from books to all of e-commerce is the canonical example.

4. **The People Question:** Do you have the right team? Technology and markets are not enough; execution requires an exceptional team. This framework rejects the notion of the interchangeable professional manager and elevates the founder. The ideal is a "Founder as Visionary," a leader who is deeply mission-driven, possesses a unique insight, and is capable of building a "cult-like" culture dedicated to a long-term vision. Strong founding teams often have a deep, pre-existing history of working together.
5. **The Distribution Question:** Do you have a way to not just create but deliver your product? Superior technology does not sell itself. Many brilliant engineers fail because they neglect the challenge of distribution. A company must have a clear and effective plan for sales, marketing, and getting its product into the hands of customers.
6. **The Durability Question:** Will your market position be defensible 10 and 20 years from now? This question forces a long-term perspective, looking beyond the initial technological advantage to the other pillars of monopoly: powerful network effects, economies

of scale, and a strong brand that can sustain dominance over decades.

7. **The Secret Question:** Have you identified a unique opportunity that others don't see? This brings the analysis full circle. The company must be built around a specific, non-consensus truth—its own private secret—that is the source of its unique vision and strategy.

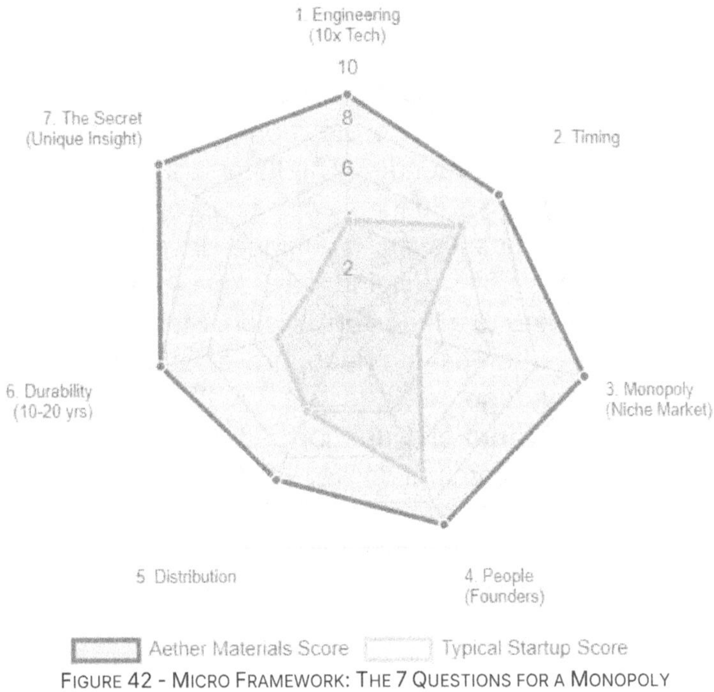

FIGURE 42 - MICRO FRAMEWORK: THE 7 QUESTIONS FOR A MONOPOLY

To make this evaluation more concrete, the framework employs a practical tool: the Monopoly Grading Rubric. This operationalizes the abstract concept of a durable monopoly, forcing an analyst to move beyond gut feelings and assess a company based on specific, evidence-backed criteria.

TABLE 19 - MONOPOLY GRADING RUBRIC

Characteristic	Definition	Evidence	Score (1-10)
Proprietary Tech	A 10x improvement over the closest substitute on a key dimension.	Performance benchmarks; Patent portfolio strength; Independent reviews; Customer testimonials quantifying the leap.	
Network Effects	The product's value increases with each new user.	Viral coefficient (k) > 1.0; High user-to-user engagement rates; Evidence of a self-reinforcing community.	
Economies of Scale	High fixed costs but low/zero marginal costs per additional user.	Gross margins > 80%; Declining Customer Acquisition Cost (CAC) at scale; Scalability of core infrastructure.	
Branding	A strong, defensible brand that inspires loyalty and pricing power.	Net Promoter Score (NPS); Premium pricing vs. competitors; "Cult-like" user base; Cohesive mission and narrative.	

This rubric, combined with the seven questions, provides a comprehensive blueprint for identifying a company with true monopoly potential.

Case Study: The Rise of Aether Materials

To see how this two-part framework operates in practice, consider the case of a hypothetical company, Aether Materials. The analysis is a narrative that moves from the abstract discovery of a secret to the concrete evaluation of a company poised to monopolize it.

Finding the Secret (The Macro Framework) The process begins with an analyst mapping the consensus view on artificial intelligence. The dominant narrative is clear: AI is about bits. The consensus is that the primary impact of LLMs will be the automation of cognitive labor—writing code, summarizing documents, and displacing white-collar workers. Applying the contrarian question, the analyst inverts this belief: "What if the most valuable application of AI is not for bits, but for atoms?". This generates a powerful new hypothesis: that AI's greatest impact will be in augmenting our ability to engineer the physical world.

The search for weak signals begins. The analyst discovers a cluster of recent papers on arXiv demonstrating the use of diffusion models for creating novel protein structures and stable metallic alloys, tasks that previously required years of painstaking lab work. Patent filings from several stealth startups reveal a focus on "generative physical design" for aerospace components. The number of open-source projects related to "materials informatics" is found to be growing exponentially.

Finally, the "AI for Atoms" thesis is subjected to the "Bad Contrarian" check. It survives. The underlying principles—using computation to navigate a vast chemical search space—are sound. The potential for a 10x+ improvement in material properties addresses a massive pain point in industries from aerospace to energy. The thesis is validated. The secret has been found.

Validating the Monopoly (The Micro Framework)

With the "AI for Atoms" secret in hand, the analyst begins searching for a company that embodies this thesis and discovers Aether Materials. The company is now evaluated against the seven questions.

- **The Secret:** Aether's foundational belief is that new materials with bespoke properties can be *designed on-demand* by a generative AI platform, rendering the traditional R&D lab model obsolete. This is a definitive "Zero to One" innovation.
- **The Engineering:** The company's internal benchmarks show its AI platform can discover novel, stable alloys at a simulated speed over 100 times faster than human-led experimentation. This is a clear 10x+ advantage. The technology is rated 9/10.1
- **The Monopoly:** Aether is not targeting the entire global materials industry. Its initial beachhead market is Formula 1 racing teams and aerospace defense contractors—a small, concentrated group of customers with an almost infinite

willingness to pay for marginal gains in material strength and weight. This is a perfect niche to monopolize.

- **The Durability:** The company's path to a durable monopoly begins with its overwhelming technological advantage. This will be reinforced over time by a powerful data network effect: as each AI-designed material is physically manufactured and tested, the real-world data is fed back into the platform, improving its predictive power for all future clients.
- **The People:** The founder is a PhD in materials science with a clear, 20-year vision to "end the age of scarcity by making the physical world programmable." Her motivation is not a quick exit but a desire to solve global challenges like climate change. Her co-founder was her lab partner for five years, demonstrating a strong, pre-existing relationship. They have successfully recruited top researchers from major AI labs, who reportedly took pay cuts to join the mission. The founder's visionary quality is rated "High".
- **Distribution & Timing:** The timing is right, as advances in AI and cloud computing have made the platform feasible. The distribution strategy is sound, focusing initially on high-value enterprise sales to the niche beachhead customers.

The Final Test (The Power Law)
All the pieces of the analysis are now synthesized to answer the single, definitive question: "If this company fully realizes its vision, does it have a credible chance of returning the entire fund?". The conclusion is clear. Aether Materials is founded on

a true "Zero to One" secret. Its path to monopoly is secured by a 100x technological advantage that is highly defensible. The market it aims to create is colossal, potentially redefining global manufacturing and exceeding $1 trillion in value. The founder is a high-conviction, mission-driven visionary with deep domain expertise. The combination of a revolutionary technology, a massive future market, a defensible monopoly, and a visionary founder gives Aether Materials a credible chance to become one of the most valuable and important companies in the world. The answer to the definitive question is an unequivocal "Yes." The investment is made.

Key Takeaways: The Zero to One Mandate

The Thiel framework is more than an investment strategy; it is a worldview and a mandate for building the future. Its core principles can be distilled into a set of actionable commands for any entrepreneur, investor, or thinker seeking to create lasting value.

- **Think for Yourself:** The search for value begins with the contrarian question. What important truth do you know that others don't? The most valuable insights are found where consensus is absent.
- **Escape Competition:** Do not compete. Create. Build a business so unique in its category that you have no direct competitors. Competition is a path to zero profit.
- **Build a Monopoly:** Aim to dominate a small, specific market first, then expand. A durable monopoly, built on proprietary technology,

network effects, scale, and brand, is the only source of long-term profits and the only condition for long-term innovation.

- **Look for Secrets:** Believe that there are still undiscovered truths about the world. These secrets—about nature and about people—are the foundation of every great company.
- **Obey the Power Law:** Understand that outcomes are not evenly distributed. A tiny handful of companies will generate more value than all others combined. Focus all your energy on finding the one company that can change everything. The greatest risk lies in missing the great, not in backing the mediocre.
- **Technology Matters:** True progress comes from "Zero to One" technological breakthroughs. Aim for a quantum leap—a solution that is at least 10 times better than the alternative. Incrementalism is the enemy of value.
- **Founders are Paramount:** Bet on mission-driven, visionary founders who possess a unique secret and are capable of leading a team on a decades-long quest to build the future. Great companies are led by prophets and cult leaders, not by interchangeable managers.

Chapter 15: The All-Weather Framework (Ray Dalio)

The Futility of Forecasting

For most of modern finance, the central challenge has been prediction: forecasting earnings, anticipating interest rate moves, and projecting economic growth. Yet, history is a relentless chronicle of forecasts proven wrong. Major market movements, the kind that define an investor's long-term success or failure, are not driven by what is known and expected. They are driven by what surprises us—events that deviate from the consensus reality already discounted and embedded in asset prices. Since these surprises are, by their very nature, unpredictable, any investment strategy built upon a foundation of forecasting is ultimately built on sand.

This fundamental truth is the starting point for understanding Ray Dalio and the firm he founded, Bridgewater Associates. The All-Weather philosophy is not the product of a better crystal ball. It is the result of a profound paradigm shift: a decision to stop trying to predict the future and instead engineer a solution to its inherent unpredictability. It is an approach born not of market wizardry, but of systems engineering.

Bridgewater's Epiphany: From Prediction to Preparation

The All-Weather strategy was not designed to outperform the market in any single year or economic environment. Its objective is far more ambitious and, for the long-term investor, far more important: to be structurally resilient across all possible economic futures. The goal is not to win any single game but to stay in the game forever, preserving capital through any storm and allowing the inexorable power of compounding to work its magic. This is achieved by minimizing the catastrophic drawdowns that derail most investment plans, which are almost always the result of a portfolio being positioned for one economic reality only to be blindsided by another.

This approach requires a radical redefinition of both "risk" and "success." In the All-Weather framework, risk is not simply volatility. The true risk is being structurally unprepared for a change in the economic environment. A traditional 60/40 portfolio of stocks and bonds, long considered the bedrock of conservative investing, is a case in point. While it appears diversified on a capital basis, it is dangerously concentrated from a risk perspective. Because equities are historically about three times more volatile than high-quality bonds, the 60% allocation to stocks can contribute over 90% of the portfolio's total risk. This is not a balanced portfolio; it is an implicit, highly leveraged bet on a single economic outcome: a future of stable, non-inflationary growth.

Success, therefore, is not measured by short-term outperformance or beating a benchmark in a bull market. It is measured by the long-term consistency and stability of returns and, most critically, by the preservation of capital through any market "weather." The strategy's genius lies in its humility—its profound acknowledgment that avoiding large losses is mathematically more powerful for long-term wealth creation than capturing spectacular but volatile gains.

How the Economic Machine Works: A Guide for the Perplexed

To build a portfolio that can withstand any environment, one must first understand the timeless and universal mechanics that govern those environments. Dalio's foundational insight is that the economy is not a mysterious "black box" but a logical machine composed of a few simple parts, driven by a series of cause-and-effect relationships that have repeated throughout history.[89]

THE ENGINE OF TRANSACTIONS

At its most elemental level, the economy is simply the sum of all the transactions made within it. A transaction is a simple exchange: a buyer gives money or credit to a seller in exchange for goods, services, or financial assets. While money is a medium of exchange, it is credit that acts as the ghost in the machine. Credit is a promise to pay in the future, and unlike money, which is controlled by central banks, it can be created out of thin air between any two willing parties. Consequently, the amount of credit in a modern economy dwarfs the amount of money, making the expansion and contraction of credit the primary driver of economic cycles. Since one person's spending is another person's income, credit is the fuel that powers the economic engine.

THE THREE PRIMARY FORCES

The complex movements of the economy can be deconstructed into the interplay of three primary forces, each operating on a different timescale.[90]

- **Productivity Growth (The Unrelenting Climb):** Over the very long run, the single most important driver of prosperity and rising living standards is productivity growth. This represents the accumulated knowledge, innovation, and efficiency gains that allow us to produce more per person over time.
    - **Analogy:** Productivity growth is like the slow, steady, grinding ascent of a mountain. It is not a straight line day-to-day, but over generations, its upward trajectory is undeniable and is the ultimate source of real wealth creation.[91]

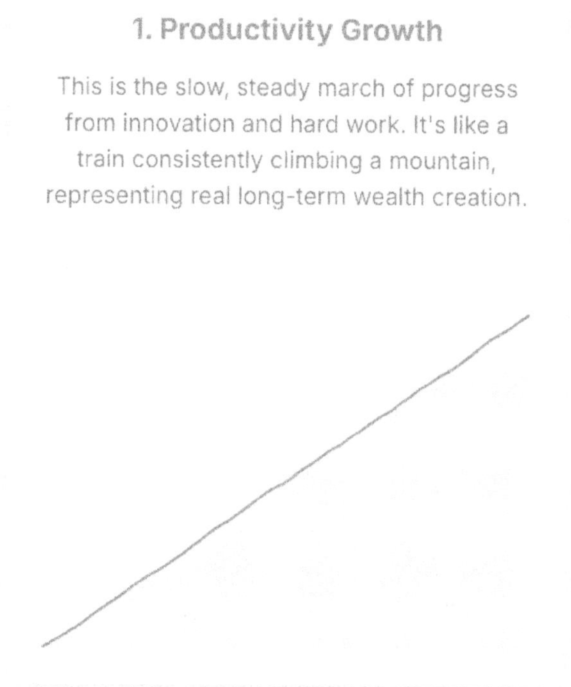

FIGURE 43 - ECONOMIC FORCE - PRODUCTIVITY GROWTH

- **The Short-Term Debt Cycle (The Business** Cycle's Tide): This is the familiar 5 to 8-year cycle of boom and bust, often called the business cycle, which is primarily managed by the central bank.[92]
    - **Analogy:** The central bank acts as a coastal engineer managing the economic tide. To stimulate growth, it lowers interest rates, which is like opening the floodgates to make credit cheaper. This encourages borrowing and spending, causing the economic tide to rise. As spending grows faster than production, inflation appears. To combat this, the

central bank raises interest rates, closing the gates and causing the tide of spending to recede, which can lead to a recession. This cycle of opening and closing the gates creates the familiar ebb and flow of the economy.

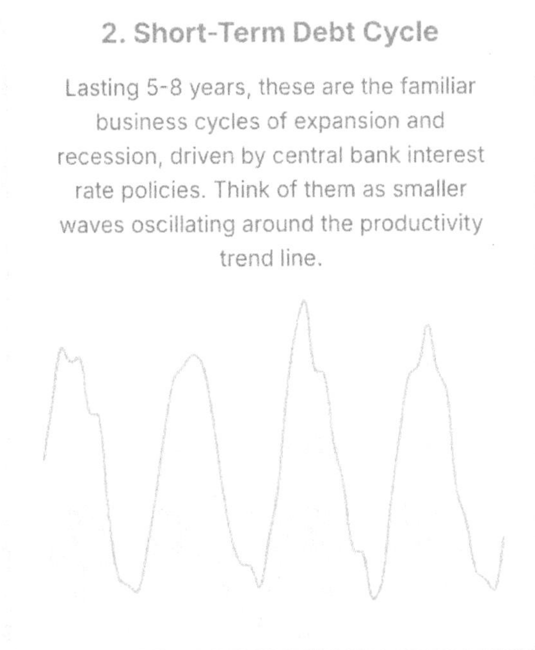

FIGURE 44 - - ECONOMIC FORCE - SHORT-TERM DEBT CYCLE

- **The Long-Term Debt Cycle (The Generational Wave):** This is the most powerful and least understood force, playing out over 75 to 100 years. It occurs as debt burdens rise faster than incomes over successive short-term cycles. In the upswing, a self-reinforcing process takes hold: rising incomes and asset prices make borrowers seem more creditworthy, allowing them to borrow more, which fuels more spending and pushes asset prices even higher. This continues for decades until debt service costs become so large that they can no longer be supported by incomes. At this point, with interest rates typically at or near zero, the central bank's primary tool (lowering rates) becomes ineffective, and the cycle peaks.

- **Analogy:** The long-term debt cycle is like a massive, slow-moving tsunami that builds over a lifetime. For decades, the water slowly rises, lifting all boats and creating a sense of permanent prosperity. But eventually, the wave reaches its maximum height and must break. The subsequent deleveraging is a powerful, system-altering event that defines an entire economic era.

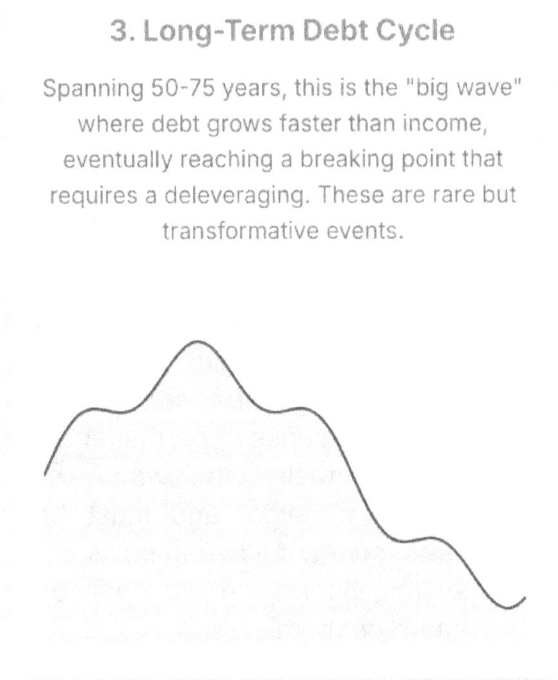

FIGURE 45 - ECONOMIC FORCE - LONG-TERM DEBT CYCLE

The current phase of this long-term cycle is not just another data point; it is the “game board” on which the short-term cycles play out. A recession that occurs early in the long-term cycle, when debt is low and central banks have plenty of room to cut rates, is typically manageable. A recession that occurs at the peak of the long wave, with debt at maximum capacity and interest rates at zero, is a systemic crisis that requires extraordinary and painful measures. Understanding our position in this long wave is the most crucial piece of contextual information for any investor.

A "BEAUTIFUL DELEVERAGING": THE FOUR LEVERS

When a long-term debt cycle peaks and debt burdens become unsustainable, they must be brought down relative to income. This process is called a deleveraging. Policymakers have four levers they can pull to manage this painful process 1:

1. **Austerity:** Cutting spending by people, businesses, and governments. This is deflationary and painful, as one person's spending is another's income.
2. **Debt Defaults/Restructuring:** Debts are wiped out or reduced. This is also deflationary and destroys the wealth of lenders.
3. **Wealth Redistribution:** Taxing the "haves" to help the "have-nots." This can reduce the pain but often leads to intense social and political conflict.
4. **Money Printing:** The central bank prints money to buy financial assets (especially government bonds), offsetting the deflationary forces of austerity and defaults. This is inflationary and stimulative.

A "beautiful deleveraging" is a rare and difficult political feat where policymakers use a balanced and aggressive mix of all four levers. The goal is to spread the pain and bring the debt-to-income ratio down without causing either a catastrophic deflationary depression or hyperinflation.

The Four Seasons: Mapping Assets to Environments

The All-Weather framework translates this mechanistic understanding of the economy into a practical investment map. It simplifies the complex economic world into four fundamental environments, or "seasons," based on how two key variables behave relative to what the market already expects: Economic Growth and Inflation.[93]

THE 2X2 MATRIX: GROWTH AND INFLATION

This elegant framework creates four distinct quadrants:

- **Quadrant 1: Rising Growth, Rising Inflation** (An "overheating" economy)
- **Quadrant 2: Rising Growth, Falling Inflation** (A "Goldilocks" or disinflationary boom)
- **Quadrant 3: Falling Growth, Rising Inflation** (Stagflation)[94]
- **Quadrant 4: Falling Growth, Falling Inflation** (A recession or deflationary depression)

It is essential to grasp that this framework is not about the absolute levels of growth or inflation. It is about *surprises* relative to the consensus expectations already discounted in asset prices. An economy growing at 4% will not necessarily be good for stocks if the market was expecting 5% growth. This focus on surprises is precisely why the strategy does not rely on prediction; it simply prepares for the four fundamental ways in which predictions can be wrong. The portfolio isn't betting that growth will be high or low; it is structurally balanced against the *possibility* of a growth surprise (positive or negative) and an inflation surprise (positive or negative).

THE FOUR SEASONS ASSET PERFORMANCE MATRIX

This matrix is the Rosetta Stone of the All-Weather philosophy. It translates the abstract economic seasons into the concrete performance of different asset classes, forming the logical basis for the portfolio's construction.

TABLE 20 - THE FOUR SEASONS ASSET PERFORMANCE MATRIX

Asset Class	Quadrant 1: Rising Growth, Rising Inflation	Quadrant 2: Rising Growth, Falling Inflation	Quadrant 3: Falling Growth, Rising Inflation (Stagflation)	Quadrant 4: Falling Growth, Falling Inflation (Recession)
Global Equities	+/-	++	--	-
Long-Term Treasuries	--	+	+/-	++
Intermediate-Term Treasuries	-	+	+	++
Inflation-Linked	++	0	++	+

Asset Class	Quadrant 1: Rising Growth, Rising Inflation	Quadrant 2: Rising Growth, Falling Inflation	Quadrant 3: Falling Growth, Rising Inflation (Stagflation)	Quadrant 4: Falling Growth, Falling Inflation (Recession)
Bonds (TIPS)				
Gold	+	-	++	+
Commodities (Basket)	++	+	+	--

Performance Key: ++ (Very Positive), + (Positive), 0 (Neutral), - (Negative), -- (Very Negative)

DECONSTRUCTING THE MATRIX

The logic behind the matrix is rooted in the fundamental drivers of asset returns:

- **Quadrant 2 (Rising Growth, Falling Inflation):** This is the "Goldilocks" environment, the ideal season for traditional financial assets. Strong economic growth drives corporate earnings higher, while stable or falling inflation means central banks don't need to raise interest rates. This is the best environment for **Equities (++). Bonds (+)** also perform reasonably well, offering positive real returns without significant price pressure from rising rates.
- **Quadrant 4 (Falling Growth, Falling Inflation):** This is a classic recession or deflationary bust.

Falling economic activity crushes corporate profits, making it a poor environment for **Equities (-).** In response, central banks aggressively cut interest rates to stimulate the economy. This causes bond prices to soar, making **Long-Term Treasuries (++)** the premier safe-haven asset. They provide a powerful offset to stock market losses.

- **Quadrant 1 (Rising Growth, Rising Inflation):** In an overheating economy, demand is strong, which is good for industrial and energy **Commodities (++).** The principal value of **Inflation-Linked Bonds (TIPS) (++)** adjusts upward with inflation, providing a direct hedge. The outlook for **Equities (+/-)** is mixed; earnings growth is positive, but rising inflation and the threat of higher interest rates can compress valuation multiples. This is the worst environment for **Long-Term Treasuries (–),** as rising inflation erodes the real value of their fixed payments and rising interest rates cause their prices to fall.
- **Quadrant 3 (Falling Growth, Rising Inflation):** Stagflation is the most toxic environment for a traditional portfolio. Falling growth hurts corporate earnings, while rising costs compress profit margins, making it the worst season for **Equities (–).** At the same time, high inflation erodes the value of nominal **Bonds (-).** In this environment, where conventional financial assets fail, real assets and inflation havens shine. **Gold (++)** and **TIPS (++)** perform exceptionally well, protecting purchasing power as fiat currencies are devalued by inflation.

By holding a balanced mix of assets that are structurally biased to perform well in each of these four environments, the All-Weather portfolio is engineered to be prepared for any season.

The Engineering Blueprint: Building the All-Weather Portfolio

The All-Weather philosophy is translated from theory into practice through a set of rigorous engineering principles. This section details how the portfolio is constructed to achieve its goal of true balance and resilience.

THE "HOLY GRAIL": THE POWER OF RADICAL DIVERSIFICATION

Ray Dalio refers to the discovery of radical diversification as the "Holy Grail of Investing". The principle is to combine 10 to 15 good, uncorrelated return streams. "Good" means the assets have a positive expected return over cash, and "uncorrelated" means their returns are driven by fundamentally different economic factors. By doing so, an investor can dramatically reduce portfolio risk (volatility) without a commensurate reduction in expected return. This can improve the portfolio's return-to-risk ratio by a factor of five—an improvement that is nearly impossible to achieve by trying to pick better individual investments.

The mathematical power of this principle is evident in the formula for the variance of a two-asset portfolio:

$$\sigma_p^2 = w_a^2\sigma_a^2 + w_b^2\sigma_b^2 + 2w_a w_b \rho_{ab}\sigma_a\sigma_b$$

The final term, which includes the correlation coefficient (ρ_{ab}), is the key. As the correlation between assets A and B decreases toward 0 or becomes negative, the total portfolio variance (σ_p^2) drops significantly. With a large number of uncorrelated assets, the individual, idiosyncratic risks of each component begin to cancel each other out, leaving a much smoother, more reliable overall return stream.

RISK PARITY VS. 60/40: A REVOLUTION IN DIVERSIFICATION

This principle leads to a revolutionary approach to portfolio construction that stands in stark contrast to traditional methods.

- **The 60/40 Illusion:** As noted, a traditional 60/40 portfolio allocates 60% of its *capital* to stocks. But this apparent balance is an illusion. Because of their higher volatility, stocks contribute over 90% of the portfolio's *risk*. It is not a diversified portfolio; it is a concentrated bet on the "Goldilocks" season of non-inflationary growth.
- **The Risk Parity Solution:** Risk Parity inverts this logic. Instead of allocating capital, it allocates *risk*. The objective is to engineer a portfolio where each asset class or, more importantly, each economic environment contributes an equal amount to the total portfolio volatility. This is the mechanical implementation of the Four Seasons philosophy. The goal is not just to balance stocks and bonds, but to systematically ensure the portfolio has a roughly 25% risk contribution from assets that thrive in a boom, a

bust, an inflationary shock, and a stagflationary malaise. The asset weights are not arbitrary; they are the solution to an engineering problem: how to build a portfolio that is maximally indifferent to the future economic state of the world.

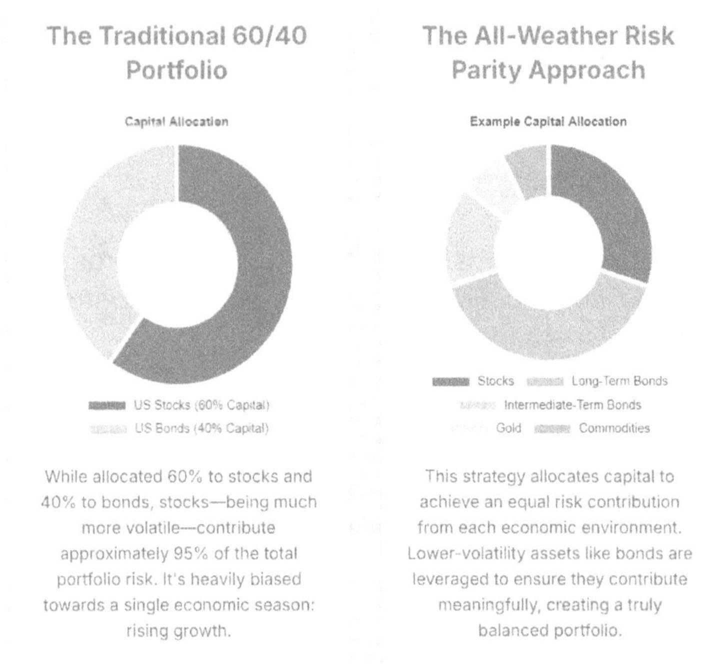

FIGURE 46 - BALANCED CAPITAL ALLOCATION

THE ROLE OF LEVERAGE: A TOOL FOR NORMALIZATION

A direct consequence of allocating risk equally is that less volatile assets, like long-term government bonds, require a much larger capital allocation than highly volatile assets like equities to achieve the same risk contribution. To make this capital-efficient and ensure that low-volatility assets contribute meaningfully to the portfolio's overall return, leverage is systematically applied.

It is critical to understand that this is not the speculative leverage used to juice returns on a directional bet. In the All-Weather framework, leverage is an engineering tool for normalization. Instruments like futures or swaps are used to increase the notional exposure to lower-risk assets (like bonds), effectively scaling their volatility up to match that of the higher-risk components (like stocks). This allows for true risk diversification across economic environments without sacrificing expected returns. It is a necessary instrument to achieve genuine risk balance.

Case Studies in Resilience: The Machine Under Stress

A framework's true worth is revealed not in calm seas but in violent storms. Stress-testing the All-Weather strategy against the most challenging economic crises of the last half-century demonstrates how its engineering was designed to function when it mattered most.

THE GREAT STAGFLATION (1970S)

This period represented a crucial test case. A toxic mix of falling growth and rising inflation (Quadrant 3) decimated traditional portfolios, as both stocks and bonds delivered punishing negative real returns. A 60/40 portfolio would have suffered significant losses in purchasing power. The All-Weather portfolio's performance during this period was critically dependent on its strategic, risk-balanced allocations to inflation-hedging assets.

Gold and a broad basket of **Commodities** delivered exceptional returns, soaring as the value of the dollar eroded. The strategy's inclusion of these real assets was designed to provide a powerful buffer, preserving capital far more effectively than portfolios composed solely of stocks and bonds.

THE GLOBAL FINANCIAL CRISIS (2008)

The 2008 crisis was a classic deflationary bust (Quadrant 4). As the global financial system seized up and equity markets crashed, a massive flight to safety occurred. This environment was ideal for the portfolio's large, risk-balanced allocation to

Long-Term U.S. Treasury bonds. As the Federal Reserve aggressively cut interest rates, these bonds experienced one of their strongest rallies in history. This bond performance was designed to almost completely offset the severe losses in the equity portion of the portfolio, resulting in minimal drawdowns at a time when the S&P 500 lost over half its value from its peak. This outcome perfectly validated the principle of balancing risk between growth-sensitive and deflation-sensitive assets.

THE INFLATION SHOCK (2022)

This period exposed the primary vulnerability of any portfolio reliant on a negative stock-bond correlation. Faced with the highest inflation in 40 years, the Federal

Reserve embarked on an aggressive rate-hiking cycle. This created a toxic environment (Quadrant 3) where rising rates crushed the value of long-term bonds while the prospect of a recession hammered equities. For the first time in decades, stocks and bonds fell in tandem for a sustained period, breaking the core diversification relationship that underpins the 60/40 portfolio.

This event, however, should not be viewed as a failure of the All-Weather framework but as a validation of its core premise. The framework exists *precisely because* the stagflationary quadrant is a real and dangerous possibility. The painful drawdown was an expected outcome in that environment. As a post-mortem analysis of the event would conclude, the simultaneous decline in stocks and bonds powerfully reinforced the critical importance of maintaining a full, strategic allocation to the portfolio's dedicated inflation-hedging assets: **Gold, Commodities, and TIPS**. While not all performed positively, they provided crucial diversification when the traditional stock-bond engine failed, behaving as designed and underscoring the necessity of being prepared for all four seasons, not just the most recent ones.

PERFORMANCE IN HISTORICAL CRISES (ILLUSTRATIVE SUMMARY)

The following table summarizes the strategy's designed behavior during these key historical periods, contrasting it with a traditional 60/40 portfolio.

TABLE 21 - ALL-WEATHER PERFORMANCE IN HISTORICAL CRISES (ILLUSTRATIVE)

Historical Event (Prevailing Season)	All-Weather Est. Max Drawdown	60/40 Portfolio Est. Max Drawdown	Key Takeaway
1973-1981 Stagflation (FG/RI)	Low	-28%	Real assets are essential to hedge stagflationary risk when stocks and bonds fail.
2000-2002 Tech Bust (FG/FI)	-5% to -10%	-21%	Long-term bonds provide a powerful hedge against equity drawdowns in a deflationary recession.
2008 Financial Crisis (FG/FI)	-4% to -10%	-34%	Risk-balanced exposure to high-quality government debt is critical for navigating systemic financial crises.
2022 Inflation Shock (FG/RI)	-15% to -20%	-21%	Simultaneous decline in stocks and bonds highlights the vulnerability of traditional portfolios and the necessity of dedicated inflation hedges.

Key Takeaways: Principles of Financial Engineering

The All-Weather framework is more than a portfolio; it is a new mental model for navigating financial markets. Its core tenets can be distilled into a set of timeless principles for sound financial engineering.

- **Embrace Humility: The Future is Unknowable.** The foundation of robust portfolio construction is the acceptance that you cannot accurately or consistently predict the future. The most successful investors do not try to be prophets; they act as engineers, building systems that are resilient to a wide range of outcomes.
- **Build a Machine for All Seasons.** Do not make a concentrated bet on a single economic outcome. The only truly robust defense is to own a balanced portfolio of assets designed to perform well in each of the four economic environments: rising growth, falling growth, rising inflation, and falling inflation.
- **Balance Risk, Not Capital.** True diversification comes from equalizing the risk contribution from each economic environment, not from allocating capital according to arbitrary rules like 60/40. The central question is not "How much money do I have in stocks?" but "How much of my risk is dependent on stocks doing well?".
- **Diversify Across Environments, Not Just Asset Classes.** The "Holy Grail" of investing is to own 10 to 15 uncorrelated return streams. Correlation should be defined by how assets behave in different economic seasons. This is the single

most powerful tool for improving long-term, risk-adjusted returns and the power of compounding.

- **Understand the Machine.** The economy is not a random black box. It is a system driven by logical, timeless, and universal cause-and-effect relationships, primarily the interplay between long-term productivity growth and the long- and short-term debt cycles. Understanding this machine provides the map you need to navigate it successfully.

The Quantitative Revolution

This is the final frontier. In these chapters, the investor as a discretionary, intuitive human is systematically removed from the day-to-day decision-making process. We leave the world of "feel" and "narrative" and enter the cold, hard domain of data, algorithms, and the scientific method. This is the story of how finance evolved from an art into a science.

Our entry point is with **Cliff Asness**, the academic-turned-practitioner who codified the harvesting of "factors" like Value and Momentum. His framework provides an accessible and transparent look into the world of quantitative investing, showing how persistent, academically-vetted market anomalies can be systematically captured.

We conclude our journey inside the ultimate black box with **James Simons** and Renaissance Technologies. This is the most complex, secretive, and successful application of pure quantitative trading the world has ever seen. The Simons doctrine rejects financial theory entirely, using advanced mathematics and an army of scientists to find faint, fleeting patterns in petabytes of data. This chapter is not a "how-to" guide, but a look inside the most powerful money-making machine ever built, asking the ultimate question: what happens when the machine becomes the master?

Chapter 16: The Factor Investing Framework (Cliff Asness)

The Professor and the Playground: A Quant Revolution

In the world of investing, a great philosophical divide separates two camps. On one side stands the academic temple of the Efficient Market Hypothesis (EMH), whose chief proponent, Nobel laureate Eugene Fama, argues that market prices reflect all available information, making it futile to try to consistently outperform through stock selection. On the other side is the bustling playground of Wall Street, where active managers live and die by the conviction that their unique insights can, and will, beat the market. For decades, these two worlds spoke different languages. It took a student of the professor to build a bridge between them—and in doing so, to launch a quantitative revolution.

That student was Clifford Asness. During his Ph.D. at the University of Chicago in the early 1990s, Asness served as Eugene Fama's teaching assistant, absorbing the principles of market efficiency from its source. Yet, his doctoral dissertation focused on a topic that was a direct challenge to the strictest form of EMH: price momentum, the empirical fact that stocks that have performed well recently tend to continue performing well, and vice versa. When Asness nervously presented his findings to Fama, expecting a rebuke, the professor's response was simple and profound: "If it's in the data, write the paper". This moment captured the intellectual honesty that would become the bedrock of Asness's future firm: ultimate authority rests not with theory or dogma, but with rigorous, long-term empirical evidence.

This dynamic—the tension between a deep respect for market efficiency and an unwavering belief in data-driven anomalies—gave rise to the core philosophy that defines AQR Capital Management: markets are "mostly efficient, but not perfectly". This is not a simple compromise but a carefully calibrated worldview. The "mostly efficient" part acknowledges that markets are formidable information-processing machines. Prices are not random; they reflect a vast amount of collective knowledge, making it exceedingly difficult for a discretionary manager to consistently out-think the entire market. This belief fosters a deep humility and a preference for systematic, diversified, and low-cost approaches.

The "not perfectly" part, however, carves out a fertile middle ground for active management. These imperfections do not arise from random noise but from persistent, structural sources. AQR posits two main pillars supporting these market anomalies:

1. **Risk-Based Premia:** Some strategies, like buying cheap "value" stocks, may outperform over the long run because they are genuinely riskier. These stocks might be more vulnerable during economic downturns, and the excess return is simply the rational compensation investors demand for bearing this non-diversifiable risk.
2. **Behavioral Biases:** Other anomalies arise from the predictable, systematic errors in judgment that investors make. Humans tend to over-extrapolate recent trends (giving rise to

momentum), get seduced by exciting "glamour" stocks while ignoring boring but stable ones (aiding the quality and low-volatility factors), and anchor on past narratives. A systematic investor can profit by being the rational counterparty to these predictable biases.

After leaving the University of Chicago, Asness and his colleagues, including future AQR co-founders John Liew and Robert Krail, put this philosophy into practice at Goldman Sachs. They were tasked with building a quantitative research group, where they developed models that combined the value insights of Fama and French with Asness's own research on momentum. The results were exceptionally strong. In 1998, they left to found AQR—Applied Quantitative Research—a firm built entirely around this philosophy. Their goal was to industrialize the process of harvesting these persistent factor premia, moving it from an artisanal craft to a scalable, repeatable, and transparent science. In doing so, they challenged the opaque, high-fee model of traditional active management, creating what some have called a "Vanguard of hedge funds": a firm dedicated to delivering systematic sources of return in a more efficient and transparent way.

The Building Blocks of Return: What is a Factor?

At the heart of the AQR framework is the concept of a "factor"—a broad, persistent, and academically vetted characteristic that helps explain and predict asset returns over the long term. Rather than focusing on the idiosyncratic story of a single company, factor investing focuses on the common attributes that successful and unsuccessful investments share. This approach is built on a few foundational mental models.

The primary factors can be understood through simple analogies:[95]

- **Value:** This is the systematic application of "bargain hunting." It involves buying assets that are cheap relative to a fundamental measure of their worth, such as earnings, book value, or cash flow. The core belief is that paying less for a stream of future cash flows is a reliable way to generate higher returns.
- **Momentum:** This is the principle of "betting on the hot hand." It involves buying assets that have demonstrated strong recent performance and selling (or shorting) those that have performed poorly. It operates on the observation that trends, once established, tend to persist in the medium term.
- **Quality:** This is the idea of "investing in sound businesses." It means preferring companies that are profitable, stable, growing, and well-managed over those that are speculative, heavily indebted, or have volatile earnings. It is a bet that financial health is ultimately rewarded by the market.

The persistence of these factor premia is supported by the two pillars of the AQR philosophy: risk and behavior. The firm's pragmatic approach does not require choosing one explanation over the other; in fact, the most robust factors are likely supported by both. For example, the Value premium may exist because cheap stocks are often associated with financially distressed companies, making them inherently riskier (the risk-based story). Simultaneously, it may persist because investors irrationally extrapolate past poor performance into the future and are overly pessimistic about these companies' prospects (the behavioral story). The presence of both a rational risk premium and an exploitable bias makes the factor more likely to be a durable feature of markets rather than a temporary anomaly.

This intellectual framework was powerfully solidified in the seminal 2013 paper, "Value and Momentum Everywhere," by Asness, Moskowitz, and Pedersen. This research demonstrated through exhaustive empirical evidence that these two factors are not confined to U.S. stocks. They are pervasive, appearing across dozens of countries and, critically, across entirely different asset classes, including government bonds, currencies, and commodities.

The "everywhere" thesis is the master key to the AQR approach and its most potent defense against the primary criticism leveled at quantitative strategies: data mining. A skeptic might argue that any pattern can be found if one tortures a single dataset for long enough. However, if a factor like Value works not only in U.S. stocks but also in Japanese equities, German government bonds, the British pound, and crude oil, it is exponentially less likely to be a statistical fluke. The pervasiveness of a factor across such disparate markets provides strong, independent, out-of-sample validation that it is tapping into a fundamental economic driver or a deeply ingrained human bias.

The AQR Toolkit: A Dictionary of Factors

Translating abstract concepts like "Value" and "Quality" into a practical, investable strategy requires precise, quantitative definitions. The real art of the "everywhere" framework lies in adapting the core essence of a factor to different domains where the data and fundamentals are completely different. The central hypothesis is that these systematically defined factors provide persistent risk premia across all major asset classes, challenging the common misconception that a concept like "Value" is something that only applies to picking stocks.

What does "Value" mean for a currency, which has no earnings or book value? The insight is to find an analogous concept of a fundamental anchor. For currencies, that anchor is Purchasing Power Parity (PPP)—the idea that, in the long run, exchange rates should adjust to equalize the price of a basket of goods between two countries. A currency trading below its PPP is thus considered "cheap". What does "Quality" mean for a government bond? It is not about profitability but about the stability and creditworthiness of the issuing nation.

The following table serves as a blueprint, or "Factor Dictionary," detailing how AQR defines its core factors across the global multi-asset landscape. A key feature is the use of **composite metrics**—combining several related indicators for each factor—to create a more robust and stable signal, reducing the risk of being misled by the idiosyncrasies of any single measure.

TABLE 22 - AQR CORE FACTORS

Factor	Asset Class	Rationale (Risk-Based / Behavioral)	Primary Metrics & Construction
Value	Equities	**Risk:** Compensation for holding distressed firms. **Behavioral:** Over-extrapolation of past growth, overpricing "glamour" stocks.	Composite of multiple valuation ratios (e.g., Price-to-Book, Price-to-Earnings, Free-Cash-Flow Yield), often calculated intra-industry.
	Gov't Bonds	**Risk:** Compensation for inflation or monetary tightening risk. **Behavioral:** Overreaction to recent economic data.	**Real Yield:** The bond's nominal yield minus expected inflation. Higher real yields are considered "cheaper."
	Currencies	**Risk:** Compensation for holding currencies of weaker economies. **Behavioral:** Over-reliance on short-term sentiment.	**Purchasing Power Parity (PPP):** Deviation of the current exchange rate from its long-term, inflation-adjusted fair value.

Factor	Asset Class	Rationale (Risk-Based / Behavioral)	Primary Metrics & Construction
	Commodities	**Risk:** Compensation for risk of shifts in supply/demand. **Behavioral:** Herding based on recent price trends.	**Long-Term Reversal:** Relative cheapness based on long-term (e.g., 5-year) price underperformance.
Momentum	Equities	**Risk:** Captures time-varying market risk; subject to "crashes." **Behavioral:** Underreaction to news followed by overreaction.	**Price Momentum:** Total return over the past 12 months, skipping the most recent month (t-12 to t-2) to avoid short-term reversals.
	Gov't Bonds	**Risk / Behavioral:** Trends in inflation and growth expectations tend to persist.	**Price Momentum:** Total return of the constant-maturity bond future over the past 12 months (skipping the most recent month).
	Currencies	**Risk / Behavioral:** Trends in	**Price Momentum:** Total return of

Factor	Asset Class	Rationale (Risk-Based / Behavioral)	Primary Metrics & Construction
		interest rate differentials and capital flows often persist.	the currency over the past 12 months (skipping the most recent month).
	Commodities	**Risk / Behavioral:** Trends in supply, demand, and inventory levels often persist.	**Price Momentum:** Total return of the commodity future over the past 12 months (skipping the most recent month).
Quality / Defensive	Equities	**Risk:** Provides insurance against downturns. **Behavioral:** Aversion to leverage and preference for "lottery tickets" underprices safe firms.	Composite of metrics for **Profitability** (e.g., ROE), **Growth** (profitability growth), **Safety** (low leverage), and **Payout** (net issuance).
	Gov't Bonds	**Risk / Behavioral:** "Flight-to-quality" premium for holding bonds of more	**Sovereign Quality:** Composite score based on credit ratings, fiscal

Factor	Asset Class	Rationale (Risk-Based / Behavioral)	Primary Metrics & Construction
		stable sovereigns.	balance, and inflation stability.
	Currencies	**Risk / Behavioral:** Preference for currencies backed by stable economies with low inflation.	**Carry & Defensive:** Often combines the "Carry" factor (high vs. low yield) with measures of economic stability and low inflation.
Low Volatility	Equities	**Risk / Behavioral:** Same as Quality/Defensive.	**Low Beta / Low Volatility:** Rank stocks based on historical beta and/or standalone price volatility over the past 1-3 years.

The Scientific Method: A Framework for Factor Investing

For AQR, the investment "product" is not a collection of stocks but the rigorous, repeatable, and intellectually honest *process* used to select them. This process is a systematic framework designed to distinguish true, persistent economic phenomena from spurious, data-mined patterns. It can be broken down into four key steps.

STEP 1: THE GAUNTLET OF VALIDATION

Before any factor is allowed into the firm's models, it must pass through a demanding intellectual gauntlet. This framework serves as a quality control checklist to protect the portfolio from the "factor zoo"—the thousands of purported market anomalies that fail to hold up to serious scrutiny. A potential factor must clear five critical hurdles 8:

1. **Persistence:** The factor must have worked over a long period of time, spanning different economic regimes, market bubbles, and crashes. A strategy that only works in a single decade is likely a fluke.
2. **Pervasiveness:** It must work across a wide range of countries, markets, and asset classes. As noted, this is the most powerful defense against data mining.
3. **Robustness:** The premium should not be fragile or dependent on one hyper-specific definition. A Value premium, for instance, should be evident whether measured by price-to-book, price-to-earnings, or cash-flow-to-enterprise-value.
4. **Investability:** The factor must be profitable *after* accounting for real-world transaction costs, commissions, and market impact. A high-turnover strategy like Momentum is subjected to particularly intense scrutiny on this front.
5. **Intuitive Rationale:** There must be a plausible, economically grounded story—either risk-based or behavioral—to explain *why* the factor should exist and persist. A statistical pattern without a

coherent theory is treated with extreme suspicion.

STEP 2: AVOIDING STATISTICAL SINS

A beautiful backtest can be dangerously misleading. The AQR process is designed with an obsessive focus on statistical hygiene to avoid the common traps that plague quantitative research.

- **Data Mining:** The risk of torturing the data until it confesses is primarily mitigated by the pervasiveness and intuitive rationale hurdles. AQR also employs formal statistical techniques to adjust performance metrics for the number of strategies tested, providing a more honest assessment of a finding's true significance.
- **Survivorship Bias:** This occurs when a backtest only includes companies that survived to the present day, ignoring those that went bankrupt or were acquired. This systematically inflates returns. To combat this, AQR uses high-quality, point-in-time databases that include all historical companies, including the "dead" ones.
- **Look-Ahead Bias:** This is a subtle but critical error where a model uses information that would not have been available at the time of the decision (e.g., using full-year accounting data on December 31st, when it is not released until months later). The use of point-in-time databases, which record data as it was known on a specific date, is essential to prevent this.

STEP 3: TO TIME OR NOT TO TIME?

A common question is whether investors should tactically rotate between factors, overweighting the one that looks most promising. AQR's position is one of deep and empirically grounded skepticism: **strategic diversification is a more robust source of returns than tactical factor timing.** The firm argues that timing models have historically shown weak predictive power and, more importantly, that attempting to time factors can destroy the very diversification benefits one seeks from a multi-factor portfolio.

The power of this diversification is best illustrated by the low and often negative correlation between factors.

TABLE 23 - HYPOTHETICAL CORRELATION MATRIX BASED ON STYLIZED FACTS FROM AQR RESEARCH

Factor	Value	Momentum	Quality	Low-Vol
Value	1.00			
Momentum	-0.55	1.00		
Quality	0.15	0.20	1.00	
Low-Vol	0.25	-0.30	0.45	1.00

The powerful negative correlation between Value and Momentum (-0.55) is the classic example. It means that the periods when Value struggles are often the periods when Momentum shines, and vice versa. Holding a strategic, balanced allocation to both provides a natural, built-in hedge that is far more reliable than any attempt to predict which one will outperform next.

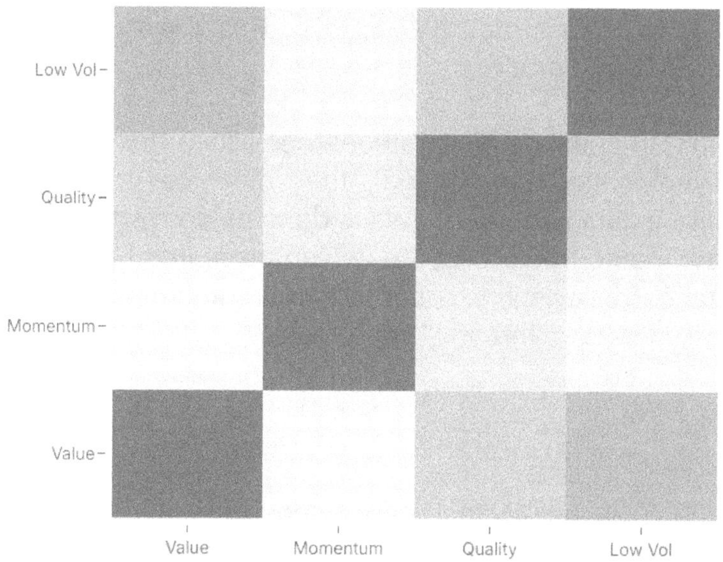

FIGURE 47 - ILLUSTRATIVE FACTOR CORRELATION MATRIX

There is, however, one rare exception to this rule: the "Value Spread." This metric measures the valuation gap between the cheapest and most expensive securities in the market. When this spread is at a historical extreme (e.g., wider than it has been 95% of the time, as it was at the peak of the dot-com bubble), it is interpreted as a strong signal of high expected future returns for the Value factor. In these rare circumstances, AQR may tactically increase its allocation to Value. This, however, is treated as a rare, opportunistic adjustment, not a continuous timing strategy.

STEP 4: BUILDING THE MACHINE

Once a robust set of factors has been validated, the final step is to construct the portfolio. This is a systematic, rules-based process.

First, to combine disparate metrics (like a P/E ratio and a momentum percentage), they must be normalized onto a common scale. This is done by converting each raw metric into a **z-score**, which measures how many standard deviations a security's characteristic is from the universe average. The formula is:

$$z = \frac{(x - \mu)}{\sigma}$$

where x is the raw metric for a security, μ is the average for the universe, and σ is the standard deviation. A z-score of +2.0 for quality means a company is two standard deviations more "quality" than average.

Next, AQR strongly advocates for an "integrate" approach to portfolio construction over a "mix" approach.

- **Mix:** Build separate portfolios for each factor (a Value portfolio, a Momentum portfolio, etc.) and then mix them together.
- **Integrate:** For each individual stock, calculate a single composite score by creating a weighted average of its z-scores across all factors. Then, build one portfolio based on this integrated score.

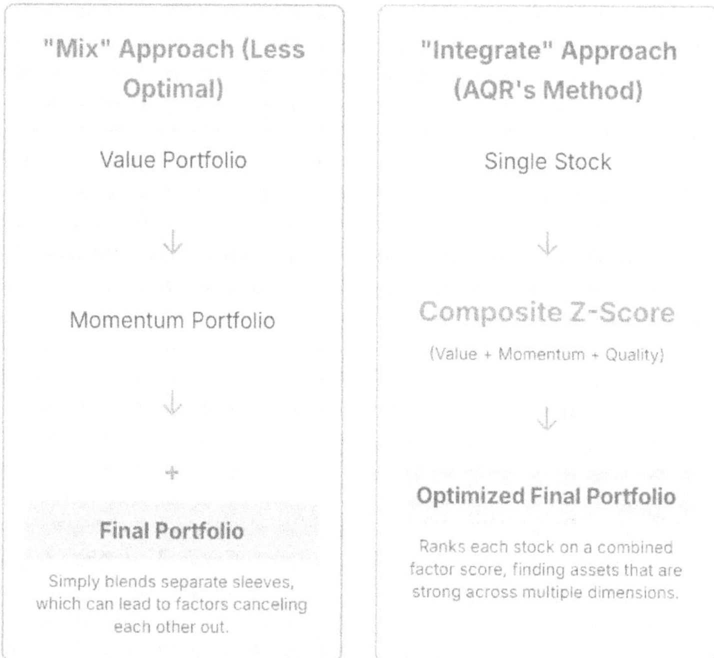

FIGURE 48 - MIX VS. INTEGRATE APPROACHES

The "integrate" method is superior because it resolves conflicts at the security level. The "mix" approach might want to buy a stock for its extreme value but short it for its terrible momentum. The "integrate" approach gives this stock a mediocre composite score, and it is likely excluded. This method naturally favors stocks with a good all-around profile, leading to a more robust portfolio with a smoother risk profile and lower turnover.

Finally, the portfolio is built by ranking all securities on their final integrated score. In a typical long/short market-neutral strategy, the portfolio goes long the top-ranked securities and short the bottom-ranked securities. The positions are constructed to be dollar-neutral (longs equal shorts) and beta-neutral (hedged against broad market movements), with the goal of isolating the return stream of the factors themselves.

Key Takeaways: The Quant's Credo

The AQR framework is more than a collection of strategies; it is a coherent philosophy for navigating financial markets. Its core tenets can be summarized as a "Quant's Credo":

- **Be a Skeptic, Trust the Data:** Start from a position of "mostly efficient" markets, but follow the long-term, pervasive, and robust empirical evidence wherever it leads.
- **Diversification is the Only Free Lunch:** Your primary defense against uncertainty is not prediction, but radical diversification across thousands of securities, multiple lowly correlated factors, and global asset classes.
- **The Process is Everything:** A disciplined, systematic, and repeatable process is more valuable than any single "great idea." The quality of the investment machine is more important than any one of its outputs.
- **Pervasiveness is the Best Defense:** An idea that works "everywhere"—across markets, assets, and time—is far more likely to be true than one that works in a single, isolated backtest.
- Know Why You're Winning: Insist on an intuitive economic rationale—be it risk-based or behavioral—for every strategy you implement. A statistical pattern without a plausible story is a trap.

- Integrate, Don't Just Mix: Build portfolios based on a holistic view of a security's characteristics, not by stapling together separate, potentially conflicting strategies.
- **Embrace Intellectual Honesty:** Relentlessly fight against statistical sins like data mining, survivorship bias, and look-ahead bias. The goal is to find the truth, not to create a beautiful but ultimately false backtest.

Chapter 17: The Black Box: Inside the Alpha Factory of Renaissance Technologies (James Simons)

The Codebreaker Who Solved the Market

Before James Simons became the most successful investor in modern history, he was a codebreaker. A brilliant geometer who chaired the mathematics department at Stony Brook University, Simons spent years working for the Institute for Defense Analyses, a secretive nonprofit that served the National Security Agency. His job was to find hidden patterns in coded messages, to see the order concealed within chaos. He was not an investor who learned math; he was a mathematician who came to see the financial markets as the most complex and lucrative code ever created.

Simons's initial forays into trading were unremarkable. He tried his hand at fundamental investing, the classic Wall Street approach of analyzing company balance sheets and economic trends. But these early, less successful ventures led him to a profound realization: human intuition, narrative, and emotion were flawed guides in the maelstrom of the market. The stories we tell ourselves about why a stock should go up or down are often just that—stories. They are susceptible to bias, herd mentality, and the seductive allure of a simple explanation for a complex phenomenon.

This failure was not a footnote in his career; it was the catalyst for his entire philosophy. Simons hypothesized that within the seemingly random torrent of market data—the endless stream of prices, volumes, and news—there must be hidden structures, faint but persistent patterns that could be exploited for profit. The market was not a story to be understood, but a complex dynamical system to be modeled. This was a problem for a geometer, who studies abstract structures, and a codebreaker, who assumes an intelligent order exists within a noisy message. Collaborating with other mathematicians like James Ax and building upon models first developed by cryptographer Leonard Baum, Simons set out not to interpret the market's message, but to crack its code. He approached the ticker tape not by asking, "Why is this stock moving?" but by asking, "What are the statistical regularities in this stream of data that predict its next move?" The "why" was irrelevant; only the predictive pattern mattered.

The Anti-Wall Street Philosophy

Before a single line of code for the legendary Medallion Fund was written, Simons engineered a unique intellectual culture—a carefully prepared soil in which all subsequent success would grow. He understood that to solve a problem differently, you had to think differently. This meant building a company that was the philosophical antithesis of a typical Wall Street firm.[96]

THE REJECTION OF FINANCIAL ORTHODOXY

The first and most famous pillar of the Renaissance culture is its systematic rejection of conventional financial expertise. The firm is known to "frown on" Wall Street experience, viewing it not as an asset but as a potential "contaminant." This is not born of arrogance, but of a deliberate and disciplined strategy of intellectual risk management. Traditional finance is laden with established theories, narratives, and biases—from the Efficient Market Hypothesis to behavioral heuristics—that can unconsciously shape how a researcher approaches data. A trader with a background in fundamental analysis might instinctively try to find an economic story to explain a statistical anomaly, potentially dismissing a valid signal simply because it doesn't "make sense."

By creating an intellectual vacuum free of this financial dogma, Renaissance allows the data to speak for itself. This enforces a "narrative-agnostic" posture where the only source of truth is the statistical significance of a pattern. The system is designed to find correlations that work, not correlations that can be easily explained. In science, a contaminated sample can invalidate an entire experiment. In quantitative finance, a biased researcher contaminates the model. The firm's hiring policy is therefore not about the skills of the candidates, but about ensuring the purity of the experimental environment. It is a systematic control against the variable of human bias, making it a risk management strategy at the most fundamental level.

THE SCIENTIFIC ASSEMBLY

Having created a space free from the constraints of financial orthodoxy, Simons filled it with a diverse assembly of brilliant minds from non-financial backgrounds. The firm became a Noah's Ark of scientists, actively recruiting top-tier mathematicians, statisticians, theoretical and experimental physicists, astronomers, computer scientists, and signal processing experts.

Each of these disciplines brought a unique analytical toolkit and a distinct mental model for problem-solving, creating a multi-faceted "attack surface" on market data. For instance, signal processing experts, many recruited from IBM, are trained to view market data as a noisy signal from which a coherent message must be extracted. A physicist might approach the market as a complex dynamic system of interacting agents, applying concepts from statistical mechanics. A computational linguist sees it as a language to be deciphered, searching for hidden patterns in a seemingly random stream of information.

This created a form of "methodological arbitrage." While competing funds might vie for an edge through superior data or faster execution, Renaissance competes on the diversity of its analytical frameworks. A subtle market pattern might be invisible to standard econometric time-series analysis but become readily apparent when subjected to a Fourier transform common in signal processing or a state-space model from physics. By assembling a team that can apply multiple, disparate analytical methods, Renaissance is effectively arbitraging these different viewpoints to find patterns their competitors, who are mostly using the same standard financial toolkit, cannot see.

COLLABORATION AND SECRECY

The internal environment at Renaissance is characterized by a paradox: radical internal transparency protected by a wall of extreme external secrecy. All code is reportedly visible to every researcher, and ideas are shared and vetted openly in regular meetings. This structure is deliberately designed to prevent the formation of intellectual silos, ensuring that an improvement in one part of the system can be leveraged by the entire organization, maximizing the rate of internal discovery.

This radical openness is made possible only by the firm's legendary secrecy. Employees are bound by ironclad non-disclosure agreements and are famously discouraged from media appearances or industry conferences. These two policies are not contradictory; they are two sides of the same coin. The intense secrecy creates a high-trust, psychologically safe "trusted garden." Inside this sealed environment, brilliant scientists can propose, debate, and critique unconventional, nascent, and even absurd-sounding ideas without fear of external theft or ridicule. Radical ideas are fragile and easily dismissed. Open collaboration on such ideas requires an immense level of trust. The external secrecy is the necessary precondition for the internal openness; the wall of the garden is what allows the delicate plants inside to grow. It protects not only the final, profitable algorithms but also the fragile, iterative, and often messy scientific process of their discovery.

The Foundation: Building the Data Universe

In the Simons doctrine, the first commandment is "There's no data like more data." The firm's most valuable asset is not a particular algorithm or a secret formula, but its petabyte-scale data warehouse—an immense repository of information gathered obsessively over decades. This data is the raw material from which all profits are extracted, and the process of refining it is a core component of Renaissance's competitive advantage.

This process is best understood through the analogy of an oil refinery. Raw data, like crude oil, is messy, full of impurities, and largely useless in its raw state. It is riddled with errors, misprinted trades, gaps in time series, and inconsistencies across sources. The acquisition strategy is expansive, extending far beyond traditional market data like price and volume. Renaissance is known for amassing a wide array of "alternative data" to find predictive signals in unconventional places: historical weather patterns, satellite imagery of shipping lanes, news wire feeds, and global economic indicators.

This raw material then enters the "data refinery," a resource-intensive endeavor that constitutes a significant and often underestimated competitive moat. The cleansing process is painstaking: every historical price is adjusted for stock splits, dividends, and mergers to create a continuous, comparable time series. Missing data points are handled with robust statistical methods. And crucially, all data from disparate sources are accurately timestamped and synchronized, sometimes to the nanosecond level, to correctly reconstruct the sequence of events.

This obsessive focus on data purity is a direct consequence of the types of signals they hunt. The Medallion Fund's edge often comes from strategies with a win rate reported to be as low as 50.75%—a mere three-quarters of a percent better than a coin flip. In an environment with such an extremely low signal-to-noise ratio, a single data error can easily introduce enough noise to overwhelm the faint, true signal, turning a profitable model into a losing one. Imagine trying to hear a whisper in a loud, crowded room. The data refining process is the equivalent of soundproofing that room. Pristine data is not a desirable feature; it is the absolute, non-negotiable prerequisite for this entire style of trading.

The Engine: Inside the Alpha Factory

At the heart of Renaissance Technologies is the "Alpha Factory"—a sophisticated, multi-pronged engine for the systematic discovery of predictive signals, or "alphas." This process is entirely quantitative, replacing human judgment with mathematical models. It operates across several distinct but complementary families of strategies.

STATISTICAL ARBITRAGE: THE LAW OF AVERAGES ON STEROIDS

The foundational strategy is statistical arbitrage, which seeks to exploit temporary market inefficiencies based on the principle of mean reversion. In simple terms, this is the idea that prices, or the relationships between prices, tend to return to their historical average after a temporary divergence.

The most intuitive example is "pairs trading." Imagine the stock prices of Coca-Cola and Pepsi, which historically move in near-perfect lockstep due to their similar business models. If a temporary event causes Pepsi's stock to surge while Coke's stays flat, the historical relationship is broken. The "spread" between them widens, like a stretched rubber band. A statistical arbitrage strategy would bet on this relationship reverting to its mean by shorting the outperformer (Pepsi) and buying the underperformer (Coke). When the rubber band snaps back, the trade is profitable.

The rigorous mathematical term for this stable, long-run relationship is "cointegration," and the tendency to revert to the mean can be described by stochastic differential equations like the Ornstein-Uhlenbeck process. This core concept can be expanded from simple pairs to complex baskets of securities or the relationship between an index and its underlying stocks, as shown in the table below.

TABLE 24 - STATISTICAL ARBITRAGE

Strategy Name	Core Principle	Number of Securities	Typical Holding Period	Key Risk
Pairs Trading	Cointegration between two related stocks.	2	Minutes to Days	Pair relationship breakdown.
Basket Trading	Mean reversion of a spread	Many (10s to 100s)	Days to Weeks	Correlation regime shift.

Strategy Name	Core Principle	Number of Securities	Typical Holding Period	Key Risk
	between two portfolios.			
Index Arbitrage	Price discrepancy between an index future and its stocks.	Many (100s)	Seconds to Minutes	Basis risk; execution leg risk.

AUTOMATED FACTOR DISCOVERY: AN EVOLUTIONARY SYSTEM

This approach moves from trading relationships between specific securities to identifying broad, systematic characteristics—or "factors"—that explain the cross-section of stock returns. While academic finance has identified persistent factors like Value and Momentum, the true competitive advantage lies in the discovery of novel, proprietary factors.

This is not a manual process of a researcher testing a pet theory. Instead, Renaissance built an automated, brute-force search engine that can be conceptualized as a powerful evolutionary system. The system programmatically generates millions of "formulaic alphas"—mathematical expressions combining various data inputs, such as rank(close/open)*correlation(volume,returns,10)rank(close/open) * correlation(volume, returns,

10)rank(close/open)*correlation(volume,returns,10). These are the "candidate organisms." They are then subjected to a harsh selection environment: a rigorous backtest against decades of historical data. Only the "fittest" alphas—those that demonstrate statistically robust predictive power—survive to be included in the final trading model.

This represents a paradigm shift from human-led discovery to machine-led evolution. A human analyst tests a hypothesis: "I believe X affects Y." The Renaissance system doesn't start with a hypothesis. It creates a machine that evolves millions of hypotheses and lets the data determine which ones are valid. The genius is not in finding the answer, but in building the engine that can find its own answers. This evolutionary framework is the firm's primary defense against the inevitable decay of its signals.

ADVANCED MACHINE LEARNING: THE ROSETTA STONE

The final family of strategies leverages modern machine learning (ML) techniques to capture complex, non-linear patterns that are often missed by traditional linear models. Algorithms like neural networks and gradient boosting machines can model highly intricate relationships between a large number of inputs and future returns.

Perhaps the most powerful application is in Natural Language Processing (NLP), which is used to extract quantitative signals from unstructured text data. The firm feeds a torrent of human language—news articles, regulatory filings, social media feeds—into its NLP models. These models act as a "Rosetta Stone," translating the nuanced, messy, and often emotional language of humans into the precise, quantitative language of the machine. A news headline is converted into a sentiment score; a corporate filing is parsed for key topics. This turns text into numbers that can be correlated with market movements, representing the ultimate expression of the firm's narrative-agnostic philosophy. The machine reads the story, but it feels no emotion and draws no conclusion—only statistical inference.

The Crucible: A Gauntlet of Validation

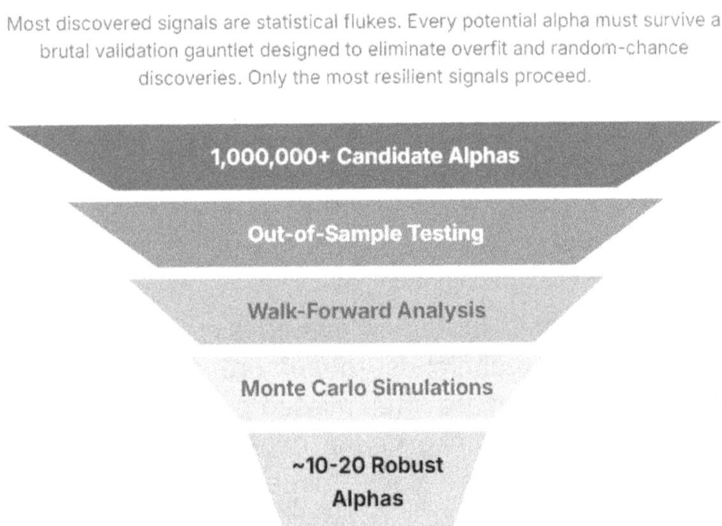

FIGURE 49 - THE CRUCIBLE: FORGING ROBUST SIGNALS

The Alpha Factory is a prolific generator of ideas, but most of what it produces is fool's gold. The vast majority of discovered signals are statistical flukes—patterns that appear significant in historical data but have no real predictive power. To separate these ghosts from genuine signals, every candidate alpha must pass through the "Crucible"—a brutal and systematic validation process rooted in deep scientific skepticism.

This process is designed to combat the twin perils of quantitative finance: **overfitting** and **data mining bias**. Overfitting occurs when a model learns the specific noise and random fluctuations in the training data too well, effectively memorizing the past instead of learning generalizable rules. Such a model will exhibit spectacular performance on historical data but fail catastrophically when deployed in the real world. Data mining bias is a related issue that arises from testing millions of hypotheses on a single dataset. By pure chance, some will appear profitable.

The validation gauntlet is an adversarial framework whose purpose is not to confirm a strategy's value but to actively try to falsify it. An alpha must survive a multi-stage battery of tests:

- **Out-of-Sample Testing:** This is the cardinal rule. A strategy is developed and optimized exclusively on one period of historical data (the "in-sample" period). Its performance is then evaluated on a completely separate, unseen chunk of data (the "out-of-sample" period). It is the equivalent of studying for an exam with one textbook and then being tested on material from another. If performance collapses, the model was overfit.
- **Walk-Forward Analysis:** This is a more realistic simulation of live trading. The model is trained on years 1-5 and tested on year 6; then, the window rolls forward to train on years 2-6 and test on

year 7, and so on. This process ensures the model remains robust and can adapt as market conditions change over time.
- **Monte Carlo Simulations:** These methods stress-test a strategy against luck. The computer creates thousands of alternative market histories by shuffling past returns, destroying any real temporal patterns. A truly predictive strategy should show no profitability on this randomized data. If it does, its logic is flawed, as it is finding patterns in randomness.

Confidence in an alpha is not derived from a single good backtest but from its survival after being subjected to a battery of tests designed to destroy it. Only the most battle-hardened signals proceed to the next stage.

The Assembly Line: Constructing the Portfolio

Once a diverse set of alphas has survived the validation crucible, the next stage is to assemble them into a coherent, risk-managed portfolio. This is the "Assembly Line," a sophisticated optimization process that combines thousands of individually weak signals into a single, robust, money-making machine.

MARKET NEUTRALITY: ISOLATING SKILL FROM LUCK

A central tenet of the Renaissance approach is the pursuit of market neutrality. The objective is to construct a portfolio whose performance is uncorrelated with the broader market's movements, such as the S&P 500. This is a critical step to isolate the returns generated by the firm's proprietary signals (alpha) from the returns generated by simply being exposed to a rising market (beta). Success becomes a pure function of predictive skill, independent of whether the market is bullish or bearish.

However, market neutrality is more than just a defensive risk management technique; it is the critical offensive enabler of the entire strategy. By hedging out the primary sources of systematic risk, the overall volatility of the portfolio is dramatically reduced. This lower volatility, in turn, allows for the judicious use of leverage to amplify the very small but consistent returns generated by the individual alpha signals. Applying high leverage to a volatile, market-correlated portfolio would be a recipe for disaster. But by first neutralizing market risk, Renaissance transforms the portfolio's risk profile, making high leverage a viable, managed strategy rather than a reckless gamble.

EXTREME DIVERSIFICATION: THE LAW OF LARGE NUMBERS

The Renaissance portfolio is the antithesis of the concentrated, high-conviction style of investors like Warren Buffett. Instead of a few large bets on deeply understood companies, the Medallion fund reportedly holds thousands of long and short positions simultaneously, spreading its capital across a vast number of assets and signals.

This approach is a direct and logical consequence of the nature of the alphas being traded. Each individual signal is weak, with a win probability only slightly better than a coin flip. Relying on any single one of these predictions would be highly unreliable. However, by placing thousands of small, uncorrelated bets, the law of large numbers begins to take effect. The randomness of the individual outcomes starts to cancel out, and the small positive statistical expectation—the 0.75% edge—can manifest itself as a smooth and consistent stream of returns at the portfolio level. The firm's conviction is not in any single trade, but in its statistical process as a whole.

POSITION SIZING: THE KELLY CRITERION

The final piece of the assembly line is determining how much capital to allocate to each individual trade. This critical decision is not left to human discretion but is governed by a mathematical formula designed to maximize the long-term geometric growth rate of the portfolio. The theoretical foundation for this process is the Kelly Criterion. The formula calculates the optimal fraction ($f*$) of capital to risk on a bet:

$$f^* = \frac{bp - q}{b}$$

where p is the probability of winning, q is the probability of losing (1-p), and b is the win/loss ratio. The inputs for this formula—the win probability and the expected payoff—are direct outputs from the validated alpha models. In practice, firms often use a "fractional Kelly" approach (e.g., betting half the recommended amount) to reduce volatility. This use of a rigorous, mathematical approach to position sizing is the final element in creating a fully systematic trading machine. It removes the destructive emotional biases of greed and fear from the crucial decision of how much capital to put at risk, making the size of each bet an objective function of its statistical attractiveness.

The Black Box in Action: Surviving the Quant Quake

In August 2007, the quantitative investing world was rocked by a sudden and violent event that came to be known as the "Quant Quake." It was not triggered by an external geopolitical shock but by an internal crisis within the quant ecosystem itself. A large fund, likely facing losses from the burgeoning subprime mortgage crisis, was forced to rapidly liquidate its highly leveraged quantitative equity portfolio to raise cash.

Because many quant funds had independently discovered similar factors (like value and momentum), they held overlapping positions. The forced selling from one large player pushed down the prices of "good" quant stocks and pushed up the prices of "bad" quant stocks, generating massive losses for all firms in this crowded trade. This triggered margin calls and stop-losses at other funds, forcing them to sell the same securities and creating a death spiral of deleveraging.

Renaissance was not immune; the Medallion fund reportedly suffered a 20% drawdown in a matter of days. However, in a move that has become legendary, its leadership did not manually override their models. The system, which was designed with a mantra of "Never place too much trust in trading models," had pre-programmed risk controls that automatically reduced leverage and cut positions as volatility surged and its strategies began to fail. This automated de-risking acted as a shock absorber. When the market violently reverted a few days later, the system was able to participate in the recovery. By the end of the year, Medallion was reportedly up an astonishing 85.9%.

The crucial lesson is that Renaissance survived not by predicting the unpredictable, but by having a pre-built, automated immune response for when its models were catastrophically wrong. The risk management system was not a report that a human reads; it was an integrated set of reflexes embedded in the trading code itself.

This dynamic risk management is essential because no predictive signal, or alpha, retains its efficacy forever. This erosion of predictive power is known as "alpha decay." It occurs either because markets evolve, rendering old patterns obsolete, or because the alpha becomes too widely known and other participants arbitrage away the inefficiency. To combat this, the entire Renaissance framework is built to win the "Red Queen Race"—a concept from evolutionary biology where a species must constantly adapt and evolve not just to gain an advantage, but to simply survive against opposing organisms that are also evolving. In finance, firms must run as fast as they can (discover new alphas) just to stay in the same place (maintain profitability) as the market constantly adapts to their strategies. The continuous operation of the Alpha Factory to generate new signals and the risk system to retire old ones is the embodiment of this race. The firm's true, enduring alpha is not any single strategy but the superior efficiency of this entire, integrated, evolutionary process.

Key Takeaways: The Simons Doctrine

The principles that animate the Renaissance Technologies black box are not easily replicable, but they offer profound lessons for any investor, trader, or decision-maker. The core tenets of the Simons Doctrine can be summarized as follows:

- **Reject Orthodoxy, Embrace First Principles:** Value freedom from bias over industry experience. Analyze data without the constraint of conforming to a pre-existing economic story.
- **Compete on Methodology:** The most durable edge comes not from what you know, but from the diversity of how you think. Assemble multidisciplinary teams to attack problems from every conceivable angle.
- **Trust the Process, Not the Person:** Remove human emotion and intuition from every critical decision—from signal generation to validation to position sizing and risk management.
- **Data Quality is the Ultimate Moat:** A strategy built on faint signals is impossible without a foundation of pristine, meticulously cleansed data. This unglamorous work is a primary source of competitive advantage.
- **Build an Evolutionary System:** Don't search for a single magic formula. Build an engine that can constantly generate, test, and evolve new strategies to survive in an ever-changing environment.
- **Isolate Skill and Amplify It:** Use market-neutral construction to strip away market luck (beta),

and then use leverage to amplify the remaining, pure signal (alpha).

- **Prepare for Model Failure:** The most dangerous risk is that your models are wrong. Embed automated, pre-programmed risk controls directly into your system to act as an immune response during a crisis.

The Red Queen's Race: Alpha Decay

No signal lasts forever. As markets evolve and competitors adapt, alphas decay. The system must constantly discover new signals faster than the old ones fade, just to stay profitable.

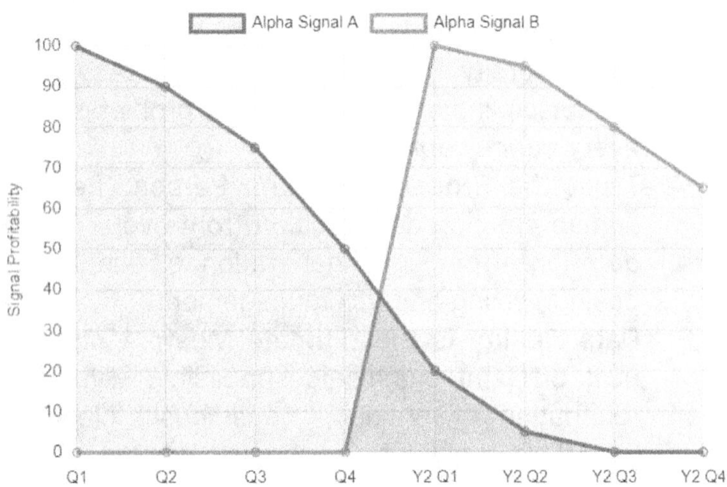

Figure 50 - The Red Queen's Race: Alpha Decay

Part III: Synthesis and Application

Having journeyed through 15 distinct philosophies of wealth creation, we arrive at the final, and most important, stage: turning knowledge into wisdom, and wisdom into action. This concluding section is designed to help you synthesize the universal lessons of the masters and forge them into a framework that is uniquely your own. In "The Grand Synthesis," we will perform a grand comparative analysis, identifying the "golden threads"—the unifying principles of risk management and psychological discipline that connect every great investor. We will also examine the great philosophical divergences that define the core strategic choices every investor must make. Finally, in "Building Your Own Framework," we turn the lens inward. This chapter is your personal workshop, a guided process to help you assess your own psychology, resources, and goals. It will provide the tools to construct a personal investment charter—a system built not to replicate any single master, but to become the best possible version of yourself as an investor. For it is here, at the intersection of their wisdom and your reality, that your own journey to alpha truly begins.

Chapter 18: The Grand Synthesis

After an expedition through fifteen unique architectures of alpha, we pause at the summit. From this vantage point, we can survey the entire landscape of investment mastery. We see the common bedrock upon which all these formidable structures are built, the foundational principles that are non-negotiable for success. We also see the distinct, often competing, philosophical peaks that define the strategic choices every investor must confront. This chapter is the cartography of that landscape. First, we will distill the "golden threads"—the universal laws of alpha generation that bind a deep-value investor like Warren Buffett to a quantitative codebreaker like James Simons. Then, we will explore the "Great Divergences"—the fundamental, and at times irreconcilable, battles of philosophy that frame the essential questions of investment strategy. This grand synthesis is the final step in understanding the masters before turning to the ultimate task: constructing a framework of your own.

The Unifying Principles: The Bedrock of Alpha

Despite the breathtaking diversity of their methods, a set of common intellectual and psychological DNA strands runs through every master profiled in this book. These are not tactical similarities but deep, structural pillars that support any and every successful investment framework. They are the bedrock of alpha.

AN OBSESSION WITH ASYMMETRIC RISK

The single most powerful unifying concept across all fifteen masters is the relentless pursuit of asymmetric risk, or convexity. This is the art of structuring investments where the potential for gain is orders of magnitude greater than the potential for loss. It is a systematic effort to find bets where the downside is small, fixed, and known, while the upside is large and potentially unlimited. This is not merely about being right; it is about ensuring that when one is right, the payoff is disproportionately massive, capable of underwriting the inevitable small losses that are a cost of doing business.

The source of this asymmetry is a direct reflection of each investor's core philosophy. For **Warren Buffett**, the mechanism is his mentor Benjamin Graham's foundational principle: the "Margin of Safety". By purchasing a business for significantly less than its intrinsic value—buying a dollar of assets for sixty cents—he creates a structural buffer. The downside is cushioned by the discount, but the upside is the full realization of the business's value, plus its future growth. Buffett's famous bridge analogy perfectly captures this: one designs a bridge to hold 30,000 pounds but only ever drives 10,000-pound trucks across it. The asymmetry arises from the fact that the loss is capped at the purchase price, while the gain from a "wonderful company" compounding over decades is theoretically infinite.

For **George Soros**, asymmetry is engineered by identifying "fertile fallacies" within global macroeconomic structures. His legendary 1992 bet against the British pound was a textbook asymmetric trade. The pound was already languishing at the bottom of its mandated band within the Exchange Rate Mechanism (ERM), so the risk of it strengthening was minimal and capped. The potential reward, however, was a catastrophic devaluation if the flawed political peg were to break. The payoff profile was skewed entirely in his favor, a bet on economic reality overwhelming a flawed political perception.

Finally, **Peter Thiel**'s entire venture capital framework is built on the "Power Law," the ultimate expression of asymmetry. He argues that in any venture portfolio, the single best investment will outperform all the others combined. This unforgiving mathematical reality dictates that every investment must have the potential to be that fund-returning outlier. The downside is capped at one times the capital invested, but the upside can be 100x, 1,000x, or more. He is explicitly hunting for investments with the most skewed payoff distribution possible. Where Buffett finds asymmetry in a valuation discrepancy, Soros in a political discrepancy, and Thiel in a technological discrepancy, the underlying quest is identical: to structure bets where heads, I win big; tails, I lose little.

PROFOUND PSYCHOLOGICAL DISCIPLINE

If there is one variable that every master identifies as the single most important determinant of long-term success, it is temperament. The ability to master the powerful internal enemies of fear and greed, to act with rational conviction when the crowd is hysterical, is the ultimate edge. Their meticulously constructed frameworks are not just analytical tools; they are elaborate psychological defense mechanisms designed to insulate their decision-making from the emotional chaos of the market.

Seth Klarman's discipline is epitomized by his strategy of "patient opportunism". His willingness to hold enormous cash reserves—at times exceeding 50% of his fund's assets—is a structural defense against the fear of missing out (FOMO) that plagues most investors. He views cash not as a performance drag but as strategic ammunition, a call option on future volatility. This patience allows him to deploy capital aggressively at the point of maximum pessimism, when others are paralyzed by fear and forced to sell.

Stanley Druckenmiller embodies what can be called the "capital preservation paradox". His philosophy of "preservation of capital and home runs" reconciles relentless conservatism with selective, hyper-aggression. By being ruthlessly disciplined in cutting small losses and avoiding low-conviction trades, he preserves the capital and, just as importantly, the psychological firepower needed to bet the ranch when a generational opportunity appears. His devastating mistake in the 2000 tech bubble, where he abandoned his own correct analysis and bought billions at the top due to FOMO, serves as his most powerful and frequently cited lesson on the primacy of emotional control.

Meanwhile, **Howard Marks**'s entire framework is an exercise in controlling emotion by understanding context. His focus on "taking the market's temperature" and knowing where we are in the cycle is a cognitive tool designed to create emotional distance. By understanding that investor psychology swings like a pendulum between the extremes of euphoria and depression, he can view the current market mood with detachment, allowing him to execute the classic contrarian creed: "Be fearful when others are greedy, and greedy when others are fearful". This discipline is not an innate personality trait but an engineered outcome of a robust process. A rigorous analytical system builds earned conviction, which in turn provides the psychological armor needed to execute with discipline under extreme pressure.

A COMMITMENT TO INDEPENDENT, FIRST-PRINCIPLES THOUGHT

The mathematical definition of alpha is a return stream independent of the market. To achieve it, one must, by definition, think and act independently from the market consensus. The core of every master's alpha is a systematic process for deconstructing conventional wisdom and building a unique, "variant perception" from the ground up. They are not merely contrarian for the sake of it; they are intellectual purists who insist on verifying every assumption themselves, starting from first principles.

Michael Burry is the ultimate financial detective. His edge in shorting the subprime mortgage market came from his refusal to accept the "official story" peddled by ratings agencies and Wall Street banks. Instead, he engaged in painstaking first-principles research: personally reading thousands of pages of mind-numbing, complex bond prospectuses. This forensic analysis allowed him to see the toxic reality of the underlying loans—a truth completely obscured by the pristine AAA ratings. His variant perception was not an opinion; it was the hard-won conclusion of a deep, independent investigation.

George Soros's entire reflexive framework is a machine for generating variant perceptions. He actively hunts for what he calls "fertile fallacies"—widely held beliefs that are fundamentally at odds with reality and are actively shaping it in a self-reinforcing loop. His analysis of the ERM in 1992 was a classic example. The consensus view was that political will would sustain the currency peg. Soros's first-principles analysis concluded that the underlying economic fundamentals made this a physical impossibility. He bet on reality over the flawed perception. The most powerful of these variant perceptions challenge not just the market's view on a single asset, but its view on the fundamental rules of the game. Soros's theory of Reflexivity is a direct challenge to the Efficient Market Hypothesis, the core "rule" of modern finance.

A DEDICATION TO A REPEATABLE PROCESS

Sustained, multi-decade success is never the product of a few brilliant, disconnected "calls" or lucky streaks. It is the output of a coherent, systematic, and deeply personal framework—an "Investment Operating System"—that is executed with relentless consistency. The masters are not just brilliant investors; they are the architects of a superior process. This process serves a dual function: analytically, it filters the infinite noise of the market into a finite set of high-probability opportunities; psychologically, it provides a rock of stability in the emotional storm of the market.

Ray Dalio is the ultimate systems architect. His All-Weather strategy is the physical manifestation of a repeatable process. It is a machine engineered to be resilient to all possible economic futures by balancing risk across four economic "seasons." The decisions are not discretionary; they are the output of a pre-defined, rules-based system designed to be robust against the unknowable.

Peter Lynch's legendary success at the Magellan Fund was not a series of lucky stock picks but the consistent application of his framework. His process of classifying every stock into one of six categories, performing the "two-minute drill" to articulate the story, and checking the numbers (especially the PEG ratio) was a repeatable filtering mechanism he applied to thousands of companies, allowing him to process information systematically and make consistent decisions.

Finally, **James Simons** and Renaissance Technologies represent the apotheosis of process over prediction. The Medallion Fund is a "black box" that explicitly rejects human intuition and narrative. Its success is derived entirely from a scientific process of data collection, signal discovery, rigorous validation, and automated execution. It is the ultimate repeatable system, where the most important thing an investor can build is not a portfolio, but a process. The portfolio is merely the temporary output; the process itself is the enduring source of alpha.

The Great Divergences: The Battle of Philosophies

While the masters are united by their foundational principles, their strategic frameworks diverge sharply on several key philosophical questions. These are not matters of right and wrong, but of deeply held beliefs about how markets work and where an edge is most reliably found. They represent the critical forks in the road where every investor must make a choice.

CONCENTRATION VS. DIVERSIFICATION

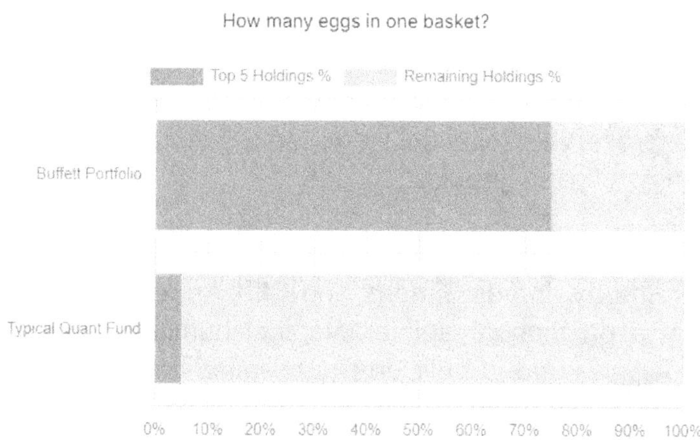

Concentration (Buffett): "Diversification is protection against ignorance. It makes very little sense for those who know what they're doing." The big, multi-bagger ideas are rare, so bet big when you find one.

Diversification (Simons/Asness): No single idea should be able to sink the ship. A portfolio of many small, statistically advantageous bets with low correlation is the path to smooth, consistent returns.

FIGURE 51 - CONCENTRATION VS. DIVERSIFICATION

The first great divergence is a debate about the nature of achievable knowledge in financial markets. Is it better to know a few things with near certainty and bet big, or to accept that certainty is impossible and spread bets across a wide array of statistical probabilities?[97]

The argument for concentration, championed by investors like **Warren Buffett** and **Stanley Druckenmiller**, is rooted in the belief that truly great ideas are rare. As Buffett famously quipped, "diversification is protection against ignorance." This school believes that deep, qualitative understanding of a business or macro theme is possible, but only for a handful of opportunities. When such an opportunity is identified, it is a mistake to dilute its potential impact by spreading capital across dozens of inferior ideas. Druckenmiller's "home run" philosophy is the epitome of this: preserve capital until a generational trade appears, then "go for the jugular".

The argument for diversification, practiced to its extreme by **James Simons** and **Cliff Asness**, operates from a position of epistemological humility. Simons's Medallion Fund is built on the premise that any single predictive signal is only slightly better than a coin flip. The only way to reliably profit is to make thousands of uncorrelated bets, allowing the law of large numbers to smooth out the randomness and let the small statistical edge prevail. Similarly, Asness's factor investing is a systematic application of this principle, diversifying not just across thousands of stocks but across lowly correlated factors like Value and Momentum, which provide a natural, built-in hedge against each other.

MACRO VS. MICRO

This is a fundamental disagreement about the primary causal force driving returns. Is it the top-down tidal wave of liquidity and economic cycles, or the bottom-up, idiosyncratic story of an individual company?[98]

The macro school, led by **Druckenmiller** and **Soros**, believes that central bank liquidity is the tide that lifts or sinks all boats. For them, the first and most important question is always, "What is the Fed doing?" Company-specific fundamentals are secondary to the overwhelming force of the macro environment. Their analysis starts with a global view of interest rates, capital flows, and geopolitics to form a thesis, and only then do they select the best instruments—currencies, bonds, or stock indices—to express that top-down view.

The micro school, exemplified by **Peter Lynch** and the deep value hunters, starts from the opposite end of the telescope. Lynch's mantra to "invest in what you know" is the anthem of this philosophy. They believe that a great company with a superior product and a strong balance sheet can thrive regardless of the macro environment. Their analysis begins from the bottom up, with a forensic examination of a single company's financial statements, competitive position, and management quality. The broader economy is a secondary consideration, a backdrop to the specific corporate drama unfolding on center stage.

PASSIVE VALUE VS. ACTIVE CATALYST

This divergence separates the analyst from the surgeon. When an undervalued asset is identified, does one wait patiently for the market to recognize its mistake, or does one intervene and force the value to be realized?

The passive value school, rooted in the teachings of **Benjamin Graham** and practiced by disciples like **Seth Klarman**, believes the investor's job is to identify the gap between price and intrinsic value. They operate with faith in Graham's "weighing machine"—the idea that, over time, the market will inevitably correct the mispricing. Their process involves buying assets at a deep discount and then waiting with disciplined patience for an external, and often unpredictable, catalyst to emerge. Their edge lies in superior valuation skills and the psychological fortitude to wait.

The activist school, defined by figures like **Carl Icahn** and **Bill Ackman**, views waiting as a dereliction of duty. They believe the most reliable catalyst is the one they create themselves. They see undermanaged companies not just as mispriced assets, but as fixable problems. Their process involves taking a large, concentrated stake and then waging a public campaign—through letters, media appearances, and proxy fights—to force changes like selling non-core assets, replacing the CEO, or returning cash to shareholders. The activist *is* the catalyst.

QUALITATIVE VS. QUANTITATIVE

This is the ultimate battle of philosophies: man versus machine, art versus science. Where does true investment edge reside? In the nuanced, artistic judgment of unquantifiable factors, or in the rigorous, scientific analysis of vast datasets, free from human bias?

The qualitative camp, led by **Warren Buffett**, believes the most important factors in long-term success cannot be reduced to a number. His focus on the width of a company's "economic moat," the integrity of its management, and the power of its brand are all qualitative judgments. The process relies heavily on "scuttlebutt" and deep, subjective analysis of a business's long-term competitive dynamics. It is an art form honed over decades of experience.

The quantitative camp, whose high priest is **James Simons**, views all qualitative judgment and narrative as sources of dangerous human bias. Renaissance Technologies was explicitly built to be a "black box" that trusts only statistical patterns in the data. The "why" behind a correlation is irrelevant; only its predictive power matters. The process is entirely systematic, with computers sifting through petabytes of data to find faint patterns and executing trades automatically. The edge lies in superior mathematical models and a culture of radical scientific skepticism.

The Master Matrix: A Comparative Schematic

This matrix provides a concise, at-a-glance schematic of the investment frameworks detailed in this book. It serves as a powerful comparative tool, allowing for a quick grasp of the core tenets and stylistic differences of each master.

TABLE 25 - INVESTORS COMPARATIVE MATRIX

Investor(s)	Core Philosophy	Primary Edge	Time Horizon	Portfolio Style	Defining Psychological Trait
Graham & Buffett	Value Investing: Buy wonderful companies at a fair price.	Business Acumen & Long-Term Perspective	Decades ("Forever")	Highly Concentrated	Extreme Patience
Peter Lynch	GARP: Growth at a reasonable price.	"Local Knowledge" & Categorical Analysis	Medium-Term (1-3 Years)	Highly Diversified	Pragmatic Flexibility
Templeton & Klarman	Contrarian Value: Buy at the point of maximum pessimism.	Crisis Investing & Risk Aversion	Medium to Long-Term	Diversified	Disciplined Pessimism

Investor(s)	Core Philosophy	Primary Edge	Time Horizon	Portfolio Style	Defining Psychological Trait
Howard Marks	Credit Cycle Awareness: "Take the market's temperature."	Second-Level Thinking & Risk Control	Cycle-Dependent (Years)	Diversified	Intellectual Humility
Michael Burry	Forensic Deep Value: "Ick investing."	Forensic Accounting & Independent Research	Medium-Term (Years)	Highly Concentrated	Obsessive Skepticism
Icahn & Ackman	Shareholder Activism: "Be the catalyst."	Corporate Warfare & Strategic Negotiation	Event-Driven (1-3 Years)	Highly Concentrated	Unrelenting Combativeness
George Soros	Global Macro: Exploit "fertile fallacies."	Theory of Reflexivity	Short to Medium-Term	Concentrated	Philosophical Detachment
Stanley Druckenmiller	Global Macro: "Liquidity is the prime mover."	Top-Down Forecasting (18-month view)	Short to Medium-Term	Highly Concentrated	Decisive Aggression

Investor(s)	Core Philosophy	Primary Edge	Time Horizon	Portfolio Style	Defining Psychological Trait
Jim Rogers et al.	Commodity Supercycles: "Buy cheap and hated."	On-the-Ground Research & Historical View	Decades	Concentrated	Adventurous Contrarianism
Peter Thiel	Venture Capital: "Competition is for losers."	Identifying "Zero to One" Monopolies	Very Long-Term (10+ Years)	Highly Concentrated (Power Law)	Contrarian Vision
Ray Dalio	All-Weather: Prepare for all economic seasons.	Risk Parity & Systems Engineering	Perpetual	Highly Diversified	Systematic Objectivity
Cliff Asness	Quantitative Factor Investing: Harvest persistent premia.	Systematic Harvesting of Value & Momentum	Long-Term	Highly Diversified	Empirical Rigor
James Simons	Quantitative Trading: "The 'why' is	Statistical Modeling & Data Processing	Milliseconds to Days	Extremely Diversified	Narrative Agnosticism

Investor(s)	Core Philosophy	Primary Edge	Time Horizon	Portfolio Style	Defining Psychological Trait
	irrelevant."				

Conclusion: The Character of Alpha

The journey through these fifteen frameworks reveals a profound truth. While the strategies diverge wildly—from the decades-long holding periods of Buffett to the millisecond trades of Simons, from the tangible assets of Graham to the abstract secrets of Thiel—the source code of their success is remarkably consistent. The methods are tools, but the true edge lies in the character of the architect wielding them. It is the **patience** of Klarman holding cash for years while others chase a euphoric market, the **intellectual honesty** of Druckenmiller publicly dissecting a catastrophic, ego-driven mistake, the **courage** of Burry holding his short position against an investor revolt, and the **discipline** of Simons trusting his algorithm over his own gut instincts.

Alpha, in the end, is not a financial metric. It is the quantifiable shadow cast by a disciplined mind. The final challenge for any investor is not to copy these masters' methods, but to cultivate their character.

INVESTOR(S)	CORE PHILOSOPHY	PRIMARY EDGE	TIME HORIZON	PORTFOLIO STYLE	DEFINING PSYCHOLOGICAL TRAIT
Graham / Klarman	Deep Value / Margin of Safety	Forensic Valuation	Medium-Term (1-5 Years)	Diversified	Extreme Patience
Buffett / Munger	Wonderful Companies at Fair Prices	Assessing Quality & Moats	Generational (Decades)	Concentrated	Rationality & Inactivity
Soros / Druckenmiller	Global Macro / Reflexivity	Identifying Unstable Equilibriums	Short-Term (Weeks-Months)	Concentrated & Leveraged	Aggressiveness & Flexibility
Simons (RenTech)	Quantitative Signal Processing	Data Science / Pattern Recognition	Very Short-Term (ms to days)	Highly Diversified	Emotional Detachment
Peter Lynch	GARP / "Invest in what you know"	Scuttlebutt Research	Medium-Term (3-5 Years)	Highly Diversified	Open-mindedness & Curiosity
Icahn / Ackman	Activist Investing	Forcing a Catalyst	Event-Driven (1-3 Years)	Highly Concentrated	Combative & Relentless

FIGURE 52 - THE MASTER MATRIX: A COMPARATIVE SCHEMATIC

Chapter 19: Building Your Own Framework

We have reached the end of our expedition. For eighteen chapters, we have journeyed through the minds of the masters, deconstructing the unique architectures of alpha that placed them in the pantheon of the world's greatest investors. We have explored the bedrock value principles of Graham and Buffett, the global macro chessboard of Soros and Druckenmiller, the venture philosophy of Thiel, and the quantitative black box of Simons. You have been given the blueprints, the tools, and the historical context of their genius.

But this final chapter is not about them. It is about you.

The knowledge of their frameworks is necessary, but it is not sufficient. The final, and most critical, piece of the architecture is the one you bring to the table: yourself. Let me state the book's final and most important lesson as clearly as I can: The single greatest mistake an investor can make is to adopt a strategy, no matter how brilliant, that is fundamentally misaligned with their own personality, circumstances, and psychological makeup. A borrowed framework, like a borrowed suit of armor, is ill-fitting and clumsy. It will protect you from nothing and will fail you in the heat of battle, just when you need it most.

The purpose of a personal framework is not just analytical; it is primarily psychological. Its main job is to function as a pre-committed defense system against your own worst emotional instincts—the primal fear and reflexive greed that surface during periods of extreme market stress. A market crisis triggers a fight-or-flight response. An investor operating with a strategy that feels unnatural will experience intense cognitive dissonance, which inevitably leads to emotional decision-making. This is the path to panic selling at the bottom and FOMO-chasing at the top. A framework that is aligned with your nature reduces this dissonance, allowing your rational, pre-committed plan to override the emotional impulse. This chapter is about building that framework. It is the final and most important act of architecture.

The Mirror Test: A Framework for Self-Assessment

Before you can build, you must take your own measurements. The following is not an exam with right or wrong answers. It is a guided journaling exercise, a diagnostic of your unique investor DNA. Find a quiet time, take out a notebook, and answer these questions with the brutal honesty you would give a trusted doctor. These answers are for your eyes only, and they will form the bedrock of your entire investment future.

WHAT IS YOUR PSYCHOLOGICAL TEMPERAMENT?

We begin with the most crucial element: your gut. Your innate emotional response to risk, loss, and uncertainty will determine which strategies you can successfully execute and which will break you.

- When a stock you own falls 20% on no new information, what is your very first, unfiltered instinct? Is it a flicker of excitement to buy more

because it's cheaper? Is it a knot in your stomach urging you to sell and cut your losses? Do you freeze, paralyzed by indecision? Or do you feel a compulsive need to check the news and find a reason for the drop?
- Are you more comfortable being part of a winning crowd, or standing alone against it? Does the idea of buying a hated, discarded stock at the "point of maximum pessimism," as John Templeton and Seth Klarman did, fill you with a sense of intellectual excitement or a deep sense of dread? 1
- Conversely, does the idea of riding a powerful trend, even if an asset seems expensive, feel more natural? An honest answer here reveals whether you are a natural contrarian, comfortable with Benjamin Graham's "Mr. Market" and his manic swings, or if your psychology is better suited to a trend-following approach, like the Momentum factor identified by Cliff Asness.
- How do you process being wrong? Does a losing investment motivate you to find the flaw in your analysis, or does it paralyze you with regret and self-doubt?

An honest assessment of your temperament is the foundational data point. A born contrarian will tear their hair out trying to be a trend-follower, and a person who craves social validation will never survive the profound isolation of a deep-value strategy.

WHAT IS YOUR TRUE TIME HORIZON?

A mismatch between your strategy's required time horizon and your personal goal's time horizon is the source of most unforced errors and catastrophic losses in investing.

- What is the specific, tangible goal for this capital? Is it for a retirement that is 30 years away? A down payment on a house in seven years? A child's university tuition that starts in four years? Write down the specific date.
- Can you truly stomach a 50% drawdown and not touch the money for five years? Be ruthlessly honest. You cannot adopt the decade-plus patience of a venture capitalist like Peter Thiel, waiting for a Power Law return, if your capital is earmarked for a short-term goal. The pressure to sell will become unbearable.
- Imagine your portfolio is cut in half tomorrow. How would your life concretely change? If the answer is "It would derail a critical life plan," then your true time horizon is shorter than you think, and your tolerance for risk is lower. A shorter horizon may demand a more catalyst-driven approach, like that of an activist, or a strategy focused on navigating shorter-term cycles, like that of Howard Marks.

WHAT IS YOUR INFORMATIONAL EDGE? (YOUR CIRCLE OF COMPETENCE)

As Warren Buffett taught us, the size of your Circle of Competence is not important, but knowing its boundaries is vital. Peter Lynch called this the "amateur's advantage". This is where you possess an unfair edge over the professionals on Wall Street. It is time to map it.

- What industry do you work in? What are the trade magazines on your desk? What jargon, trends, and key players do you understand better than 99% of the population?
- What are your most obsessive hobbies and passions? Are you a gamer who intimately understands the ecosystem of game developers and publishers? A doctor who can evaluate the clinical trial data of a new medical device? A homebuilder who sees shifts in housing demand months before they appear in government statistics?
- Where do you possess "local knowledge"? What stores in your town are always packed while others are empty? What new software are all your colleagues adopting? What products are your friends raving about? This is the scuttlebutt that forms the foundation of a true informational edge.
- Conversely, and just as importantly, what do you *not* understand? Be explicit. Write down your "Too Hard" pile. Is it biotechnology? Complex derivatives? Chinese macroeconomics? Acknowledging the boundaries of your knowledge is an act of supreme wisdom, not ignorance.

WHAT IS YOUR REQUIRED "ACTIVITY LEVEL"?

The masters in this book ranged from obsessive, full-time investigators to patient, systems-driven architects. Your available time and energy are finite and precious resources. Your strategy must honor them.

- How many hours per week can you realistically and consistently dedicate to investment research? Not in an initial burst of enthusiasm, but averaged over an entire year.
- Is that number closer to the 20+ hours a week required for the forensic, detective-like deep-value analysis of a Michael Burry or the corporate warfare of a Carl Icahn? 1
- Or is it closer to two or three hours a month, a budget far better suited for the patient, low-maintenance, systems-based approach of Ray Dalio's All-Weather framework? 1

Do you genuinely enjoy the process of deep research—of digging through dense 10-K filings and footnotes—or does it feel like a burdensome chore? The answer will determine whether an active, discretionary strategy is sustainable for you over the long run. Attempting a Burry-level analysis on a Dalio-level time budget is a surefire recipe for superficial work and disastrous results.

Your available time is a critical constraint. Your chosen philosophy must align with the hours you can dedicate to research and portfolio management. An honest assessment prevents burnout and strategic drift.

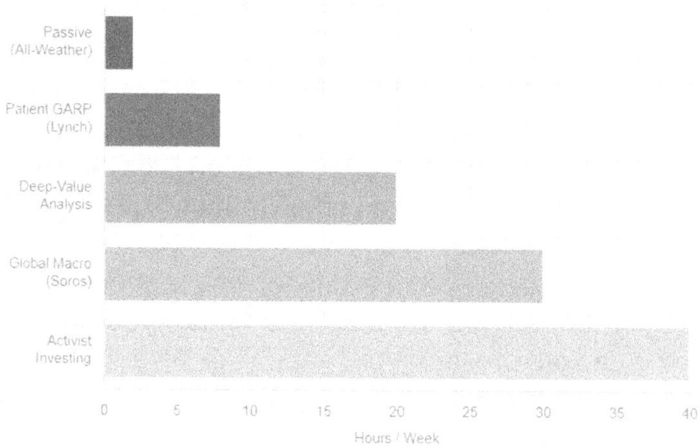

FIGURE 53 - ACTIVITY LEVEL VS. PHILOSOPHY

The Synthesis Toolkit: Assembling Your Operating System

Having taken your own measurements, you are now ready to build. This is an act of creative architecture, not rote imitation. We will assemble your personal investment operating system by choosing a core "base model" and then enhancing it with specialized "plugins" from the masters.

STEP 1: CHOOSE YOUR PHILOSOPHICAL CORE (YOUR "BASE MODEL")

Your answers from the Mirror Test point toward a natural philosophical home. This will be the chassis of your investment vehicle, your intellectual and psychological center of gravity. It is the default lens through which you will view the market and the anchor you will return to in times of uncertainty. Review your journal and select the single framework from this book that feels most aligned with your DNA.

- If the Mirror Test revealed you are a patient pessimist with a long time horizon, a contrarian temperament, and a passion for business analysis, your core is the **Graham/Buffett Value Framework**.
- If you are a systems-thinker who is humble about your ability to forecast the future, you prioritize capital preservation above all else, and your available time is limited, your core is the **Dalio All-Weather Framework**.
- If you are a global thinker, fascinated by the interplay of politics, economics, and human psychology, and you are comfortable making a few large, concentrated bets on major trends, your core might be the **Soros/Druckenmiller Macro Framework**.
- If you have a clear informational edge in a specific industry, enjoy the investigative hunt for growing companies, and have the time for active research, your core is the **Peter Lynch GARP Framework**.

STEP 2: INTEGRATE YOUR "PLUGINS"

Now we customize the chassis. The greatest investors are not dogmatic purists; they are synthesizers. Buffett evolved Graham's rigid value by integrating a focus on quality. Druckenmiller enhanced Soros's philosophy with a relentless focus on liquidity. The most robust frameworks are hybrids. You can, and should, enhance your core philosophy by integrating specific tools—"plugins"—from other masters to cover your blind spots.

- **Plugin for the Value Investor:** Even if you are a bottom-up, Buffett-style stock picker, you are not investing in a vacuum. You can integrate Howard Marks's "Credit Cycle Thermometer" as a macro overlay. This tool doesn't change *what* you buy, but it helps you decide *when* to be aggressive (when the thermometer is "frigid" and fear is high) or defensive (when it's "scorching" and greed is rampant).
- **Plugin for the Macro Investor:** You may have a brilliant top-down thesis like Stanley Druckenmiller, but you need the right instrument to express it. If you're looking to short a vulnerable sector, you can integrate **Michael** Burry's forensic accounting checklist. Use his microscope to find the single company with the weakest balance sheet and most questionable earnings quality, adding a powerful micro-level precision to your macro bet.
- **Plugin for the Growth Investor:** You're hunting for "ten-baggers" like Peter Lynch, but the biggest risk is overpaying for a great story. You can integrate Seth Klarman's rigorous **insistence on a margin of safety**. This forces you to ask: "Even for this amazing growth company, at what price would I be buying with a built-in cushion against disappointment?" It is a defensive tool that protects an offensive strategy.

STEP 3: DEFINE YOUR NON-NEGOTIABLES (YOUR HARD-CODED RULES)

This is where you write the unalterable source code for your operating system. These are the bright-line rules you will not cross, the circuit breakers designed by your rational self to protect you from your future, emotional self in the heat of the moment.

- **Valuation:** What is my personal "Margin of Safety"? Will I only buy a stock if it trades at a 30% discount to my conservative estimate of its value? Will I use a PEG ratio below 1.0 as a firm rule?
- **Risk Management:** What is the maximum percentage of my portfolio I will ever allocate to a single idea? Am I a concentrator like Buffett or a diversifier like Simons? What is my absolute, non-negotiable stop-loss rule that triggers an automatic sale or review?
- **Leverage:** Will I ever use leverage or buy on margin? If so, under what exact, pre-defined conditions? Or is my rule simply "Never"?
- **Behavioral Rules:** What is my specific, pre-written plan for a market crash? My rule might be: "During a market decline of 20% or more, I am forbidden from selling any existing positions. I am only authorized to review my pre-made watchlist of high-quality companies and deploy a set amount of cash."

Your Personal Charter: Writing an Investment Policy Statement

My Investment Policy Statement

My Financial Goals & Time Horizon:

[e.g., Achieve financial independence by age 55, fund children's education in 15 years. My time horizon is long-term, 20+ years.]

My Core Philosophy:

[e.g., I am a long-term, bottom-up value investor focused on wonderful companies at fair prices, based on the Buffett framework.]

My "Plugin" Tools:

[e.g., I will use Marks's cycle awareness to adjust position sizing and Lynch's "local knowledge" framework to source ideas.]

My Non-Negotiable Rules:

- Never use leverage.
- Require a minimum 30% margin of safety at time of purchase.
- Maximum 5% of portfolio in any single stock at cost.
- Re-evaluate thesis if a stock drops 50%, but do not sell automatically.

Pre-Investment Checklist:

- Can I explain this investment idea to a ten-year-old?
- Have I read the last three annual reports?
- What is the primary bear case, and can I refute it?
- Does this investment align with my core philosophy and rules?

FIGURE 54 - INVESTMENT POLICY STATEMENT

All of this work—the self-reflection, the synthesis, the rule-setting—must be codified. A philosophy that isn't written down is just a collection of vague intentions, and vague intentions are the first casualty in a market panic.

The Investment Policy Statement (IPS) is the tangible output of your journey. It is the most important single page you will ever create as an investor.

Think of this document as a contract with your future self. It is a Ulysses Pact. In the ancient myth, Ulysses had his sailors tie him to the mast of his ship so he could hear the beautiful, deadly song of the Sirens without steering his ship onto the rocks. Your IPS is the rope you will use to tie yourself to the mast when the siren songs of market panic and euphoria try to lure you to your financial ruin. It must be written down, printed, and signed. Its purpose is to be read during periods of maximum stress to remind you of the promises you made to yourself when you were thinking clearly.

Below is a template. Fill it out. Make it your own. It is your charter.

My Investment Policy Statement

- **My Primary Financial Goal & Time Horizon:**

  (Example: To fund a comfortable retirement beginning in 2055. This is a 30+ year horizon, allowing for a high tolerance for near-term volatility.)

- **My Core Investment Philosophy:**

(Example: I am a long-term, bottom-up value investor in the mold of Buffett. My core strategy is to buy wonderful companies with durable economic moats at a fair price, operating strictly within my Circle of Competence (Technology and Consumer Retail). I will enhance this by using Howard Marks's credit cycle analysis to guide the timing and aggression of my capital deployment.)

- **My Non-Negotiable Rules:**
    - I will never invest outside my defined Circle of Competence.
    - I will only purchase a stock if it trades at a minimum 25% discount to my conservative estimate of its intrinsic value (my Margin of Safety).
    - No single position will ever exceed 15% of my portfolio at cost.
    - I will never use leverage or margin. Period.
    - During a market decline of 20% or more, I am forbidden from selling. I am only authorized to review my watchlist and buy.
- **My Pre-Investment Checklist:**

☑ Can I explain this investment idea simply in a two-minute drill (the "Lynch Test")?

☑ Does this investment fall squarely within my defined Circle of Competence?

- ☑ Have I completed a forensic check of the balance sheet for red flags (the "Burry Test")?
- ☑ Does the purchase price satisfy my required Margin of Safety?
- ☑ Does this investment violate any of my Non-Negotiable Rules?

Signed: John Doe

Date: 2025-11-21

The Architect of You

The journey through "Wall Street's Greatest Minds" was never about imitation. It was about apprenticeship. You learned the principles of sound structure from Buffett, the importance of a firm foundation from Graham, the art of seeing what others miss from Burry, and the discipline of systems-thinking from Dalio. You have been given the blueprints of the masters not to copy them, but to learn the timeless principles of sound construction.

The goal was never to be the next Warren Buffett, but to be the first and best version of *yourself* as an investor—disciplined, thoughtful, and playing a game you are uniquely suited to win. You have passed the Mirror Test. You have assembled your toolkit. You have drafted your personal charter. You are no longer just a student of the great architects. You are now one of them. You are prepared to build something durable, something resilient, something uniquely and powerfully your own.

The quest for Alpha is over. Your life's work as an architect begins now.

Image Index

Table Index

References

1. Benjamin Graham - Wikipedia, accessed September 17, 2025, https://en.wikipedia.org/wiki/Benjamin_Graham; Benjamin Graham (investor) | Research Starters - EBSCO, accessed September 17, 2025, https://www.ebsco.com/research-starters/business-and-management/benjamin-graham-investor; Ben Graham Collection - Ivey Business School, accessed September 17, 2025, https://www.ivey.uwo.ca/bengrahaminvesting/resources/ben-graham-collection/; Benjamin Graham - The History of Economic Thought Website, accessed September 17, 2025, https://www.hetwebsite.net/het/profiles/bgraham.htm

2. Warren Buffett | Biography, Education & Age - Lesson - Study.com, accessed September 17, 2025, https://study.com/academy/lesson/warren-buffet-biography-education-quotes.html; Video: Warren Buffett | Biography, Education & Age - Study.com, accessed September 17, 2025, https://study.com/academy/lesson/video/warren-buffet-biography-education-quotes.html

3. Why the Margin of Safety is Important When Performing Stock ..., accessed September 17, 2025, https://stablebread.com/margin-of-safety/; Margin of safety as a concept - Redeye Capital, accessed September 17, 2025, https://www.redeyecapital.se/margin-of-safety

Benjamin Graham - Wikipedia, accessed September 17, 2025, https://en.wikipedia.org/wiki/Benjamin_Graham

5. stablebread.com, accessed September 17, 2025, https://stablebread.com/circle-of-competence/#:~:text=The%20%22circle%20of%20competence%2C%22,concept%20is%20important%20to%20discuss.

6. Circle of competence - Wikipedia, accessed September 17, 2025, https://en.wikipedia.org/wiki/Circle_of_competence

7. What did Buffett mean with "Boy, if I had listened only to Ben (Graham), would I ever be a lot poorer."? - Reddit, accessed September 17, 2025, https://www.reddit.com/r/AskEconomics/comments/186mret/what_did_buffett_mean_with_boy_if_i_had_listened/

8,9. Cigar Butt Investing: Your Ultimate Guide - Net Net Hunter, accessed September 17, 2025, https://www.netnethunter.com/cigar-butt-investing-ultimate-guide/

10. The evolution of Warren Buffett's investment style - Trustnet, accessed September 17, 2025, https://www.trustnet.com/investing/13445213/the-evolution-of-warren-buffetts-investment-style; Making the moat of it - Federated Hermes Limited, accessed September 17, 2025, https://www.hermes-investment.com/us/en/professional/insights/stewardship/making-the-moat-of-it/

11,12. Economic moat - Wikipedia, accessed September 17, 2025, https://en.wikipedia.org/wiki/Economic_moat

13. Assessing Leadership in Business: A Critical Investigation of Warren Buffett - Digital Commons @

UConn - University of Connecticut, accessed September 17, 2025, https://digitalcommons.lib.uconn.edu/cgi/viewcontent.cgi?article=1946&context=srhonors_theses

14. Assessing Management Quality | Value Investing Course | Safal ..., accessed September 17, 2025, https://www.safalniveshak.com/value-investing-course-assessing-management-quality/

15. New Coke: The Most Memorable Marketing Blunder Ever? - The Coca-Cola Company, accessed September 17, 2025, https://www.coca-colacompany.com/about-us/history/new-coke-the-most-memorable-marketing-blunder-ever

16. Benjamin Graham (investor) | Research Starters - EBSCO, accessed September 17, 2025, https://www.ebsco.com/research-starters/business-and-management/benjamin-graham-investor; Ben Graham Collection - Ivey Business School, accessed September 17, 2025, https://www.ivey.uwo.ca/bengrahaminvesting/resources/ben-graham-collection/; Revisiting Buffett / Coca-Cola in 1988 - GuruFocus, accessed September 17, 2025, https://www.gurufocus.com/news/205476/revisiting-buffett-cocacola-in-1988; Breakdown of Warren Buffett's Valuation of Coca Cola in 1988 - Investing for Beginners 101, accessed September 17, 2025, https://einvestingforbeginners.com/warren-buffett-coca-cola-valuation-daah/

17. The Coca-Cola Company - Wikipedia, accessed September 17, 2025, https://en.wikipedia.org/wiki/The_Coca-

Cola_Company; Revisiting Warren Buffet's Investment in Coca-Cola - CIBC Wood Gundy, accessed September 17, 2025, https://woodgundyadvisors.cibc.com/documents/555091/1942438/Revisiting+Warren+Buffet%27s+Investment+in+Coca-Cola+%28August+2013%29.pdf/3b63ca5a-0122-4fb6-8b7b-e0dc69adcf34; Roberto Goizueta - New Georgia Encyclopedia, accessed September 17, 2025, https://www.georgiaencyclopedia.org/articles/business-economy/roberto-goizueta-1931-1997/; The Lasting Legacy of Roberto C. Goizueta - EmoryBusiness.com, accessed September 17, 2025, https://www.emorybusiness.com/2019/06/03/the-lasting-legacy-of-roberto-c-goizueta/; The Goizueta Legacy, accessed September 17, 2025, https://goizueta.emory.edu/about/legacy

18. Revisiting Warren Buffet's Investment in Coca-Cola - CIBC Wood Gundy, accessed September 17, 2025, https://woodgundyadvisors.cibc.com/documents/555091/1942438/Revisiting+Warren+Buffet%27s+Investment+in+Coca-Cola+%28August+2013%29.pdf/3b63ca5a-0122-4fb6-8b7b-e0dc69adcf34; Breakdown of Warren Buffett's Valuation of Coca Cola in 1988 - Investing for Beginners 101, accessed September 17, 2025, https://einvestingforbeginners.com/warren-buffett-coca-cola-valuation-daah/

19. Breakdown of Warren Buffett's Valuation of Coca Cola in 1988 - Investing for Beginners 101, accessed September 17, 2025, https://einvestingforbeginners.com/warren-buffett-coca-cola-valuation-daah/

20. How to invest like John Templeton | Trustnet, accessed September 17, 2025, https://www.trustnet.com/investing/13430515/how-to-invest-like-john-templeton; John Templeton - Wikipedia, accessed September 17, 2025, https://en.wikipedia.org/wiki/John_Templeton; Sir John Templeton, accessed September 17, 2025, https://www.templeton.org/about/sir-john-templeton

21. Seth Klarman - Wikipedia, accessed September 17, 2025, https://en.wikipedia.org/wiki/Seth_Klarman; Seth Klarman | Broad Institute, accessed September 17, 2025, https://www.broadinstitute.org/history-leadership/board-directors/bios/seth-klarman

22,57-59,61-64. Adventure Capitalist by Jim Rogers (book)

23. John Templeton: global stock picker's remarkable life story | LGT, accessed September 17, 2025, https://www.lgt.com/global-en/market-assessments/insights/financial-knowledge/how-john-templeton-reconciled-god-and-mammon-301542; John Templeton - Wikipedia, accessed September 17, 2025, https://en.wikipedia.org/wiki/John_Templeton; Sir John Templeton | William Green, accessed September 17, 2025, https://williamgreenwrites.com/wp-content/uploads/2020/11/Sir-John-Templeton.pdf

24. John Templeton - Philanthropy Roundtable, accessed September 17, 2025, https://www.philanthropyroundtable.org/hall-of-fame/john-templeton/

25,29. Seth Klarman: The Margin of Safety Master Who Found Value in Market Panic - Verified Investing, accessed September 17, 2025, https://verifiedinvesting.com/blogs/education/seth-klarman-the-margin-of-safety-master-who-found-value-in-market-panic; Margin of Safety: Risk-Averse Value Investing Strategies for the Thoughtful Investor by Seth Klarman - James Clear, accessed September 17, 2025, https://jamesclear.com/book-summaries/margin-of-safety-risk-averse-value-investing-strategies-for-the-thoughtful-investor; Margin of Safety | Summary, Quotes, FAQ, Audio - SoBrief, accessed September 17, 2025, https://sobrief.com/books/margin-of-safety

26. Investment principles of John Templeton - Value Spreadsheet, accessed September 17, 2025, https://www.valuespreadsheet.com/blog/investment-principles-john-templeton

27,34,35. Seth Klarman - Wikipedia, accessed September 17, 2025, https://en.wikipedia.org/wiki/Seth_Klarman

28. Sir John Templeton: A Legacy of Contrarian Investing and Value Principles, accessed September 17, 2025, https://valueinvestingacademy.com/sir-john-templeton-a-legacy-of-contrarian-investing-and-value-principles/

30. Seth Klarman | Broad Institute, accessed September 17, 2025, https://www.broadinstitute.org/history-leadership/board-directors/bios/seth-klarman

31. Lessons from Seth Klarman's Margin of Safety - Novel Investor, accessed September 17, 2025, https://novelinvestor.com/lessons-seth-klarmans-margin-safety/

32,33. Asymmetric Risk: How to Win Even When You're Wrong - Bonfire Financial, accessed September 17, 2025, https://www.bonfirefinancial.com/asymmetric-risk/

36. Fulcrum Security | Value-Break Analysis + Calculator - Wall Street Prep, accessed September 17, 2025, https://www.wallstreetprep.com/knowledge/fulcrum-security-primer-restructuring-and-distressed-debt-investing/

37-40,42. Marks, Howard. "Open and Shut." Oaktree Capital memo, December 1, 2010.

41. On Howard Marks' Memos, accessed September 17, 2025, https://blas.com/wp-content/uploads/2019/10/On-Howard-Marks-Memos-2.pdf

43. Business Insider. "Fantastic Michael Burry UCLA Commencement Speech on U.S. & European Financial Crises." June 24, 2012. Accessed September 25, 2025. https://www.businessinsider.com/fantastic-michael-burry-ucla-commencement-speech-on-us-and-european-financial-crises-2012-6.September 25, 2025.

44,46. Wikipedia contributors. "Carl Icahn." Wikipedia, The Free Encyclopedia. Accessed September 25, 2025. https://en.wikipedia.org/wiki/Carl_Icahn.

45,47. Verified Investing. "Carl Icahn: The Activist Investor." April 22, 2025.

48,50. Soros, George. The Alchemy of Finance. Hoboken, NJ: John Wiley & Sons, 2003.

49. Dhar, Rohin. "The Trade of the Century: When George Soros Broke the British Pound." Priceonomics, June 17, 2016. Accessed September 25, 2025. https://priceonomics.com/the-trade-of-the-century-when-george-soros-broke/.September 25, 2025.

51-56. Duprey, Rich. "Billionaire Stanley Druckenmiller Went on a Shopping Spree. Here Are 3 of His Biggest Buys." 24/7 Wall St., August 25, 2025.

60. Rogers, Jim. Investment Biker: On the Road with Jim Rogers. New York: Random House, 1994.

65. T. Boone Pickens - Wikipedia, accessed September 17, 2025, https://en.wikipedia.org/wiki/T._Boone_Pickens

66-68. Flynn, Keli. "Mesa Petroleum Corporation." Handbook of Texas Online. Texas State Historical Association. Accessed September 25, 2025. https://www.tshaonline.org/handbook/entries/mesa-petroleum-corporation.

69-81. Mobius, Mark. Mobius on Emerging Markets. 2nd ed. London: Financial Times Pitman Publishing, 1996.

82. Mark Mobius, emerging-market guru, to retire after 30 years - Mint, accessed September 17, 2025, https://www.livemint.com/Companies/VLQSc6CKZ5pFvgTjUadh0O/Mark-Mobius-emergingmarket-guru-to-retire-after-30-years.html

83. The 1990s to Today: How Privatization Shaped Modern-day Russia, accessed September 17, 2025, https://www.americansecurityproject.org/the-1990s-to-today-how-privatization-shaped-modern-day-russia

84,85,87,88. Thiel Foundation. "Thiel Fellowship." Accessed September 25, 2025. https://thielfellowship.org/

86. Thiel, Peter, with Blake Masters. Zero to One: Notes on Startups, or How to Build the Future. New York: Crown Business, 2014.

89,90,92. Dalio, Ray. Big Debt Crises. Westport, CT: Bridgewater Associates, 2018.

91,94. "Ray Dalio." Wikipedia, The Free Encyclopedia. Accessed September 25, 2025. https://en.wikipedia.org/wiki/Ray_Dalio.

93. Dalio, Ray. Principles: Life and Work. New York: Simon & Schuster, 2017.

95. Asness, Clifford S., Tobias J. Moskowitz, and Lasse Heje Pedersen. "Value and Momentum Everywhere." Journal of Finance 68, no. 3 (2013): 929–985. https://doi.org/10.1111/jofi.12021.

96. Zuckerman, Gregory. The Man Who Solved the Market: How Jim Simons Launched the Quant Revolution. New York: Portfolio/Penguin, 2019.

97. Jim Simons Trading Strategy—QuantVPS.com

98. Graham, Benjamin. The Intelligent Investor: Rev. ed. New York: HarperBusiness, 2003.

www.ingramcontent.com/pod-product-compliance
Lightning Source LLC
LaVergne TN
LVHW052026200926
848481LV00005B/1600